Art Through Religion

A Process of Character Building

BY

Mary G. McMunigle

A Teacher's Manual to be used with
Art Education Through Religion

St. Augustine Academy Press

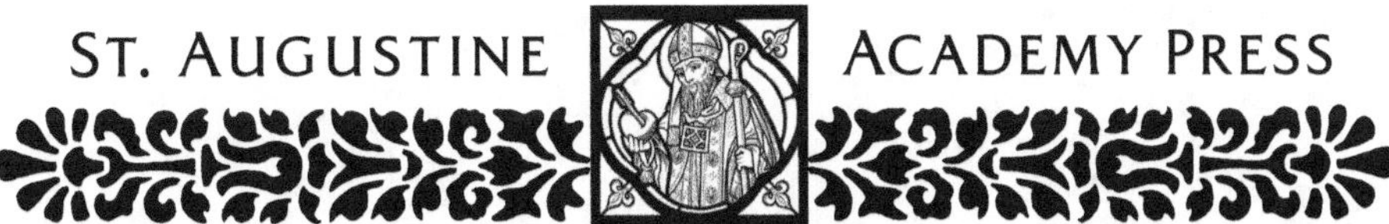

This book is newly typeset based on the 1930 edition published by Mentzer, Bush & Company. All editing strictly limited to the correction of errors in the original text, the addition of selected footnotes and supply lists, and minor clarifications in structure, punctuation or phrasing. Any remaining oddities of subject matter, spelling or phrasing are as found in the original.

IMPRIMATUR:

✠HUGH C. BOYLE, D.D.

Bishop of Pittsburgh

PITTSBURGH, MAY 28, 1930

This book was originally published in 1930
by Mentzer, Bush & Company.

All editing by Lisa Bergman

ISBN: 978-1-64051-135-4

Contents

Foreword

Art has been defined as the expression of spiritual values in terms of beauty. It is correct to say that in its inception it is always associated with the religious impulse. In the service of formal and organized religion art finds its greatest opportunity and its most ardent support. The spirit and inspiration of religion gave birth to all true art that the world has known. It is the handmaid of religion. Born of religion, art has ever been a loving and devoted child. Service after service in the cause of religion is the history of art. She has attempted to repay the debt of her creation. The painting, the sculpture, the architecture, the music of the Church have been powerful allies in impressing upon the minds of men the lessons of the Gospel. Art has supported and popularized the truths of religion, and proved herself a missionary ally of great power and effectiveness.

The Catholic Church, ever in the forefront of movements making for the social and cultural betterment of mankind, lost no time in enlisting art in her service. There had been an attempt at art in the Catacombs. Pictures—sometimes crude, it is true—conveyed the lessons of religion to the eye of the Christian at worship. When given freedom of worship, the Church immediately seized upon a human agent that could ennoble material things and make them less unworthy of the service of God. Art in all its manifestations gave concrete expression to spiritual truths and brought man nearer to God. Through the beauties of art man was made acquainted in some poor measure with the Beauty that is God.

It is not the primary purpose of this art course to produce artists. No, the first general objective of an art education is to develop in every pupil, superior, average, or inferior, his native ability to appreciate art. A true understanding of the usefulness of art recognizes creative power as a divine gift, the natural endowment of every human soul, showing itself at first in the form we call appreciation. This appreciation leads a certain number to produce actual works of art, greater or lesser (perhaps a temple, perhaps only a cup) but it leads the majority to desire finer form and more harmony of tone and color in surroundings and in things for daily use (Dow). Too long has the average or inferior student been discouraged by the conviction that talent and technical ability are necessary for any real acquaintance with art. Only about two per cent of the children of any given school or era will become producers of art or of art works. But all possess the God-given ability to recognize and to respond emotionally to the appeal of beauty. Every child can be trained to the appreciation of beauty in the thousand common things of daily life, and thus to the appreciation of beauty as a dissociated ideal. It has been said that Americans are a restless, money-grabbing people without affection for the more beautiful and finer things of life; that we have "eyes for the movies, ears for the radio, nose for news, the gentle touch—all that is lacking in taste." If we are to be as a nation redeemed of this reproach, the work must be done in the schools of the nation.

Our children and our people must, first of all, understand the principles of design and the problems of the designers, that they may choose houses that are well built and beautiful, house furnishings that are comfortable and useful as well as beautiful, pictures that are congenial in subject and good in line or color, picture frames that harmonize with picture and wall and do not kill the picture, books that are pleasing to the eye, rugs that stay on the floor, wall paper that does not jump out at one, clothing that best suits the individual figure and complexion, the automobile that is a pleasure to the eye, the house paint that does not forever annoy the neighbors, the planting of shrubbery to set the home in its natural surroundings as a jewel is set in gold, to tie it to the landscape, and so on—in other words, they must understand the beauty with which they may surround themselves, if they are to enjoy life to its fullest measure (Waldo F. Bates, Jr.).

Americans are vindicated in their profession of good taste and artistic appreciation by other art needs that are commonly enumerated. Merchants demand salespeople with fine taste and with sound, esthetic judgment. They spend money lavishly on beautiful show windows and attractive advertising, for these will sell the goods. But this can be so only when the people at large have the capacity to respond to such an appeal. Commercial sales organizations generally are demanding people and products that can appeal to an artistic sense. It is evident that they think the American people have this sense. In the fields of textiles, wall paper, carpets, rugs, furniture, pottery, glass, silverware, jewelry, lighting fixtures, and art metal products, skilled designers and artistic craftsmen are in constant demand. The development of the printing industry in the past score of years is proof conclusive to the art advocate that the taste of America is improving. The State develops artistically with the people of which it is comprised. Art is but the revelation of the spirit of man. That spirit distinguishes the State to which a given people belong. That spirit lives when the nation is dead, and the nation, though dead, lives with it. States erect beautiful and enduring buildings that give expression to the spirit of their people; they give employment to painters, sculptors, architects; they erect museums and art galleries which are not mere tombs of a spirit that is dead. The spirit lives. Greece lives in her Parthenon and her Praxiteles, Italy in her Madonnas, Raphaels, and Botticellis, France in her cathedrals.

Certainly there are in our country a large proportion of people to whom art is not without its appeal. But our greatest single artistic need is to develop a response to beauty and a real affection for the finer things of life in the soul of every citizen. This is the raison d'etre of art education. Art is a constructive force that cheers the work-day, glorifies and ennobles recreation, and gives a lasting value to leisure hours.

The seven main objectives of education are: health, command of the fundamental processes, worthy home-membership, vocation, citizenship, worthy use of leisure time, and ethical character. The making of a health poster makes the lesson in health vivid and impressive. The mere description of fly-borne infection is tedious to the young mind, but the correctly colored poster, portraying the hegira of the fly from the sick room in one home to the breakfast table in a neighboring home, creates a lasting impression. The help afforded by art in the attainment of the second objective, command of the fundamental processes, is obvious. Art affords an excellent aid in the development of the powers of attention, accuracy, observation, perception, comparison, discrimination and original thought; children learn to do, the imagination is challenged, the inventive power is stimulated, and there is ample scope for original creative work.

The part of art education in producing worthy home-membership was previously emphasized; the home is the province in which the developed good taste of the home member will exercise itself. To create a beautiful, artistic, restful environment within the home is worthy home-membership. Need we speak of the place of art in preparing one for his vocation? There is no vocation so humble that it has no need of art principles. The harmony of color and design contribute to the success of the street fruit vendor, perhaps no less than to that of the painter or sculptor. There is no vocation so exalted that it has no need of art principles. If the seminarists of a bygone age had been grounded in the principles of perspective and proportion, of color and design, they could have prevented many of the atrocities of color-daubing that masquerade as church art.

The citizen who has been trained to respond emotionally to the beautiful is the better citizen because of that training. If he lives in a congenial home atmosphere and pursues his vocation in a congenial, artistic atmosphere, he has every natural stimulation and encouragement to good citizenship. The worthy use of leisure time becomes easy to the patron of art. Art is that constructive force that glorifies and ennobles the recreation and leisure hours (Kirby). The lover of art can live in the glorious world of imagination created by the great artists of all time. He enters this world through his own imagination and his own power of appreciation. Art education aims to develop not only ability for self-expression but also understanding of the expression of others. Ethical character is the seventh and last objective of education. One who lives in the glorious world of imagination created by the artists of the world has every natural help for the practice of virtue. In fact, he lives in an atmosphere that makes the practice of virtue easy. When we accept art as the handmaid of religion and through art teach the lessons of religion, we have a character-building force that employs every natural and supernatural help.

Picture-study is an integral part of the course of study in Art of the elementary school curriculum. The Catholic Church, as a true teacher, has never failed to appeal to man through the senses. Her artists, her painters, her sculptors, her architects have been apostles of visual education. Yet, visual education is spoken of as a new development. Many an old principle of education and of other sciences, togged out in the vesture of a new terminology, is hailed as a modern discovery.

No greater single contribution to the advancement of art education in this country has been made than the establishment of the Federated Council on Art Education. The Council numbers among its members the American Federation of Arts, the American Institute of Architects, the Association of Art Museum Directors, the College Art Association, the Eastern Arts Association, the Pacific Arts Association and the Western Arts Association. They prepared as a report of the Committee on Elementary School Art (1926) a brochure descriptive of the objectives and the essentials of art instruction. The Committee says nothing of religion as a possible ally in the teaching of art, or it may be more correct to say that they do not speak of art as the handmaid of religion. With this stricture it is safe to accept the Committee's succinct and satisfactory statement of the first specific objective of art education:

> "To develop ability to appreciate and enjoy esthetically and intellectually correct arrangements of space, beauty of line, fine proportions in form and harmonious combinations of color, whether it be in the fine arts of architecture, painting and sculpture; the environments of nature, or in the arts of man's industry and genius, including the child's own work as well as that of more skilled hands."

Next in order they stress the objectives of training the judgment to keen discriminations that will function practically in later life, and of acquainting the child with materials and processes of production. The skills, habits, attitudes, and ideals which are objectives of art education are enumerated in much the same manner as previously in this article. Final emphasis among the objectives is placed on the ascertaining, conserving, and developing of the creative ability of talented pupils, and on correct vocational guidance of the talented pupil. The Committee then enumerates as minimum content essentials, and advocates formal drill and instruction in these main elements of art: design, lettering, color, form, narrative illustration, construction, appreciation, creative, and individual expression.

Religion as an element in education or in art is necessarily ignored by the patrons of a system of education that excludes religion. Our purpose must be to show the natural alliance that exists between art and religion, that art is the handmaid of religion, that art is best taught through religion.

We append the words of Doctor Chambers of State College, Pennsylvania. He writes of Art: "I believe in Art because I believe in richness of life. I believe in Art Education because there can be no complete education without it. I believe in Art Education not as another subject added to the curriculum, but as an attitude and a spirit which suffuses the whole." May we suggest that the word "Religion" be added to the word "Art" in this assertion? The Church has always combined them.

—Extract from an article by Rev. Paul E. Campbell in The Homiletic and Pastoral Review.

INTRODUCTION

The Major Objective of this series of books is to vitalize the teaching of religion through helping the child to visualize subject matter, which, because of its nature, ordinarily makes but a vague impression on his mind.

In the problems planned throughout the series, the aim has been to kindle in the mind of the child a vivid interest in, and an intimate and loving relationship with God. To engender in children a keen desire to render loving service to Him, in all their human contacts and daily activities. Service of God based on love makes for surety of love for one's neighbor and in the words of Our Lord "This do and thou shalt live." Also: "He that loveth not, knoweth not God, for God is love." (1 John 4:18) Happily this Major Objective may best be accomplished through the development of the esthetic nature of the individual. This is made possible through giving him a well balanced Art Education, wherein, while developing his physical visualization we may direct at the same time his spiritual vision, leading him to recognize reflections of The Blessed Trinity in himself, as well as when found spread over the whole face of Nature.

As pointed out by Rt. Rev. Monsignor Vaughn, these reflections may be found in the triune nature of water, ice, liquid, and steam; in plant life showing seed, flower, and fruit; in the unchangeable attributes of Time to which we are irrevocably bound, showing past, present and future, as well as numerous other examples. And this leads to the second Objective of these books, to present a well balanced Art Education, which is the study of another trinity: Line, Form, and Color—the basic elements of all visual objects both natural and man made.

To avoid confusion of terms, this series follows the nomenclature of art terms recommended by the Committee on Terminology of the Federated Council on Art Education.

Line is the defining outline, contour, or visible edge of anything visible to the eye.

Form is the mass shape or appearance of objects enclosed within its contours.

Color objectively is that quality of a thing which is perceived by the eye alone, independent of its form; subjectively a sensation peculiar to the organ of vision and arising from the optic nerve. Every person with normal vision feels its influence. This influence is based upon the stimulation of the senses which results when white light, broken by reflection or refraction into its various wave lengths, falls upon our vision so that instead of sombre grays, we see varying hues which appear to give vitality to form.

Analysis of the complete series of ART EDUCATION THROUGH RELIGION will show how completely they fulfill the objectives recommended by the Committee on Elementary School Art of the Federated Council on Art Education, which are:

I—BROAD OBJECTIVES

A—Appreciation:

1—To vigorously stimulate emotional response to graphic, plastic, and constructed forms, so there will be recognition, enjoyment and participation in art wherever it may be found in all human activities.

B—Skills:

1—To develop useful skills for graphic and glyphic communication through representation, illustration, and design, and construction in three dimensions.

C—Knowledge:

1—To give a background of facts concerning the contribution of the great masters of all time in all fields of art.

II—SPECIFIC OBJECTIVES

A—Appreciation:

1—To develop ability to appreciate and enjoy esthetically and intellectually correct arrangements of space, beauty of line, fine proportions in form, and harmonious combinations of color, whether it be in the fine arts of architecture, painting, and sculpture; the environment of nature; or in the arts of man's industry and genius including the child's own work as well as that of more skilled hands.

2—To train the judgment to keen discriminations and wise choice that will function later, as circumstances permit, in the selection of apparel, the selection and beautifying of the home and garden, and in city planning.

3—To acquaint the child with materials and processes of production.

B—Skills:

1—To develop skills which should be productive of joy in school life and give resources within, which enable one to make worthy and happy use of leisure.

2—To develop useful skills which will lay a foundation for those skills that may be gained later by more intensive vocational training.

C—Habits, Attitudes, Ideals—(To give the child opportunity for better conduct by making art a social situation)**:**

1—Good habits of accuracy, neatness, right attitudes in cooperation and responsibility, unselfishness, etc., are objectives common to all subjects of education. But art activities in education afford fields of experience especially rich in opportunity for the development and measurement of these qualities.

D—Outstanding Abilities:

1—To ascertain, conserve, and develop, creative ability of pupils with natural endowment for the production of beauty.

2—To guide the talented pupil to select the vocational field of art to which he is most naturally adapted.

Development of ability to Visualize Form will be emphasized in each succeeding step for only with the aid of really "seeing" eyes can we hope for real growth in esthetic appreciation which develops that "inward eye" so necessary for complete development.

Books 1, 2 and 3 carefully utilize the play spirit predominant in this period of childhood when expression is largely through drawing because speech has not yet become sufficient (vocabulary is limited). During this period there is a lack of coordination and the teacher must be careful of tiring the child. The real secret of technique is to get coordination without fatigue, by introducing the technique in many forms, viz.: cut in the air, cut newspaper columns, invent new games and drills with scissors.

Each period of child growth is characterized by certain interests born of instincts. In the primary stage the greatest instincts are individualism, curiosity, imitation, and play. **Play** underlies all **interest** in work and so underlies all art.

The constructive instinct develops with play, as every child loves to build (modify material) that he may enjoy the thrill of Creation.

GENERAL PRINCIPLES OF METHOD IN ART TEACHING

It is essential that the teacher keep clearly in mind the following points in all lessons:

1—The *aim* of the lesson in

- **a—Relation to other lessons** and as an aid in explaining to the child his environment.
- **b—Intellectual development** or training in judgment and reason. This requires questioning by the teacher and answers, after sufficient thought, by the pupil. This is the method of discovery, to be employed in all Art teaching, to cause pupils to determine the steps of each process. The secret of successful art teaching is thoughtful questioning and demonstration drawing.

  Intellectual development requires original application of knowledge gained. This is the **personal** expression to be sought in each lesson in the arts.
- **c—Manual or Muscular** development requires that pupils be given necessary knowledge through illustration and demonstration by the

teacher, followed by re-demonstration by the pupil, in the form of a muscular recitation. ("Scissors up, open, close.")

d—Esthetic development requires that pupils be caused to make discriminating judgments concerning form, proportions, color, both of their own work and that of their neighbors. This is the critical comparison to be secured at the end of each lesson. **Have an exhibition of work follow every lesson.**

LESSON STEPS FOR ANY LESSON IN THE ARTS

1—Introduction—with a brief reference to previous knowledge to relate the lesson.

2—The Oral Recitation (Intellectual) following the presentation of the new material, careful questions leading to the discovery of its chief elements.

3—Muscular Recitation to teach children how materials may be best handled through demonstration by the teacher, with a re-showing by the class, to be sure that technique has been understood.

4—Individual use of the technique through **original** expression by the pupil.

5—Esthetic recitation through class criticisms of exhibit at end of lesson.

Illustration by the teacher is strongly recommended for all phases of each lesson. Keep chalk constantly in hand and remember children are not critical and illustrations should not be left on the blackboard long enough to have children copy them. It is surprising how quickly a teacher may develop a fair ability to sketch rapidly on the blackboard, if a few minutes' regular practice is given to mastering a few simple subjects.

The illustrations in the books have been planned to take the place of expert blackboard illustrations, as they will place before the child the finest examples of technique and drawing to aid him in his work. They **are not** intended to be copied but to inspire **original thought** and action. From the earliest grades, make children understand that the precious germ of originality which God has planted in each of His children, will only grow strong through using it.

A THREEFOLD OBJECTIVE

Each lesson in the series will be found to have a threefold aim, viz.: **(1) Character training; (2) Spiritual training** and **(3) Art training.** The threefold objective should be constantly kept in mind by the teacher, whose watchful eye will note every possibility of strengthening one with the other.

The use of the blank page opposite each lesson page has been considered as a definite part of the complete plan of the books. Since development of creative power on the part of the child is of the utmost importance, every precaution should be taken to have him **follow** the **method** of work shown on every page, rather than slavish copy of the illustrations found there which are intended primarily to inspire original thinking along new lines, as well as to show fine standards of work. As an additional aid in training visualization and discrimination, the child should be trained in every grade, to search the magazines for pictures related to the lesson under discussion. This collection enriches his art vocabulary and helps to give him independent power in using it in creative work. **At regular periods** the arrangement of this material on the blank page in the book provides an **excellent lesson in design and pasting.** Meanwhile, the book becomes doubly useful through having a finely arranged page of colored reference material opposite each method page illustrating the text. The added color will always be found to be very stimulating. The arrangement or plan of every page should show **good composition.**

DIVISIONS OF ART TRAINING

Art Education presents four phases of work as agencies through which instruction can be given in the Elementary school: Drawing, Construction, Design, and Color.

Drawing or graphic expression may be divided into Imaginative drawing or illustration, and "Seeing," which includes nature forms, still life, figure drawing, and mechanical drawing.

Construction includes all forms of constructed models, paper cutting, and clay modeling.

Color may be studied both in Theory and experimental application.

Design shows many phases, always closely related to color. Problems in the books include Theory, applied to Commercial Art, Industrial Art, Home Decoration, Costume Design, Civic Beauty, and Stage Design.

Art Appreciation is interwoven in all the lessons, but **directed appreciation** is especially planned in the development of **picture study.**

ILLUSTRATION

This form of drawing is the natural expression of children who desire a graphic outlet for ideas. The pupil uses it best while language still lacks in vocabulary. It has a peculiar appeal to young children because of its practical value, from the child's point of view, while it meets his desire for life and action. The aim in teaching it should be to develop an easy medium of expression while strengthening the power of mental imagery. It offers a simple introduction to the study of color. It satisfies the story-telling instinct while language is deficient. The subjects chosen should deal with life and action. It is advantageous to have several lessons centered around some general interest (referring back to previous lessons). All objects of the child world may be used, i. e., his play, home, shops, industries, and other activities around him with which he has contact.

Historical incidents and stories may be used to provide a ready means of coordinating **language, nature study, history, geography, and the study of environment,** by the aid of illustration.

Colored crayon is the best medium for beginning work, as color is essential. Brush and color may be used in the higher grades. Cut paper is also interesting. Technical details are wisely taught in previous lessons, i. e., before a picture requiring the use of trees, animals, or figures, the pupils should be given a definite lesson on these separate elements.

Standards of Work: This drawing is not primarily to be judged from the esthetic standpoint. The test is "Does the picture tell the story plainly, vivaciously, and individually?" Be wary of the dictated picture. **It defeats the purpose of the lesson.** Emphasize original thinking and original work.

Excellent opportunities for group work are offered in illustrative drawing through such large subjects as "The **Picnic, Circus, Market, May Festivals** in honor of Our Lady," etc. This may take the form of a frieze for the classroom, and include a contribution from each member of the class. (This is the child's natural introduction to esthetics arising out of his life.)

At the end of every lesson have a brief exhibition of the work of the entire class so that the children may discuss the results. Their own keen criticisms will be the best indication of their **level of achievement** and set the **standards for future work.**

FREE CUTTING

The purpose of freehand cutting is to strengthen the power of visualization in children, while developing coordination. Definite exercises should first be given in cutting to line, in order to detect errors in procedure. This should be followed by the teacher's demonstration of free cutting of a very simple fruit form with which the children are familiar. Have children look carefully at the form, calling attention to important characteristics. Be careful to give pupils paper having the same proportions as the object to be cut, so that the cut form resulting will be the full size of the paper.

After cuttings have been made, have pupils hold them up and compare them with the original to discover any differences caused by errors in their seeing or visualization. After errors have been found, have them cut again to improve their forms.

White scratch pad paper makes excellent cutting or tearing paper and is much cheaper than regular cutting paper. After children have gained some facility with the scissors, have them try to complete the form with a continuous cut, so that the space remaining after the form has been cut out will also show the form. Vary cutting lessons with tearing lessons. Do not have children attempt to tear forms having smooth contours, or results will not be satisfactory. Paper cutting emphasizes form and necessarily limits the possibility of detail; for this reason it is especially valuable as a means of expression for small children. The addition of colored paper for posters and illustrations, etc., adds a new stimulation, but where regular colored paper is not available, paint or crayon may be used as a color lesson, to color paper to be used.

Cut letters are treated in detail on pages 7 and 12. Interesting lessons may be had with trees and landscapes. Here tearing will be found very effective in getting leafy edges. A valuable lesson in developing judgment may be had while the various parts of the landscape are being placed on a large classroom poster. Paste sky first in order that it may come down **back** of the trees and hills. Paste things farthest away first and continue toward the foreground or front of the picture. Remember that things **nearer** are placed **lower** in the picture and distance fades out color. When pasted forms protrude from edges of paper, trim after all pasting has been completed and mount on harmonious paper.

See text for further discussion of flowers and fruits.

CONSTRUCTION WORK

This may be best developed on a basis of the child's interest in his experiences and surroundings. Planning around some special center of interest will always be found advantageous, such as the home, the town, religious events, the farm, school, the picnic, folklore, myths, dramatization, etc. The main point to be observed is to give the child a sufficient reason for developing the constructed form. There should be no construction for construction sake, but rather as a means of better understanding the world in which we live.

Construction work is also valuable for correlation with other school work as booklets, folders, envelopes, pencil boxes, etc. **Communal** work is always valuable for assembling related forms, as a town, market, farm, etc.

The chief difficulty in teaching construction work is the technical difficulty, i. e., every new process involves a new group of muscular coordinations. These must be made familiar and in part subconscious, through drills, before the pupil puts them into actual practice. Illustration of technique should be done on a large scale before the class and motor responses should be frequently asked for. To secure individuality in construction it is necessary that the pupil make simple type forms first and then be encouraged to make a large variety of individual forms based on them. Have him keep the purpose of the model in mind, as he works out the details of construction. **Make every step a thinking process.** The element of discovery should be the special feature of each construction lesson. The teacher should use every device to induce the class to offer a means of solution. The teacher should always show some completed type of the form before the lesson is begun, as a stimulus to interest as well as for the purpose of analysis. The finished form should show a reasonable degree of accuracy. If it does not, the pupil's own judgment will condemn it. Hence the problems offered should be within the ability of the class. Commendation should be given chiefly for **ingenuity** and **originality**, rather than on technical accuracy of the form.

Construction problems develop the child's reasoning powers and his result gives him an opportunity to test his own ability to do things successfully. His keen interest in getting a satisfactory result causes him to learn accuracy in measurement more quickly than would be the case should failure not cause such keen disappointment.

CLAY WORK

Clay may be procured for two or three cents a pound from Robinson-Ransbottom Clay Company, Roseville, Ohio.† When ordering ask for modeling clay, washed and wet, in fifty or one hundred pound lots. It can be obtained in larger quantities also. Fifty pounds is the normal amount for a classroom.

CARE OF CLAY

Make a coarse bag or use a sugar bag to hold clay after it has been used for a class lesson. Place bag in a non-rusting container having about an inch of water. As clay absorbs water more should be added until whole mass is moist. Wedge the clay for use by lifting the mass and throwing down until its own

† Editor's note: We felt it was worth maintaining references like this from the original book, as they are of particular interest, despite the fact that Robinson-Ransbottom ceased operations in 2005.

Modern options for clay work can include modeling clay if desired, but because this does not harden, it may be more satisfying for the students to use an air-dry clay, or one like Sculpey, which can be hardened in the oven. But of course, good old-fashioned pottery clay is also a joy for children to work with!

weight has kneaded it into shape. Two boys in the class may be assigned to do this work. A small zinc garbage can makes an excellent container for clay.

Clay has been proven antiseptic and no germ can live in it. This makes it a healthy medium to use all through the year. Newspapers placed on the desks protect the floor from crumbs. When the lesson is over the hands are fresh and clean and do not need washing.

When making clay ready for passing it is a good plan to have it wedged into a loaf shape, like brick ice cream, then slice off each pupil's portion with a pad back or thin ruler.

Because of its plasticity, clay is an exceptionally fine medium for developing the creative instinct, as it keeps constantly changing its form, under the slightest pressure. It makes it easier for children to visualize things in the round.

From each lesson a few good models may be allowed to harden and later, if desired, they may be colored with crayon or paint.

COLOR

The fascination of color is universal and the objective of the color study planned in this series of books is to develop in children a fine and discriminating taste in color selection which will be valuable all through life.

The color page in each book is planned as **source material** for color lessons which should be distributed over the entire year.

If necessary supplies are available, work with brush and color may be started in grade one, as paint gives quick results in fresh pure color. If paints cannot be obtained, have children use a set of crayons having true colors (eight in a box). If crayons are used, the teacher should be sure that the combination of the primary colors used will produce the binary colors. Much of the color work in Books 1, 2 and 3 has been planned to be carried out in crayon, as practically all color work shown may be done beautifully with that medium. Water colors should be used above 3rd grade.

For color experiment work it is best to use white drawing paper, but for illustration, gray bogus paper is best. The gradation of color lessons presented on the color pages in the books may be summarized as follows:

1—Recognition of 6 hues and manipulation of materials.

2—Recognition of light and dark colors. Continuation of primary & binary.

3—Recognition of Intermediate colors.

4—Recognition of Neutral Values.

5—Analysis and use of Complements.

6—Color Balance—Color laws.

7—Color Harmony—Analogous.

8—Harmony of Contrast—Complementary—Relative color values.

COLOR INFORMATION

The source of color is light. Its effect is caused by different wave lengths of light affecting the optic nerve. We know the shape of objects because their color forms a contrast with another color as a background. Without light there is no color. Three colors, red, yellow, and blue, are called Primary colors because they are each indivisible, and from their combinations all other colors may be produced.

RED and YELLOW make ORANGE.
RED and BLUE make PURPLE.
YELLOW and BLUE make GREEN.

ORANGE, GREEN, and **PURPLE** are called **Binary colors** because they contain two colors. See color page, Book 3, for **Intermediate colors.** A color in its pure state is called a Normal color. When **water** or **white** is added we get a **tint** of the color. When **black** is added we get a **shade** of the color. **Hue** is the color name, as green, blue-green, etc. **Value** is the amount of light in a color. **Yellow** has the **lightest color value.** The absence of light produces black. **Purple** has the **darkest color value.** The term **Neutral Value** is used where no color can be discerned. The **Neutral Value Scale** is a scale of **grays** without color between white and black.

Colors are also noted as **warm** and **cool. Orange, red,** and **yellow** are **warm** colors. **Blue, green, and violet** are **cool colors. Chroma** or strength or intensity of color means the amount of pure color present. By **neutralizing** a color is meant reducing its strength and causing it to approach grayness by adding to it its **complement**. (See text Book 5, color page 10.)

When water colors are used in the earlier grades it is advisable to pay much attention to caring for the paints, since only clean paints will give purity of color. **Clean** the colors with **brush and water** at the end of every lesson.

Valuable beginning lessons may be had by teaching children to cover small sheets of paper with a flat tone of color. To do this, have pupils make free horizontal strokes over the paper with water, holding the brush lightly. Next take a full brush of color and repeat strokes with color, making the top of each new one connect with the bottom of the previous stroke. Be careful that strokes are made from left to right **only.**

The historic symbolism of colors will be found to coincide with their general effect upon people. Briefly they are:

Yellow—Sunshine—light and joy.
Red—Exciting—love and sacrifice.
Blue—Coolness—truth and infinity.
Orange—Combines red and yellow—gladness.
Green—Restful—hope and promise.
Purple—Mystery—mourning—royalty.
Black—Death and penance.
White—Symbol of purity.

Teach the symbolism of colors in all grades. Book 1, page 10, suggests the use of the Primary colors as a reflection of the Blessed Trinity in nature. Allow a ray of sunlight to pass through a glass prism; have children associate the three colors into which it is refracted with the Three Persons of The Blessed Trinity:

Red—Love and Sacrifice—God the Son.
Yellow—Light—God the Holy Ghost.
Blue—Infinity—God the Father.

Have children acquire the habit of direct painting, that is, lifting the color from the cake of paint instead of mixing in the box lid. Mixed color is always lifeless. Notice carefully all the directions given for the various color problems explained in the text books. **Do not draw with pencil before painting.**

When using crayon, hold it like chalk and use the beveled side of the crayon. When drawing fruits or trees draw the form in mass rather than filling in an outline of the shape. Make a flat center and work from center to outside shape or contour, comparing from time to time to get the correct shape. Brightly colored toys are always good models for a lesson in color matching.

REPRESENTATION

The purpose of Representative Drawing is twofold:

1—To train the eye to translate three dimensions in the round into two dimensions in the flat.

2—To train muscular coordinations to repeat the mental image with a reasonable degree of accuracy.

The modern idea in primary teaching is born of the conviction that all work with little children must be done in the spirit of play. It is essential therefore that models offered in drawing shall be related to the life of the child, that they shall be colorful and identifiable with activities the child will understand. In the group should be flowers, vegetables, toys, familiar objects, and the always useful live model in the form of one of the pupils, or a pet animal.

In this early stage drawings should be done in the mass, that is, rubbed with crayon from the middle to the outside until the form is completed. The simplest aspects of the form should be presented, i. e., a toy wagon in silhouette and not as a foreshortened form. The models must be numerous enough to have pupils really see the form they are drawing. To draw a form as seen from the side, when the pupil actually sees it from the front, is to defeat the whole aim of the lesson in the translation of the mental image.

Emphasize the standards to be created by suitable examples from other lessons. In making demonstration drawings, the teacher should question the class as to what she must think of, in each step she takes. Even with the youngest pupils the process should be a **reasoning** one.

The lesson should offer a fine opportunity for training individual judgment of size, placing, proportion, and direction. This is to be done with continual reference to the model as well as with many quick blackboard sketches.

In nature drawing direct attention to characteristic growth of the plant; attachment of leaves—are they alternating or in pairs? Note the shape and placing of flowers, etc. Keen observation may be trained through having children note and draw various stages of plant growth. The teacher must not dictate what the child must decide for himself.

Secure this independent action through much questioning. Criticism should be constructive, i. e., point out the well done things and keep the class striving for them. Exhibits should follow at the end of the lesson, standards should be erected by the children themselves, and it should be remembered that children's drawings **should be childlike.** When properly done they should show such progress from grade to grade that the age of the child will reveal itself in each successive stage.

ELEMENTARY DESIGN

Children have a primitive desire to decorate, not unlike the similar instinct in primitive people, who uniformly decorated their weapons and their persons. Primitive design takes the form of story-telling, which becomes formal and then symbolical.

The aim of primary design is to add interest to structure and thereby achieve structural beauty, give a sense of order and proportion, tell a story, and informally introduce the child to the study of color.

Primary design should be informal, with much emphasis on the symbol and should be done as far as possible in the spirit of play. It must be kept **alive** (not formal) by using motifs taken from life.

Principles—as principles—should not be emphasized.

The principle of Unity is illustrated by examples showing **likeness** in the forms, and relation between forms, based on this likeness, and structural relationships. One finds a lack of Unity through a lack of structural relationships.

Variety is opposed to monotony and when properly used is the spice of the design.

Design should not be applied merely for the sake of design, but the form should legitimately call for design. Simple examples of Repetition, Alternation, and Radiation should be presented over and over again, not as specific principles in design, but to familiarize children with different types of arrangement.

DRAMA

The pages devoted to drama have been especially planned to intensify the effect of desirable character traits shown in the characters of the persons to be impersonated in the play. The memory verse on the inside of the cover has been selected as a similar aid in character training. **All the English work for the drama is to be creative** through original dialogue worked out during the English period.

The setting of the stage, the planning, and the execution of necessary costume accessories will arouse inventive minds to produce original results, as keen interest in the project will continue to run high until it is completed.

RELIGION

Where religious lessons are planned for projection into the home to disseminate much needed information about things liturgical, the work should not be held until the end of the year, **but if sent immediately** and in proper season will make a deep impression on adult minds. This **impression is nullified** if all the problems in a complete book are shown at the same time.

And this suggests artistic mounting of problems to be taken home. Observation of illustrations to be found in the books of every grade will show fine arrangement and helpful suggestions in the text.

Margins should be carefully considered from the viewpoint of variety. To mount a paper longer than wide, have the bottom margin greatest, with the top medium, and the sides narrowest and alike. To mount a paper wider than long, have the bottom margin widest, the sides medium and alike and the top narrowest. Choose paper for a background that is very neutral in tone and harmonizing with the dominant color in the picture. Artistic mounting gives a finish to a piece of work, but is too expensive to consider for other than very special problems to be used as gifts or for exhibition purposes. Have a bulletin board in the room as an example of artistic arrangement.

The development of the religious objective of each lesson will be best carried out by individual teachers. The special aid to be found in the problem is that it **excites the pupil's interest** in the subject and brings to the assistance of his ears the added faculties of sight and touch and makes **concentration on the religious subject a certainty.**

> "Great teachers have differed little in their interpretation of the objectives of education. Invariably they have insisted on symmetrical development. They realize that unless it is accompanied by the cultivation of the child's spiritual nature, the training of the intellect is 'as sounding brass or tinkling cymbal'."
>
> —*Dr. Jeremiah Burke,*
> *Supt., Public Schools, Boston, Mass.*

ORGANIZATION OF WORK

Materials: The color work in Books I, II, and III has been planned for crayola, but if brush and paint are available they will be found more effective in any grade for teaching color. A good quality of crayola should be used for illustration in the lower grades.

When training for habits of carefulness it will be found an advantage if each pupil has an individual paint box. Where several rooms use the same materials, paint boxes should be carefully checked before and after use. Lack of materials need not deter any schools from carrying on art work, however, as it will be found that a large part of it **may be done on the blackboard.**

The pupil's equipment should consist of a box of crayola, a water color box containing red, yellow, blue, and black, with a number 7 brush, a small pan for water, a ruler suitable for the grade, a pair of scissors, and an eraser. To expedite the work of passing materials these may be kept in individual large envelopes made from tough wrapping paper.

Paste may be passed as needed on small pieces of paper. Pupils should be taught to paste evenly with the **third** and **fourth** fingers, in order that other fingers may be kept clean for folding. If paste cannot be bought it may be easily made from flour and water and a teaspoonful of alum boiled. A couple of drops of carbolic acid or oil of cloves will keep it from souring.†

Fibre **rulers** may be obtained with **measurements suitable for the grade,** beginning in second grade with 1 inch, third grade ½ inch, fourth grade ¼ inch, fifth and sixth grades ⅛ inch wood rulers, seventh and eighth grades 1/16 inch brass edged wood rulers. **Pencils** should be fairly **soft** for general use. Charcoal is a good medium for large, free work in any grade. Poster or show card paint (or tempera paint) is convenient to have on hand for special work in seventh and eighth grades. One 2 oz. jar of the six colors with black and white should be sufficient.

Paper: Manila drawing paper should be used for work in color study; gray bogus paper has been planned for the major part of the work in illustration and construction. Regular construction paper in soft tones of color is to be preferred if it can be obtained. It may be ordered in 12" x 18" sheets and is nice for posters. Colored poster paper in large sheets of normal colors with tints and shades may be purchased. This is nice for cut paper projects where the study of color is being emphasized. This paper is expensive and if used should be conserved by saving scraps for future lessons.

Large sheets of tough wrapping paper will be found very inexpensive and convenient. These may be bought from any wholesale paper house. Squared paper may be purchased with ¼" squares in gray or cream manila. It will be found cheaper to order paper in bulk as large sheets 12" x 18" may be cut to better advantage than smaller ones.

---

† Editor's note: We highly recommended making paste, which was common at the time, but today it is hard to find. Its properties are superior to glue sticks (which lose bond strength over time so that projects fall apart), and to bottled glue (which rarely dries flat).

To make paste, whisk together equal amounts of flour and water with a teaspoon of salt or alum until lumps are eliminated, then heat gently in a pan on the stove until it reaches the desired consistency. Store in a small jar with a lid.

It is best to make paste in small batches to fit the need for a week or two.

Cardboard may be ordered but it will be found economical to **save the backs of pads** and **boxes** for book covers, etc. Ask pupils to bring old newspapers which may be quartered into neat piles and kept for use under edges of paper being pasted. Ask pupils to bring several bricks for use as weights to press constructed articles. If these are covered with gray paper, they will present a neater appearance.

Use of Materials: For painting lessons desks should be arranged with paint box on **upper right** corner of desk in **front** of the water pan with **lid** of the box toward pupil.

Use a monitor system for passing and collecting materials quickly and orderly. There should be a monitor for each type of materials if they are to be passed separately. For passing and collecting water it will be found convenient to use a sprinkling can **with the sprinkler removed,** and if large enough, water may be passed and collected in the same vessel.

All work should be correlated with other school subjects where possible. The order of lessons as arranged in books may be changed if the teacher thinks it advisable. The lessons in the books follow the liturgical as well as the seasonal year, but many lessons suit several subjects.

Catalogues for supplies may easily be obtained and it is wise to get a number of different catalogues for comparison.

Time for Lessons: A definite time should be planned for the art lesson as well as for other lessons. A period just preceding the dismissal is convenient as it does not interfere with subjects following. The plan used in so many schools of having **the art period saved for Friday afternoon is not good,** as it detaches the work from the **regular curriculum where it belongs with religion.** In the lower grades fifteen minutes every day is advisable. Much of this might be practice work on the blackboard with two definitely planned lessons each week amounting in all to about one hundred minutes per week. In the upper grades about seventy-five minutes per week should be given to the work. Aim to find local adaptations for problems where possible. Very long art periods are not advisable for young children.

When the teacher is sure she has the attention of all pupils she should give her directions clearly and briefly. Children ignore orders which are repeated too often. **Insist on good habits** and **do not allow pupils to work in a careless, haphazard manner,** or it will be very difficult to train them into orderly habits later.

PICTURE STUDY

All children love pictures but they must be carefully guided to an appreciation of fine expressions of art.

To bring enthusiasm to the presentation of picture study to children, a teacher must first have a real appreciation of the picture herself and love it for what it means to her personally. Appreciation is enriched through the knowledge of a picture, which comes through study. It will be found that definite art principles are to be discovered in all fine pictures and a careful reading of the notes given for the beautiful large picture in each book of this series will show an analysis of these principles with suggestions as to **where and when they should be emphasized** when teaching the other pictures suggested for the grade.

When teaching the smaller pictures from the following list it is well for the **teacher to use a large picture to show to the class,** as sometimes details are not shown clearly in small reproductions. The notes given with the pictures emphasize the importance of the **individual interpretation of the picture by the children.**

By noting the Art **Objective** in the picture studies given for each book in the Manual, it will be seen that a definite addition has been made each year to the sum total of art principles learned in preceding grades, in order to add to the intellectual response pupils are expected to get from the picture. The emotional response is the natural reaction to the picture, but the more knowledge a pupil acquires about it so much more will he be interested in it.

Dramatization, particularly with primary children, will deepen the impression made by the picture and add keen interest. Merely taking positions of persons seen in the picture is sufficient to create interest.

The following pictures have been selected as additional subjects to be studied by the various grades to acquaint them with fine masterpieces of the past and present, each one of which has been carefully selected because of its universally acknowledged greatness as well as its suitability to the age of the pupils:

GRADED LIST OF SUBJECTS

Grade 1
1. Baby Stuart .... *Van Dyck*
2. Miss Bowles .... *Gainsborough*
3. Feeding Her Birds .... *Millet*
4. Hearing .... *Jessie Willcox Smith*
5. Angels' Heads .... *Reynolds*

Grade 2
1. With Grandma .... *MacEwen*
2. Children of the Shell .... *Murillo*
3. Infanta Margarita Theresia .... *Velasquez*
4. Age of Innocence .... *Reynolds*
5. Carnation, Lily, Lily, Rose .... *Sargent*

Grade 3
1. Angel with Lute (Detail) .... *Carpaccio*
2. The Boy Christ in the Temple .... *Hofmann*
3. Boy with Rabbit .... *Raeburn*
4. Pastry Eaters .... *Murillo*
5. The Storage Room .... *Hooch*

Grade 4
1. Aurora .... *Guido Reni*
2. The Holy Night .... *Correggio*
3. Song of the Lark .... *Breton*
4. The Mill .... *Ruisdael*
5. Miraculous Draught of Fishes .... *Vogel*

Grade 5
1. Venetian Waters .... *Tito*
2. The Gleaners .... *Millet*
3. Artist and Daughter .... *Vigee-Lebrun*
4. The Blue Boy .... *Gainsborough*
5. Neapolitan Boy .... *Mancini*

Grade 6 1. The Horse Fair .... *Bonheur*
2. The Vigil .... *Pettie*
3. Icebound .... *Metcalf*
4. The Fog Warning .... *Homer*
5. Christ Washing the Feet of the Disciples .... *Brown*

Grade 7 1. The Angelus .... *Millet*
2. Avenue of Trees .... *Hobbema*
3. The Syndics .... *Rembrandt*
4. The Solemn Pledge .... *Ufer*
5. The Crucifixion .... *Rubens*

Grade 8 1. The Artist's Mother .... *Whistler*
2. Galahad the Deliverer .... *Abbey*
3. The Jester .... *Hals*
4. Dance of the Nymphs .... *Corot*
5. The Last Supper .... *Da Vinci*

All of the pictures listed here may be obtained from Mentzer, Bush & Co., 2210 South Park Way, Chicago or 31 East 10th Street, New York. They are included in their list of SUNRAY PRINTS.†

† Editor's note: These pictures and others were incorporated into a series of art appreciation readers by Mentzer, Bush and Company entitled *Great Pictures and Their Stories.*

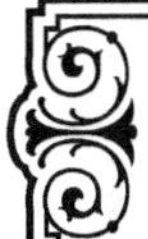

Book One

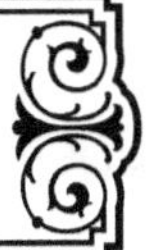

BOOK I—THE COVER

Spiritual Objective: To arouse in children a consciousness of the protective watchfulness of a Guardian Angel, who, suffused with the Light pouring downward from a loving God, keeps close to them while life lasts.

The cross on the open book suggests Catholic education being absorbed by the little girl in grade one, and her big brother in grade eight.

Art Objective: To teach children that the picture or decoration on the cover of a book should tell them something about what is inside the book.

Procedure: Through questioning have children tell what they understand from the picture. "What are the children in the picture seeing in the book? Are they pleased? Does the Angel seem happy to be with the children? Why is the Angel a different color? Why are two angels not shown in the picture?" (The artist was making a decoration for the cover and did not have space for two, so used the large beautiful Angel as a symbol of all guardian angels.)

Teach the following verses:

1—Angel of God my Guardian dear,
To whom God's love commits me here
Ever this day be at my side
To light, to guard, to rule and guide.

2—Guardian Angel, shining and fair,
Close at my side, do you hear my small prayer?
Please take it to Jesus who once was small, too,
And tell Him my love is in all that I do.

BOOK I—END PAPER—THE ARK

Character Objective: Gratitude—Love of God

Spiritual Objective: To associate God's love with His every expression found in Nature.

Art Objective: Training in visualization and memory through learning to cut and draw the animals found in the Ark.

Procedure: Read the verse to the children and have them memorize it. Turn to lining paper at back and have class study and discuss the forms. Demonstrate the drawing of the animals at the blackboard.

Have children develop a graphic vocabulary by drawing them from memory at the blackboard and when form is sufficiently familiar, cut from paper without drawing.

BOOK I—PAGE 1—YOUR PICTURE

Picture Study and Appreciation—*The Madonna of the Chair*, by Raphael

Character Objective: Love of Parents

Spiritual Objective: To teach children that Prayer is thinking about God and talking to Him.

Art Objectives:

1—To develop sensual appreciation of the picture through the human interest expressed by the artist.

2—To develop observation through recognition of colors and related objects in the picture.

Preparation: As a preparation for your teaching, study the picture and analyze its individual appeal to yourself. Is its strongest message that of loving, protective motherhood? Do you find its greatest beauty in the rhythmic lines of the unusual composition, which is one of the world's greatest renderings of beautiful rhythms? Notice how easily the eye travels from the veil of our Blessed Mother to the red stripe of the shawl, down the sleeve to the fold of the Infant's dress, thence along the leg until caught by the lovely curve of the blue skirt and around to include the figure of St. John, then back to the center of interest, the faces of Mary and her Son. Notice how many minor rhythms are found in the beautiful curves of the Baby's body and elsewhere.

Do you find its greatest beauty in the loveliness of its color, which remains unsurpassed? The original picture seems to be suffused with a golden light coming from within, through which comes the beautiful red, yellow, blue, orange, green, and violet. Notice that the light colors are near the center of the picture, and emphasize the Center of Interest by contrast with the dark background.

Raphael Santi, the artist, was a great master of both color and composition. He lived in Italy about 1500 and painted beautiful pictures on the walls of the

Stanza or reception room of the Vatican for Pope Leo X. His great love of our Blessed Mother was shown by painting hundreds of beautiful pictures of her.

Legend gives us a reason for the round shape of the picture in the following story: One day Raphael was out in the country and happened to stop at a wayside inn. He saw the wife of the innkeeper with her two beautiful boys sitting by the side of the house and was so struck with their beauty that he asked permission to paint them. Not having canvas, he picked up the top of a wine cask and quickly sketched the group within its circular shape. It is now one of the prized possessions of the Pitti Palace in Florence, where it is placed in a prominent place and is always surrounded by an admiring crowd.

Procedure: Have the children open books and enjoy the picture a few moments before reading the text to them. Primarily, the beauty of the picture should be allowed to make its own appeal. Have the children begin a discussion of the picture. What do they like best? What have they noticed about the Baby? About St. John? Our Blessed Mother? Where are they? What are they looking at? Is it cold? What time is it? What might St. John see if he turned his head? Whose hands are hiding? What colors can be recognized? Have discussion continued as long as children are interested. Questions should be planned to develop **thoughtful** observation and **individual** answers.

Lesson 2: During the Christmas season, after children have had sufficient practice with scissors, cut picture, leaving a little margin outside the gray. Do not cut off title. Mount on heavy construction paper 9 x 12 about the tone of the background. Have margins widest at bottom, slightly narrower at top and narrowest at sides. Review previous lesson to test color knowledge. If picture is placed on a calendar, cover the date pad with construction paper of the same color as background to make it more harmonious.

For additional picture study, see page xxx.

CORRELATED WORK

Number Work: Count hands, fingers, pairs of hands, feet, heads, eyes, etc.

Language: Oral reproduction of how Raphael painted the Madonna of the Chair.

Word Study: Selected words from text or discussion. Each new reference to the picture helps it to become an integral part of the child's thought content.

BOOK I, PAGE 3—YOUR NAME

Character Objective: Reverence

Spiritual Objective: To have children acquire a knowledge of the significance of the Cross and recognize it as a symbol of Christianity. This will be developed while teaching children to make the Sign of the Cross. They should understand that when making the Sign of the Cross they are asking God in a very intimate way to listen to what they are going to tell Him.

Art Objective Lesson 1: To have children acquire muscular coordination through learning to cut on a line.

Supplies: Scissors, old newspapers, lined paper, Cross

Procedure: Have children place thumb and second finger in scissors holes and then give an animated quick drill in the air, to show imaginary cutting. This helps to strengthen the muscles of the fingers. Try keeping the scissors on the track by cutting column lines on old newspapers. Cut columns or ruled paper into narrow strips. Place strips to form Cross. Place cross bar above middle. Observe real Cross again and make changes where necessary. Follow Cross suggestions, by free placing for fences, houses, chairs, etc. Note carefully different ability levels, while distributing words of praise for each new form created.

The result of the lesson should show that the children have learned the technique of cutting and the use of line in building forms through placing strips of paper.

Spiritual Objective Lesson 2: To give children a knowledge of the Sacrament of Baptism which has made them children of God.

Read the first part of the text relating to the Sacrament, to the children, and elaborate on the religious ceremony as outlined in the *Course in Religion.* Read the second part of the text and try to have the children recognize the symbol of Baptism as the fish. Ask them to look for this symbol around the Baptismal Font in the church.

Art Objective Lesson 2:

1—Visual training by cutting fish without drawing.

2—Development of good judgment in placing arms of cross and the making of a simple booklet.

Supplies: Goldfish bowl (if possible), scissors, construction paper, thin paper, paste

Procedure: If possible have a bowl of goldfish in the room so that children may become familiar with their form and beauty. Questions should be planned to direct observation to widest parts, narrowest parts, etc. Demonstrate to class how fish may be cut without folding the paper. Select best fish to paste in book. Finish book as shown in text and add name.

Related Lessons: Bowl of Fish: Cut bowl shape as shown for page 5, from 6 x 9 construction paper. Paste thin paper over the opening left, to make a transparency. Cut, color, and paste fish in place to make a fish bowl. Ask children to find pictures of bowls to paste on the blank page, to make them familiar with many forms, as well as to accentuate their visualization when at home.

The pasting of the cut-out pictures related to textbook lessons should always be considered as an excellent opportunity for a lesson in arrangement and should be treated as a regular lesson.

BOOK I, PAGE 5—FRUIT

Character Objective: Courtesy

Spiritual Objectives:

1—To cause children to associate God's love and care for them, with the gifts nature produces for them.

2—God's plan of distribution through the year.

3—A simple form of Grace may be taught.

Art Objective Lesson 1: Visual training through comparisons and cutting fruit shapes.

Supplies: Scissors, construction paper, paste

Procedure: Direct discussion and questions to develop observation of form and colors, of like and unlike fruits, points of similarity, etc. Have children look carefully at model to be cut. Close eyes to see whether they can still "see" the model, then after looking again, cut model from paper without drawing. When finished, hold shape beside model to see whether it looks like original. Finish this lesson with a game as proposed in the text and then place cuttings in envelope until next lesson.

Art Objective Lesson 2: To direct attention to pleasing shapes of containers at home and in pictures, and to create a pleasing arrangement of fruit in a bowl.

Supplies: paint or crayons, construction paper, gray bogus paper, paste, scissors

Procedure: Observe bowl shapes collected and pasted on page 5. Decide, through questioning, what type of dish is suitable for fruit. Through questions develop different kinds of decoration a bowl may have. If colored construction paper is used for cutting bowl shape, have children select colors for bowl and decorative bands. Bands may be trimmed to correct size after being pasted. Paste fruit to bowl and then paste to gray bogus paper as a background. Additional creative work may be done through making a community harvest poster with large baskets of fruit, also large community borders with fruit repeats.

With paint or crayon make pictures of real fruits.

Ask children to find colored fruits to paste on blank page, thereby making the book of double value.

BOOK I, PAGE 7—TREES

Character Objective: Gratitude

Spiritual Objective: To help children to appreciate God's love for them through associating with it His gift of trees combining beauty with usefulness.

If the theme of Creation is being pursued, the creation of plant life will probably precede this lesson. Have children discuss the many uses of trees. Direct attention to the beauty of some neighborhood tree now changing its color. Children may show their gratitude by caring for all growing things.

Art Objective: To teach the structure, shape, and color of trees, bare and in full foliage. The addition of trees to their vocabulary, necessary for illustration.

Supplies: crayons, white chalk, gray bogus paper

Procedure: The text clearly shows the method of making the bare tree with black or brown crayon, on gray bogus paper. Later in the season it may be repeated if the locality is in a snow area, with the addition of white chalk used on the **upper** side of the branches and on the ground. Notice how much bare trunk is to be seen **below** the branches.

Lesson 2: Study the shape of the leaf and note similarity to tree shape. Hold yellow crayon like chalk and make shape with short vertical strokes like the picture. To show the sunny side of the tree add green strokes over the yellow strokes. To show the shady side of the tree add blue strokes over yellow strokes. To make the grassy ground under the tree make short scribbling lines.

BOOK I, PAGE 9—COLOR

Character Objectives: Responsiveness to Beauty—Purity

Spiritual Objective:

1—To cause children to associate God's love with recognition of color wherever it may be found, through knowledge of its source in His creation of light.

2—To impress on childish minds that the reason for thinking only pure beautiful thoughts, is to keep their souls bright and beautiful for God.

Art Objective:

1—To teach children the true source of color.

2—To teach the recognition of the three primary colors, red, yellow, and blue.

3—To teach recognition of the binary colors, orange, green, and purple, through their experience in combining any two of the primaries.

4—To teach the spectrum as found in the rainbow.

5—To develop in children a responsiveness to color in nature and elsewhere.

Supplies: Glass prism, construction paper, crayons, scissors, paste

Procedure: Each objective should be considered as one complete lesson.

Read the text and use large sheets of colored paper if possible to demonstrate the primary colors. Have children find them on the color page.

Having aroused sufficient curiosity about "the sunbeam's secret," place a glass prism in the sunlight and show the sunbeam passing through and being broken up into the three beautiful colors, red, yellow, and blue, which form a band on the floor. Where red overlaps yellow, the orange is formed, where yellow overlaps blue, the green is formed, and where blue overlaps red, the violet band is formed. Many devices may be formulated to develop recognition of **colors,** but one very effective way is to make large **classroom color charts,** about

22 x 28. A **yellow** chart might receive special attention on the bright sunny days through the year. Children should bring for the chart anything they can find that is yellow—paper, strings, flowers, etc. It will be interesting to note that children will often recognize a color where adult eyes have missed it. There is an additional value in the training children receive in independent research. To carry out the sequence of color charts, a **red chart** may be made during the **Christmas season,** since red is the symbol of love; **blue** may be saved for **cold** days; **green** in the **Spring; orange** in the **Autumn; purple** on **gray days** or during the **Lenten** season.

Color appreciation may be developed by encouraging children to observe beautiful color in nature as well as in the works of man. The color page is to be used as source material for all color lessons in the book.

Suggested Additional Lessons:

1—Cut and paste colored circles for balloons.

2—Cut and paste colored lanterns, add black bands, top and bottom.

BOOK I, PAGE 11—YOUR LETTERS

Character Objective: Accuracy

Spiritual Objective: To cause children to associate letters with their use in messages about God's love.

Art Objective: Development of ability to visualize form, and to correct errors in coordination.

Supplies: 6 x 9 paper, scissors

Procedure: Read the text for the children. Demonstrate folding 6 x 9 paper for letter strips, by folding long edges together and creasing with **fingernail.** Cut or tear on crease. Fold short edges together, then crease and fold again. Cut on folds as shown on picture, to make letter blocks of uniform size. Make all cuts on **inside** of block. When smaller letters are desired have children fold for narrower strips.

Teach as the first group of letters L C D O U, as all cuts used are repetitions. Demonstrate L as "level" cut, "vertical" cut (if vertical has become part of their vocabulary with its meaning of up and down like the wall, and "level" like the floor).

Demonstrate C: "Hold letter block vertical. Level cut at top; level cut at bottom; vertical cut **inside."** Demonstrate U: "Fold long edges together; crease, hold **closed,** (fingers on edges). Repeat the cuts for L."

Demonstrate O: Repeat fold for U and hold **closed;** repeat cuts for C; open; result is O. O is changed to D by clipping upper and lower **right** corners.

Demonstrate T: Repeat the fold for U; hold **open** (fingers on crease, edges free) and repeat cuts for L.

Teach related groups of letters as separate lessons:

(1) L C O D G U J I

(2) E F S T H

(3) P B Q

Combinations of letters may be made to form words related to other activities.

Use letter blocks for demonstration work twice as large as those used by children, but be sure to have them the same **proportion**.

BOOK I, PAGE 13—YOUR CHURCH

Character Objective: Reverence

Spiritual Objective: To develop a spirit of reverence for all things related to the worship of God.

Art Objectives:

1—To have children acquire control of materials through facility in folding, cutting, and pasting.

2—To develop a consciousness of local architecture through collecting pictures of houses to be pasted on the blank page.

3—To develop a vocabulary for illustration.

Supplies: Construction paper, paste

Procedure: Read the text as a basis for discussion.

Follow steps in construction shown in the picture. Be sure to show a finished model before attempting to teach it, as the finished model is always an added incentive to good work. Pay special attention to the correct technique of pasting to be learned by children. Apply paste evenly with third finger to develop these muscles. An advantage in doing this is that the thumb and two fingers are kept clean for folding. Children acquire clean and orderly habits of work, as easily as careless and slipshod habits. Either type will carry over into other life activities.

Church and trees when finished may be used on a sand table or fastened to a stiff paper base to be taken home.

BOOK I, PAGE 15—YOUR FRIENDS

Character Objectives: Punctuality—Care of Health

Spiritual Objective: To teach children that God watches over all our activities, makes possible our play or our work, makes it possible for our bodies to do many things. Develop health rules. To show our thankfulness to God, we visit our Lord in Church. Discuss attendance at Mass and the necessity of being punctual.

Art Objective:

1—To enrich the graphic vocabulary through the addition of figures, houses, animals.

2—To develop imagination and observation through illustration.

Supplies: Pictures of figures and street scenes, blank paper, paste, scissors

Procedure: Read and discuss the text while children refer to the illustration. Demonstrate figures marching in single file in twos and threes, calling attention to bending places in body, arms, and legs. Always finish the line figures in mass.

Have children bring to school pictures showing figures and street scenes. These are to be well arranged on blank page and pasted neatly to enrich vocabulary and for reference for future illustrations.

Notice how simply the street and houses are shown. Distance is shown by making things smaller and placing them higher on the paper.

Show children how pictures are made, then aim to have them show individual differences. Do not have illustrations copied or the object of the lesson is lost.

Observe the following points in teaching illustration:

1—Objects in good proportion.

2—Houses, trees, animals, and people placed back in picture between the horizon and lower edge of the paper and not on a line.

3—Roads lighter than grass.

4—Water reflects the sky color.

5—Back of tall trees and houses the sky is visible. (Comes down.)

6—The beveled side of the crayon should be used.

7—Build up the vocabulary of the children, very carefully, for each new illustration.

8—Be careful of giving too much help.

9—Select stories full of interest.

10—Encourage the poorest efforts by finding something good.

The teacher should practice demonstration drawing on the blackboard as much as possible.

BOOK I, PAGE 17—FOR BABY JESUS

Character Objective: Sympathy and Generosity (applied to classroom situations, as sharing candy, etc.)

Spiritual Objective: To develop in children an intimate or personal desire to please God.

Art Objectives:

1—To develop accuracy in following directions and efficiency in cutting and pasting.

2—To increase art vocabulary as well as develop keen visualization.

Supplies: Pictures of barns/stables, 9-inch square or 9 x 12 oblong piece of gray bogus paper, scissors, cut-outs of crib, strips of paper (for straw), toy animal, chalk and blackboard (optional)

Procedure: Tell or review the story of Bethlehem. Show many pictures of barns, stables, etc., until children understand the meaning of a stable. Show and discuss pictures of ancient stables like that in which Christ was born. Show completed model given on page 17. This problem may also be made in booklet form, using model of booklet on page 3. Paste simple cut-out of crib on one page with strips of paper for straw on opposite page. Follow the suggestion given in text for filling the Crib.

Fold either a 9-inch square of gray bogus paper or a 9 x 12 oblong to make two edges meet evenly. Crease with thumb-nail. Open and fold right edge to center, crease, and fold again. Fold left edge to center and fold again. Fold upper and lower edges to meet at crease. Open and fold upper and lower edges to center and crease.

Have children cut out upper corners first, then half of the remaining squares on top row. Make remaining cuts as directed on page 17. While directing cutting, be careful to keep paper in same position, otherwise children will become confused. When model is finished, pinch the center crease at front to shape the roof. Have children make variations of this form for other problems.

Lesson 2: Use toy animal for observation. Make a quick sketch of animal at blackboard and then quickly erase. Have children dictate repetition of picture from memory. Erase again and have children go to blackboard to draw from memory, while class criticises errors. Follow with variations of position, grouping, etc. Illustrate story of Bo-Peep and other sheep stories.

BOOK I, PAGE 19—MORE LETTERS

The objectives and procedure for this page will be the same as **page 11.**

When demonstrating, have work large enough to be sure processes may be seen from all parts of the classroom.

Be sure that children understand that folded paper for letters should be held **open** for letters such as Y and **closed** for letters such as M.

Make every lesson a thinking lesson to develop carefulness.

BOOK I, PAGE 21—THE FIRST JOURNEY

Character Objective: Protectiveness

Spiritual Objective: To develop in children a reverence and love for the Divine Infant and because of Him, kindness to all helpless things, following the example of St. Joseph.

Art Objectives:

1—Adding to graphic vocabulary the representation of action in figures and animals.

2—Strengthening keen visualization through paper cutting.

Supplies: Magazines for picture cutting, chalk and blackboard (optional), scissors, paste, crayons, white or black paper, gray bogus paper, colored paper

Procedure: Tell the story of the Flight Into Egypt, placing the emphasis on the flight rather than on the cause of it. Lead children to imagine, through discussion, what could happen on the way—resting, walking, eating, sleeping, meeting other persons. Show pictures of the country, trees, etc.

See how many different pictures of the trip may be planned. Have children draw donkey on blackboard until they are familiar with the form, as shown in book, reversed, and in different positions, from other pictures collected to be pasted on the blank page.

Cut the donkey and the Blessed Virgin separately, and then paste. Later try cutting both together. Add halos with white or orange crayon. Use either white or black paper for cutting, and paste to gray bogus paper for background. Colored paper may be used if desired. Do not have children draw the picture they intend to cut before cutting, or purpose of lesson is defeated.

Lesson 2: Treat the vocabulary problem of the figures as before. Always finish the figures in solid mass. Never leave them in skeleton form or line.

Finish lesson on figures by putting them into illustration of familiar stories, or illustrations of daily activities of the children.

Lesson 3: Have children carefully arrange magazine cut-outs of horses and people, on the blank page, placing largest pictures on lower part. Tip edges with a tiny bit of paste, cover with piece of scratch paper and rub hand firmly over surface.

BOOK I, PAGE 23—WHERE JESUS LIVED

Character Objective: Helpfulness

Spiritual Objective: To develop in children an intimate love for our Blessed Mother and a desire to please her through work well done, especially helping parents.

Art Objective: To develop a sense of proportion and to stimulate creative work at home, through making strong paper construction possible without the use of paste.

Supplies: Hatbox, scissors, cardboard or construction paper

Procedure: Model should be made before lesson in order that each step in its construction may become familiar to the teacher.

Discuss homes; what furniture is necessary; how windows are dressed; added beauty given by placing of flowers. Compare modern homes with the kind of home lived in by the Holy Family. Jesus helped His Mother as well as His father.

Where are priedieus† always used?

After book model has been made, children should begin invention of entirely new models based on the double oblongs, as chair, bench, cupboard, table, chest, etc.

Make a community house for the class by using a hatbox. Only the best things may be used in the house. Have windows cut in the box. The arrangement of the windows may be made a separate lesson.

BOOK I, PAGE 25—ANOTHER PARTY

Character Objectives: Courtesy and Politeness

Spiritual Objective: To acquaint the child with God's great plan of Creation, which is the theme for the year.

Art Objective: To develop visualization of form through modeling.

Supplies: Clay, cardboard, newspapers or bogus paper, water

Procedure: When the clay has been wedged into a loaf about 12 x 4 x 4. cut slices about ½ inch thick. Use pieces of cardboard for trays when passing clay. Ask children to bring newspapers to cover desks if large sheets of bogus paper cannot be procured. Make a bird's nest by rolling a small piece of clay into a ball. Push thumb into center and press out the sides to make the shape. The cup and saucer are made the same way. Follow this with the bird as shown in the book.

Rub places of joining together until joining cannot be seen. Teach children to pick up crumbs of clay by using a larger lump of clay to do so. To flatten rounded shapes, touch the clay gently to the desk and press instead of pounding noisily. Read notes on care of clay in this manual (page xx).

† Editor's note: A prie-dieu (French, meaning 'pray [to] God') is more than just a kneeler, as it has a stand attached in front to hold prayer books or breviaries. Prie-dieus were traditionally intended for private devotional use, but may also be found in churches.

BOOK I, PAGE 27—CAN YOU DO THIS?

Character Objectives: Fair Play and Orderliness

Spiritual Objective: To help children to appreciate God's wonderful gift of sight as another reason for loving Him.

Art Objective Lesson 1: To develop acute visualization through quick comparisons of changed positions.

Supplies: Chalk and blackboard (optional), pegs, colored paper, crayons, paper towel, gray bogus paper, handkerchief or muslin, iron

Procedure: The teacher should practice quick sketches on the blackboard of the model in many different positions. Accuracy in drawing is not essential, as children are not critical, and sketch remains on the board only a moment. Aim to show a difference between a **wide top** and a **narrow bottom.** Continue the lesson as the game suggested in the text.

Art Objective Lesson 2: To introduce the principles of orderly **Repetition** and **Alternation** in Design.

Procedure: Using pegs or small pieces of colored paper, have children arrange them on desks to show their marching order. Single file, in twos, in threes, showing Repetition; boy and girl (contrasting shapes as oblong and square) to show Alternation. Have them invent new arrangements showing both these principles. Children must understand that arrangements must be **orderly.**

1—As a follow-up lesson on "Seeing" lesson, have children cut basket shape from memory, using colored or gray bogus paper. Decorate it with crayon by making an original border arrangement.

2—Fringe two ends of paper towel; decorate with crayon border.

3—Fold a square handkerchief and decorate with crayon border. (If put on muslin, color may be made permanent by pressing with hot iron.)

4—Curtains may be made for community playhouse from either paper or muslin and borders added.

BOOK I, PAGE 29—YOUR VALENTINE

Character Objectives: Thoughtfulness, Love of Parents—Patriotism

Spiritual Objective: To cause children to feel a more intimate relationship with God's love, through a knowledge of the human love exercised by His Saints because of Him.

Art Objective Lesson 1: To make an original arrangement of letters and hearts to show a well-proportioned valentine.

Supplies: Scissors, colored paper, paste, chalk and blackboard (optional), safety pins (for badges), crayons

Procedure: Tell the story of St. Valentine and how valentines originated when the good Saint sent messages from his prison cell to his followers at home. They were called "Valentine's messages of loving thoughtfulness."

In what other ways may children show their love for parents besides sending valentines?

Teach cutting of hearts as shown in the picture. Get different proportions by changing sizes of paper. Children should suggest what words are to be used in the message.

Teacher should plan size of letter strips and have children fold for number of letters needed in the proposed message. Have as many variations of the model in the book as possible, such as small heart borders, top and bottom, showing either repetition or alternation. Have children suggest many reasons why they should let their parents know how much they love them.

Art Objective Lesson 2:

1—To make a badge of the national colors, cutting and pasting harmonious shapes.

2—To teach the symbolism of the colors.

Procedure: Carry out the problem on February 12th or February 22nd to increase the interest in the teaching of patriotism.

Tell children why we honor our national colors and what each color tells us. White for purity, red for love and sacrifice; blue for truth and loyalty.

Sketch geometric shapes on blackboard—circles, squares, and oblongs. Teach children to put similar shapes of each color together to form badge arrangement. Badges are to be worn home from school.

This lesson may be reviewed on Feast days of our Blessed Mother by making badges of blue and white.

BOOK I, PAGE 31—THE LITTLE FISHES

Character Objective: Obedience

Spiritual Objective: To develop in children Faith and Trust in God.

Art Objective Lesson 1: Efficiency in planning and fitting together the parts of a basket to be made without pasting.

Supplies: Pictures of baskets of other objects, paste, scissors, paper, crayons

Procedure: Tell the Parable of the Fishes. Recall the lesson on furniture. Test memory by calling for a voluntary demonstration of making the double square. Fold the sides of the basket in half, to make inserted part strong enough to support the weight. Cut loaves and fishes to fill the basket. Enthuse over initiative shown, when new models, made at home, are shown to you. Children should be urged to make things at home, since no paste is needed.

Ask children to find pictures of baskets or other objects possible to construct through the use of the double oblong or double square. Paste these pictures on the blank page as a special lesson in arrangement.

Art Objective Lesson 2: To develop imagination and visualization through illustration.

Procedure: This lesson may be carried out either through paper cutting or crayon. If paper cutting is medium used, have children cut boat and figures separately. The illustration may be made without the figures, using the boats filled with fish. The illustration using figures is easily made with crayon, as they are built upon the action lines.

If the illustration is placed in a booklet, a repetition of fish may be used as a border, or an alternation of fish and bubbles.

Illustrate other parables or events in the life of Christ.

BOOK I, PAGE 33—THE DELUGE

Character Objective: Kindness

Spiritual Objective: Appreciation of God's great plan of Creation. His thoughtfulness for man's comfort through His creation of animal life.

Art Objective: Development of visualization through directing the child's attention to the similarity of shapes between the simplest form of the animal being studied and some other familiar shape, as oblong or square.

Supplies: Paper, scissors, paste, blank paper

Procedure: Have children give their impressions of the story of Creation if it has been told previously. Show how God prepared the earth to care for the animals before He created them. Dwell on His care and thoughtfulness for all dumb beasts. Be sure to give children paper for cutting, having the same proportions shown by the animal to be cut. Follow the steps shown in the picture, for the camel. Then try the cutting of other animals in the same manner. Ask children to bring to school pictures of animals, to be pasted on the blank page as models for other cuttings. Later have children repeat from memory.

Tell the story of Noe and have children turn to back cover to discuss the animals found there. Tell the nature myth, "Why every dog has a cold nose." While Noe was collecting all the animals in the Ark, he was helped by his faithful dog until all were inside. When the dog finally got on the Ark himself, he had to stand with his nose out in the rain during all the days of the Deluge. Ever since, all dogs have had cold noses to remind people of their faithfulness. Although children are quick to discriminate between nature myths and nature facts, the teacher should be careful to make it clear that nature myths are stories told to help fix animal characteristics. When children have learned to cut many animals, an interesting project is that of a classroom frieze showing a circus parade.

BOOK I, PAGE 35—YOUR BOOK

Character Objectives: Reverence and Attention

Spiritual Objective: An introduction to the meaning of the Mass through a knowledge of the office of the Chalice as well as to develop in children a reverence for all church ceremonies.

Art Objective: The planning and making of a strong booklet which may be varied in size for other school lessons.

Supplies: Scissors, colored paper, pencil, cord or string

Procedure: Read the text as a basis for discussion of the Mass. Emphasize the Consecration and Holy Communion in order to leave a clear-cut impression on childish minds. Emphasis on other parts of the Mass may be allowed to wait a little longer. Talk about the shape of the Chalice. The broad base protects it from overturning. The wide-mouthed bowl allows easy access for the fingers of the priest. The thick roll on the stem enables the priest to hold it firmly when he lifts it. Get responses from the class as to why the inside of the Chalice must be gold. Follow directions for cutting the shape of the Chalice. Follow directions for making the booklet. Make holes in cover as indicated by placing pencil dots about same distance from edges. Then place left finger under paper and gently bore hole with pencil. This prevents tearing. All inside double pages are placed, **one at a time,** under the holes just made as markers, and the new holes made as before. Several thicknesses of paper would prove too thick for the pencil point.

Tie booklet with cord, using the pencil to push cord through the holes. Tie cord on the outside in a double knot before attempting a bowknot.

BOOK I, PAGE 37—THE HOLY GHOST

Character Objective: Understanding

Spiritual Objective: To help children to appreciate the beautiful significance of each Person of the Blessed Trinity and to prepare the child's reasoning powers to combat future doubts.

Art Objective Lesson 1: To enrich the graphic vocabulary through memory training of the visualized form of the dove.

Supplies: Chalk and blackboard (optional), prism, scissors, paper, posterboard

Procedure Lesson 1: Follow the steps given in the textbook, then have children work quickly at the blackboard without books. Change shape to other bird forms by lengthening tail and legs. Have children collect pictures of birds in color to be pasted on the blank page.

Art Objective Lesson 2 and 3:

1—To teach symbolism of colors.

2—To train perception in arrangement of a decorative poster for Pentecost and visual coordination through paper cutting.

Procedure Lesson 2: Read the text and demonstrate the color change of one into three by placing a glass prism (three-sided piece) in the sunshine. The age and ability of the children must determine how much detail should be put into the religious aspect of this lesson. Tell them the symbolic meaning of the three colors red, yellow, and blue which can be seen coming through the prism. Red symbolizes love and speaks to them of God the Son Who is the essence of love; yellow symbolizes light, which helps them to see and know things clearly and speaks to them of God the Holy Ghost, the fount of light and understanding; blue symbolizes truth, and the Infinite, and speaks to them of God the Father, Who always was and always will be. Because of their meaning, the primary colors red, yellow, and blue should be associated in the child's mind with the Three Persons of the Blessed Trinity, and the great love God showered on the world when He sent these three colors into the world to beautify it.

Procedure Lesson 3—A poster for Pentecost: Demonstrate the cutting of dove, first with folded paper, then not folded, calling attention to the proportions of head, wing, and tail. Notice that the whole shape fills a square. Give a quick exercise in the air with scissors, getting action with a rhythmic drill of "open," "close." Errors in using scissors are quickly detected. When children have finished cutting doves, review the principles of Repetition and Alternation before they plan borders for their posters. A Community Poster involving the cutting of birds and letters, may be finished at one lesson, if some rows cut letters, while others cut birds. The arrangement then becomes a general class lesson. When this plan is followed it is well to permit children to use free time to make a small individual poster or booklet about Pentecost, to take home. Many problems are planned as a means of projecting religious truths into the home, where children can make the most effective appeal and become little missionaries.

BOOK I, PAGE 39—GOD'S RAINBOW

Character Objective: Obedience

Spiritual Objective: To develop in children a loving trust in God, through causing them to associate with the rainbow the story of God's reward of Noe's trustfulness.

Art Objective: To arouse in children an appreciative response to color as found in nature.

Supplies: Inside cover page, crayon, cut paper

Procedure: Tell the story of Noe; God's command to build the Ark; Noe's unquestioned obedience and how it helped to save so many. Turn to inside cover to illustrate a few of the animals in the Ark. Emphasize Noe's trust during the dark dreary days of the flood. After reading the text, discuss it with the children, turn back to page 9 and find the rainbow colors. With crayon draw the rainbow and finish the picture with a simple landscape of blue sky and green grass. A second lesson, using cut paper as a medium, may be used to illustrate the story of the Deluge. Children will enjoy learning the following stanzas of "Hiawatha":

Hiawatha saw the rainbow
In the Eastern sky the rainbow,
Whispered "What is that, Nokomis?"
And the good Nokomis answered:
"'Tis the heaven of flowers you see there,
All the wild flowers of the forest
All the lilies of the prairie,
When on earth they fade and perish
Blossom in the world above us."

Also:

THE RAINBOW

The sun went out to shine one day
Said he, "I'll drive the rain away."
The raindrops laughed to see him try
To drive them back into the sky.
Each raindrop caught a sunbeam white
And split it into rays of light,
Red, yellow, blue, three rays in one
And made a rainbow just for fun.

BOOK I, PAGE 41—BE CAREFUL

Character Objectives: Carefulness and Judgment

Spiritual Objective: To develop in children a consciousness of a Guardian Angel and of God's love in giving His angels to guard over us.

Art Objective: Development of color sense through (1) recognition of danger signals; (2) directing attention to colors in dress and in nature.

Supplies: Crayon, pictures of automobiles, paste, blank paper

Procedure: Have children read text and discuss the picture. "Which group of children are facing the red light?" "What does the red light tell them to do?" "When the green light tells them it is safe to cross, they must be careful to look both ways, then cross quickly without stopping." "Do children who play on the street show good judgment?" "In what other ways can children help their Guardian Angel to keep them safe?" Discuss safety in traffic in school.

Continue the development of the Guardian Angel theme. Explain why God has given each of us a Guardian Angel to stay with us through life and finally conduct us to heaven. This is another proof of His great love for us.

Turn to page 9 and find the color that is shown in the traffic light as a danger signal. Find the color that tells children it is safe to cross. Find the color that tells the children to wait until they are sure which color is to follow. Children are now ready to color the picture.

Demonstrate how the crayon should be used. It should be held like chalk and used on the beveled side. Keep strokes light and even. No scribbling. Use light tone of orange for flesh tones. Have children aim to keep color tones within the spaces allotted. When brighter color is wanted, press hard with crayon.

Have children decide on colors for costumes of children. When poster is finished, cut out and mount on heavy paper to take home, to hang up.

As a memory lesson, have children make a traffic light showing a red light on one side and a green light on the other.

Ask children to find pictures of automobiles and other vehicles. Arrange nicely on the blank page and paste. Use them to enrich vocabulary for illustration.

Original illustration may be "Coming home from School."

BOOK I, PAGE 43—OUR BLESSED MOTHER

Character Objectives: Reverence—Generosity

Spiritual Objective: To implant in the minds of children loving devotion for our Blessed Mother and a realization of God's generosity to His children.

Art Objective: Cultivation of Good Taste:

1—Fine arrangement of community poster.

2—Development of originality in Constructive Design through planning a flower container for our Lady's altar.

Supplies: Fresh flowers (if possible), colored/white paper, scissors

Procedure Lesson 1: Using a real specimen if possible, discuss flowers or blossoms as to construction, color, shape, etc. Fold small squares of paper, making two folds and cut pattern for flower. Dandelions may be made by fringing small circles and then crumpling. Flowers may be colored with crayon or cut from colored paper. Paste on strips of stiff paper. Containers may be circular or square, and decorated with crayon borders.

May baskets may also be made in this way as a following lesson, using a basket model made on page 31, or by folding and pasting an oblong folded into twelve parts as shown on page 13.

Procedure Lesson 2: Review letter folding and cutting. Have children decide whether name is to go above or below the middle. (If name is placed below, flowers must go higher.) Notice shape and color of tulips or other spring flowers used. As a quick classroom drill with scissors, have children cut strips of green paper with short jagged cuts for grass. Variety of greens will lend interest. Have children plan the placing of the garden. Class should be called on for criticism of grouping as the work progresses.

BOOK 1, PAGE 45 —YOUR CHRISTMAS PLAY

Planned for correlation with:

1. English
2. History
3. Arithmetic
4. Nature Study
5. Expression and word recognition
6. Color and Design
7. Costume
8. Creative development

Character Objectives: Love and Thoughtfulness for Others

Procedure: Early in the month tell the story of Bethlehem, describing its location and people. Use as many pictures as possible.

CORRELATED WORK

1. ENGLISH (vocabulary):
    1. Reproduction of story in easy natural tone and in related sequence.
    2. Correct forms of is, are, was, were, come, came, run, ran, do, did.
    3. Correct any errors common to a particular locality.
2. HISTORY:
    1. Class discussion of different kinds of people (nationalities) living in the neighborhood. How are they different (language, food, dress, etc.)? Lead conversation to story of the people who lived in Judea and describe the home of Mary and Joseph.
    2. Why were they in Bethlehem?
    3. Compare that hilly country with local features as to similarity or difference.
3. ARITHMETIC:
    1. Counting persons in the picture. Adding and subtracting as curtain hides some from view.
    2. Similar problems about books, letters, sheep, etc.
4. NATURE STUDY—Sheep:
    1. Size. Compare with dog.

2. Coat. Compare with dog.
3. Discuss what is done with wool—when it is necessary for clothing. What other uses has it? How do sheep live? Who takes care of them? What are the baby sheep called? Are sheep wild animals? How do we know?

5. EXPRESSION AND WORD RECOGNITION:

Begin teaching lines for angels after initial letters have been cut the proper size. Aim for clear enunciation and correct pronunciation, the sentence sense, and easy, free expression.

6-7. COSTUME AND COLOR STUDY: Suggested Questions.

1. What do you know about Bo-Peep? Boy Blue? (They are story book people. They played they were minding the sheep in a story book.)
2. Why do they wear large hats? (Protection.)
3. Why does Bo-Peep have a crook? Should her clothing be woolen? What color will be best for the angels? Why?
4. What color should be used for our Blessed Mother's veil?
5. Show picture of our Blessed Mother and have children note difference between the costume of that time and the present time.

8. CREATIVE DEVELOPMENT:

Have children illustrate different phases of their story about the play with crayon, cut paper, and clay. Have them decide what books they wish to use in the stage setting with appropriate decorations. **Have children plan their own dialogue instead of memorizing it.** Cut letters for angels. Cut crowns for angels. Plan decoration and names for books to be used on stage. Make costumes for characters.

BOOK I, PAGE 47— "THE DREAM," A CHRISTMAS PLAY

Character Objectives: Carefulness, Neatness and Orderliness

Spiritual Objective: To instill in children love for The Divine Infant. Art Objective: Development of judgment and skills in planning and making the necessary accessories needed for the play.

Supplies: Large sheets of paper, curtains, two books or two mounting boards, wire

STAGE DIRECTIONS FOR DRAMA

Location: The corner of a room next to the robery if possible is usually a convenient place to suspend a curtain. Old portieres or faded cretonne curtains when dyed make excellent stage curtains.

Fasten large sheets of paper to wall to represent books. Arrange Nativity group far enough in front to allow angels to take proper places behind them. Suspend curtain across stage to conceal them until the proper time. If curtain is not heavy material it may be suspended between two chart stands.

Inside the curtain, fasten two books to wire supporting curtain, or two mounting boards (22 x 28) may be used as book covers to stand on floor. These are sufficiently large to conceal a first grade pupil. Classroom lesson chart stands make excellent stage accessories when covered. Boy Blue and Bo-Peep are concealed behind these books. A loose end of the curtain may be pinned over them.

Little girl walks on stage outside curtain and sits down on floor in center. She talks to her mother, off stage, about Christmas, (e. g., preparations being made at home, in school, at church, helping the poor, etc.) Mother asks her about the gifts she has just wrapped up and warns her about her carelessness in not clearing things up. She falls asleep. Curtains are moved enough to show books of Boy Blue and Bo-Peep. They step from behind the books and free dialogue suggested in book follows.

During the conversation the first angel crosses the stage and stops in center to repeat line and disappears behind curtain. After the last angel has passed behind the curtain, the curtains are pulled aside, showing setting as in book.

The little girl rubs her eyes while Boy Blue and Bo-Peep repeat the memory verses from Course in Christian Doctrine.

Between verses the angels, accompanied by the whole room, may sing the Christmas Carols selected by the teacher with a finale of "Holy Night."

For variety, other familiar story book children may be used. They need not be limited to two characters. However, in order to keep the center of interest on the Nativity, care must be exercised in selection.

A CHRISTMAS PLAY, "THE DREAM"

Lines to Be Memorized by Characters

Angels: (Crossing front of stage in front of curtain before manger is visible):

C is for cold in the stable so dim.
H is for home which the oxen gave Him.
R is for road into Bethlehem town.
I is for the Infant Who from heaven came down.
S is for shepherds who came to adore.
T for Time told by Prophets before.
M is for Mary who held Jesus small.
A is for angels who came at His call.
S is for songs of praise all heaven raised,
For this tiny Babe was the great God they praised!

WHAT LOVELY INFANT CAN THIS BE?

Boy Blue and Bo-Peep after the manger is uncovered:

Bo-Peep: "What lovely Infant can This be
That in the little crib I see?"
Boy Blue: "So sweetly on the straw It lies
It must have come from Paradise."
Bo-Peep: "Who is that Lady kneeling by
And gazing down so tenderly?"
Boy Blue: "Oh, that is Mary ever blest
How full of joy her holy breast."
Bo-Peep: "What man is that who seems to smile
And looks so blissful all the while?"
Boy Blue: "'Tis holy Joseph, good and true
The Infant makes him happy, too."
Bo-Peep: "What makes the crib so bright and clear
What voices sing so sweetly here?"
Boy Blue: "Ah, they are baby angels sweet
Who came from heaven their King to greet."

Bo-Peep: "Who are those people kneeling down
With crooked sticks and hands so brown?"
Boy Blue: "The shepherds from the mountain top,
The little angels woke them up."
Bo-Peep: "Hail holy cave tho' dark thou be
The world is lighted up from thee."
Boy Blue: "Hail Holy Babe! Creation stands
And moves upon Thy little hands."

(*Course of Christian Doctrine, Dolphine Press, Philadelphia, Grade 1, Page 53*)

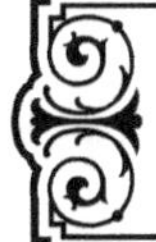

Book Two

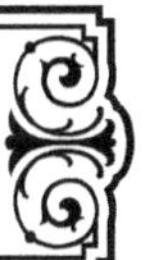

BOOK II—COVER

See page 3 of this manual.

END PAPER: FIRST COMMUNION

Character Objective: Purity

Spiritual Objective: To develop in children a desire for a close intimacy with Jesus in the Blessed Sacrament.

Art Objective: To develop observation through costume study of the children of many lands.

Supplies: Student Book Two, scissors, paper

Procedure: Have children memorize the poem and understand its meaning.

Turn to the end paper at the back of the book to study the many costumes found there. Have children practice figures at the blackboard in order to enlarge their vocabulary for illustrations. Figures may be developed as they are needed for stories about children of other lands.

The little American children symbolize love and friendship as opposed to quarreling.

Have children compare the costumes to discover similarities and striking differences. After forms have become familiar have children cut paper dolls and add costumes to suit. End papers throughout the series have been planned for blackboard use in building a graphic vocabulary.

BOOK II, PAGE 1—INFANT SAMUEL

Character Objective: Reverence (Courtesy to God)

Spiritual Objective: To develop in children a realization of God's love for them in providing them with loving parents. This gives a concrete reason for their gratitude.

Art Objective:

1—To develop imagination as an aid in picture appreciation.

2—To develop observation through recognition of colors and related objects in the picture.

Teacher's Preparation: Before the lesson, study the picture and analyze the individual appeal the picture may have for you.

Do you find its strongest appeal in a message of the sweet seriousness of childhood which the artist, Sir Joshua Reynolds, so loved to portray in his pictures?

Are your senses captured by the golden tones of its rich color harmonies of such mystifying depth? The artist was a great experimentalist in the field of color. He labored incessantly to reproduce the sensuous colors of the early Venetian painters, by laying as many as nine colors, one over the other.

Notice how the artist has kept the attention centered on the boy's face: the hands lead up to it; the rays of light coming from the upper left corner slant toward it; the dark crease in the material on the chair leads to it; the dark lines of the hair curve around it; and the face holds the message of the picture.

Notice how the two light spots on the left are balanced by the large light panel on the right. This is another means of keeping the attention directed to the boy.

The Artist, Sir Joshua Reynolds, was one of the founders of the English School of painting in the 18th century. He specialized in fashionable portrait painting, but is best beloved for his exquisite renderings of children, among which are "Angels Heads," "Age of Innocence," "Miss Bowles," and "The Strawberry Girl."

Supplies: Scissors, neutral brown or any other neutral paper

Procedure: Have children open the book and enjoy the picture for a few minutes undisturbed. The beauty of the picture should always be permitted to make its own appeal.

Read the text to open the discussion of the picture. Where is the little boy? What time is it? At what do you think he is looking? From where does the warm light come, which makes the little boy so much brighter than the room? What may cause the light in the upper left corner? Is the little boy poor? Why do we think he is not? Does he seem afraid of the dark? Why not? Is he alone? How do you know?

Call on different pupils to reconstruct the room as it will look when the sun shines next morning. Ask children to imagine the kind of home in which the little boy lives. (Suggested by the bit of furniture shown.) Name the many things that possibly happened during the day, for which he is thanking our Dear Lord.

Emphasize his reverence. Discuss courtesy to people and how shown when speaking to them.

Continue the discussion as long as children are interested. Questions should be planned to develop **thoughtful** observation and **individual** answers.

After the picture study is finished, have children cut the picture about half inch from the binding and put it away for use as a gift at Christmas time, when it should be mounted nicely on a neutral brown or other harmonious paper.

For additional picture study, see page xxx.

CORRELATED WORK

Language: Oral reproduction of imaginary story of the boy.

Word Study: Recognition of selected words from text or discussion. Religion: Prayer—in its various forms—morning and evening prayers, etc.

History: Something about the far away homes of little English children.

BOOK II, PAGE 3—FALL FLOWERS

Character Objective: Understanding

Spiritual Objective: To help children to understand a little of God's great plan of the Universe in the reproduction of plant life with a resulting reaction on the part of child, of love and appreciation for God's unending care for His children.

Art Objective:

1—To visualize shape of mass and note characteristic structure of seed pod.

2—To gain experience in technique of surface rendering through the use of crayon.

Supplies: Bogus paper, black crayon, white chalk, real plant model (if possible)

Procedure: Pass gray bogus paper of suitable proportions, black crayola, and white chalk. Using real plant as model, have children observe its structure and freely discuss their individual discoveries while observing it.

After discussion of real model has been carried far enough, place it on a strip of paper harmonizing in shape, to make a pleasing composition. Have children first take a few minutes to practice with chalk and crayon, following procedure shown in plate, to learn the rendering.

Now, with all attention on the real model, note where main masses (pod shapes) are placed on the paper; where divisions of branch may appear, etc. Use the major part of the lesson to direct observation into right channels, allowing children to use only a short period for their actual work. Their results will have more freshness and vitality. Use chalk and crayon very lightly.

Supplies: A Cosmos flower (if possible) or any other fall flower available, paper, crayons

Lesson 2: The procedure for the Cosmos or any other fall flower which may be used, will change only so much as the characteristics of the flowers may vary.

In demonstrating the rendering of the Cosmos petals, make flower center first, then quick strokes from the **outside** toward the center. Heavy pressure at the **beginning** of the stroke, **lifting** the chalk as it approaches the center.

Always give children paper having proportions similar to model. More vitality is given to plant rendering when stems cut the bottom edge of paper, as the impression of continued growth is thus given.

Supplies: 6 x 9 gray bogus or colored construction paper, scissors, pictures of flowers and fall leaves, crayons

Lesson 3: A nature study booklet may be made from 6 x 9 gray bogus or colored construction paper, repeating the model made in Book I.

Fold small squares or oblongs, for practice work in leaf cutting. Select one and proceed as suggested on plate. Always have children try different plans for decorating cover, using lettering, etc.

The work in nature study should be closely correlated with these lessons.

Ask children to find pictures of fall flowers and leaves, to paste on the blank page. All individual research work helps to make undirected observation more acute and enriches art vocabulary.

BOOK II, PAGE 5—LETTERS

Character Objective: Thoughtfulness for Others.

Spiritual Objective: To implant in children a desire to help the souls of the departed because they cannot help themselves.

Picture the wonderful joys planned by God for His children when they return to heaven. The souls in purgatory are like wounded soldiers in a hospital. They have been crippled by the Dragon of Sin. The prayers of the children will help to make the souls perfect again, so that they may gain heaven and see the King of Glory. The natural generosity of childhood will respond voluntarily and an excellent habit will have been started.

Art Objective: Development of keen observation and reasoning powers in the selection from the three types of holding and folding, for various letters as required.

Supplies: Paper, colored or plain; scissors, crayons

Procedure: Before beginning lesson, review method of letter cutting, Book I.

Demonstrate to the class what is meant by cutting without folding. Have them select all such letters. Demonstrate what is meant by folding paper and making cuts on "open" edges ("holding open"). Have children select these letters. Demonstrate what is meant by folding paper and making cuts on the fold ("holding closed").

Cut letters in order of difficulty as shown by plate. Be careful that nothing is cut from **outside** other than corners, in order that **uniform size,** an essential of lettering, may be kept. These letters may be used for community or class posters for many subjects. The decoration should be in keeping with the subject matter of the poster. A Hallowe'en poster might have a border of pumpkins, etc.

BOOK II, PAGE 7—NEW FRIENDS

Character Objective: Friendship and Generosity.

Spiritual Objective: To kindle in children the flame of a missionary spirit, which shall aid them through life in spreading a love of God.

Theme: Develop the suggestion of the loss sustained by the pagan children through not having had knowledge of our kind Heavenly Father and His Blessed Mother. Have them realize how precious are their prayers for the missions, little love messages transmitted through Heaven to their unknown friends.

Art Objective: To teach children to plan a poster for which they have felt a definite need.

Supplies: Posterboard, crayons, colored or plain paper, scissors, paste

Procedure: A poster must advertise something with bold letters which may be quickly read. Have children suggest many slogans. Give practice work on cutting and decorating figures and lanterns.

Do not have children **copy** poster shown on the plate, but aim for an individual arrangement from each child. Posters may be arranged with lanterns, and no children, or with any number of children and no lanterns. Lettering should be very important in any arrangement and may be above or below middle of poster. If colored paper is not available, use crayola to color the paper used, with bright contrasting colors and black.

Find pictures of children to paste on the blank page to be used as models for illustrations and cuttings when making other school posters. Make the pasting of these pages a definite lesson in good arrangement.

BOOK II, PAGE 9—MORE COLOR

Character Objective: Appreciation

Spiritual Objective: To make children sensitive to beautiful color and at the same time cause them to associate it with God's marvelous love for them.

Art Objective:

1—To teach recognition of the tints of Primary and Binary colors.

2—To teach the technique of water color or crayon to produce fresh, clean color as shown in bubbles.

Supplies: Magazines, paste, paint, bubbles, crayons, white paper, pipe

Procedure: Use large sheets of colored paper corresponding to colors on color page. Have rows compete for correct selections to correspond to colors called for on color page.

Have children find colors in magazine illustrations to correspond to colors on color page. Have these neatly pasted on blank page.

Lesson 2: Have children blow bubbles in class-room before attempting to paint bubbles. Be sure that they have found the beautiful tints before permitting them to represent the colors. Emphasize the great delicacy of the colors and the necessity for a very light touch, with either brush or crayon. If paints are available be sure to read over the general directions for the use of paints. **Do not draw** the shapes, follow directions given in text and paint shape with water. Be sure that previous lessons have taught proper placing and care of materials. Emphasize cleanliness and purity of color. When painting the bubbles with either brush or crayon, white paper should be used. To keep the lesson simple, paint only bubbles, or if the pipe is desired, have stem cutting edge of paper, with little girl not included. Pipe may be painted black.

Lesson 3: Color booklet for Primary and Binary colors to show color formation.

Example: Yellow plus Blue equals Green (it is effective to place the three colored oblongs on black).

Lower part of page may show a green leaf, other pages may show basic elements of orange or red and yellow, with an orange painted below. Purple may be illustrated by a purple plum. Any of the suggestive borders shown on color page may be arranged individually, to decorate the cover.

BOOK II, PAGE 11—THE INDIANS

Character Objective: Helpfulness

Spiritual Objective: To train children to appreciate the rich heritage they possess in their knowledge of, and close relationship with God. To imbue them with a spirit of helpfulness to others wherever possible, as little distributors of God's love.

Art Objective: To teach children to express themselves graphically through the medium of cut paper.

Supplies: Gray bogus paper, different colors of paper, colorful scraps of paper, pictures of winter trees and various missionaries, scissors, paste

Procedure: Tell some story of American colonial days. Gray bogus paper may be used for background, white paper for snow, and black or dark brown for trees. Bright scraps may be used for Indian costumes.

Lesson 1: Show children pictures of winter trees bare and with winter foliage. Practice cutting and placing on large classroom poster, calling on children to express judgment in placing of the trees. Aim to avoid the monotony of equal spaces. The back edge of ground or horizon may be either high or low in picture.

Lesson 2: Show pictures of various missionaries. Note distinguishing characteristics—have free cutting. Follow with free cuts of Indians and Settlers after class discussion of both costumes. Costume parts may be pasted separately on any figure, or if silhouette is desired the completed figure may be cut from picture model. Best results are placed on class room composition. Ask children to bring in pictures of trees or figures, for blank page vocabulary. After they have been exhibited, the children are ready for an original composition on 9 x 12 paper. Call attention to the fact that figures and houses and trees must **touch** the ground. Do not cut figures off as shown in plate unless it has been necessary to cut completed figures after pasting to reduce size of finished picture. Do not copy the plate but make a variety of arrangements. It is not necessary to show three types of figures and any of them may be shown repeated.

BOOK II, PAGE 13—A PLAY HOUSE

Character Objective: Accuracy and Initiative.

Spiritual Objective: To train in children the habit of morning and evening bedside prayers, as expressions of love to their Heavenly Father.

Art Objective: To develop dexterity, accuracy, and creative power through construction work.

Supplies: Construction paper/cardboard/cardstock paper (needs to be strong enough to be made into a 3D object), scissors, paste

Procedure: Use paper sufficiently heavy to make strong furniture, 6 x 9 is a desirable size. Teach type forms which may be made by folding the oblong. When **inside** blocks are folded down and pasted over **outside** blocks, the box shape resulting may be modified for baskets, table, etc. By folding a square sheet similarly and cutting off a row of four blocks, the remaining blocks may be transformed into a highback chair. Blocks cut off may be used to strengthen back. After teaching the type of lesson as shown in plate, encourage children to modify design of shape. The bed accessories also permit simple original design units. Have children invent as many new models as possible. By using construction paper of a uniform size, a general uniformity in proportion will result. Emphasize accurate folding and cutting and careful pasting.

BOOK II, PAGE 15—LILIES

Character Objective: Purity

Spiritual Objective: To create a desire in children to please our Blessed Mother through emulation of her purity.

Art Objective: To train aesthetic judgment in planning a poster which gives a feeling of good spacing and a nice sense of order.

Supplies: Paper, scissors, posterboard, paste

Procedure: Follow steps shown on plate for practice work in making both types of lilies. When making the Easter lily cut on the folded, or dotted lines, almost to top before pasting as shown at 3.

Lesson 2: Place on blackboard a list of simple titles of Our Blessed Mother. Review quickly the method of keeping cut letters uniform in size. Have children fold strips of paper already passed, for number of letters required in each word of title. Each child should plan some variation of the poster if possible. Lilies may be cut in silhouette for decoration if desired.

Have children suggest other titles of our Blessed Mother and use most popular one on the large classroom poster to be made from the practice work on lilies. Have children compare size and placing of letters, with size of poster.

BOOK II, PAGE 17—OUR CRIB

Character Objective: Love and Sympathy

Spiritual Objective: To develop in children a responsiveness to and appreciation of the love of the Christ Child, which may be expressed by trying to make others happy.

Art Objective: To develop the creative instinct through modeling the story of Christmas.

Supplies: Clay, toothpicks

Procedure: The art objective is very necessary to the spiritual side because children in imagination are really living through the scenes they are modeling. Clay puppets become very real. A small boy who was in charge of the assembling of his classroom manger, refused to accept one of the animals because "it doesn't bow its head before Him." Read over directions on page 17 for care of clay before the lesson. Show children how easy it is to make a kneeling figure as shown at top of page. To achieve the third step make a dent in soft clay with broad part of thumb for shadowed face and arms under veil. Only talented children should be urged to carry figures further than simple silhouette. Use little models if they can be brought to school by children. When modeling animals it will be wise to use toothpicks to strengthen legs. Be careful that these do not get into the clay pile.

BOOK II, PAGE 19—A CHRISTMAS GIFT

Character Objective: Parental Love and Generosity

Spiritual Objective: To impress on the child mind the real spirit of Christmas as evidenced by the birthplace of the dear Babe of Bethlehem. To direct their thoughts into the fine philosophy of life, "It is more blessed to give than to receive."

Art Objective: To train children in elementary craftsmanship in the making of artistic and useful Christmas gifts.

Supplies: Construction paper; cardboard, scissors, paste, number pad

Procedure: Use heavy cardboard if possible, for calendar back. Have children follow steps shown in illustration for making of stable and star. Use white paper for snow and brown or gray paper for stable. Paste brown house shape in 2, to white square and cut corner to suggest snow along the edge of the roof. Paste scrap of orange paper in space of door opening to suggest light. If series of large enclosing stars are used, begin by pasting smallest one to paper, darker in tone, and cut shape freehand around it. Each succeeding size is cut in the same way. If distant hills are used keep those in distance a trifle darker than the foreground. If white is used in the foreground, very pale blue might be used in the distance. A tiny star without enclosing shapes is equally effective. The enclosing dark border line has been achieved by placing illustration and panel of similar color to hold date pad, on black panel and then trimming to desired width of border.

The completed panel is then placed on calendar back. The date pad should be covered with paper harmonizing with illustration, and numbers for year cut out and pasted. Cheap little date pads are usually garish in color and might prove a discordant note.

Other suggestions at the bottom of the page will help to suggest original creative work in the minds of the children.

The large picture which has been cut out and saved for the Christmas calendar may be used at this time as a gift for mother. The picture would look well mounted on brown or tan construction paper, with but a very narrow white edge left on picture. Warn children to be careful not to cut off title.

BOOK II, PAGE 21—TOYS

Character Objective: Responsibility

Spiritual Objective: The appreciation of God's wonderful gift of sight. Our responsibility to make the best use of each of our senses by developing them through use.

Art Objective: To develop visualization and a sense of proportion through comparisons.

Supplies: Christmas toys, gray bogus paper, crayons, chalk and blackboard (optional), pictures of toys

Procedure: Ask several children to bring to school one of the Christmas toys they like. Discuss and compare proportions and characteristics. Pass gray bogus paper and crayon and after placing the simplest toys, if possible one for each row, have children draw quickly. Rows may then exchange toys and draw again. Have children draw in mass showing the general shape only, leaving out the details. At the end of the lesson arrange drawings around ledge of blackboard and have children criticise them while comparing them with the models. Review the lesson the next day by having a memory lesson on the blackboard.

Discuss pictures in book calling attention to proportion and important characteristics that should be remembered. Allow the children to try the simple toys shown in the book by sketching them from memory on the blackboard. When they return to seats have them compare with picture and criticise. Have them find pictures of toys for the blank page.

BOOK II, PAGE 23—THE THREE KINGS

Character Objective: Faithfulness

Spiritual Objective: To acquaint children with the meaning of the Epiphany.

Art Objective:

1—To train visualization through paper cutting.

2—To review Repetition and Alternation in design.

Supplies: Chalk and blackboard (optional), Christmas cards, paper (for booklet), paste, scissors

Procedure: Tell children the story of the Three Kings and develop the spiritual objective in accordance with the current work in religion. To enrich the child's vocabulary, have a blackboard lesson to develop visualization, while familiarizing him with forms necessary for the illustration. Ask children to bring Christmas cards showing illustrations of the Wise Men to paste on the blank page.

Make a simple booklet to hold the story and illustrate with cut paper forms showing strong contrast of light and dark. An effective result is obtained by silhouetting white forms against dark trees or other landscape forms. Any part of the units shown at the bottom of the page may be used as repeats or alternating forms to decorate the cover of the booklet planned.

BOOK II, PAGE 25—AGNUS DEI

Character Objective: Sacrifice

Spiritual Objective: To teach children the meaning of the Agnus Dei of the Holy Mass.

Art Objective: To have children acquire a sense of fine spacing on a poster, with decoration suggestive of lettering.

Supplies: Scissors, images of animals

Procedure: The development of the spiritual objective will lead the children into a careful study of lambs and sheep. Review a similar lesson in Book I, Page 17.

As the Agnus Dei poster does not allow much modification, it should be followed with cut paper illustration of any story involving sheep, as nursery rhymes, etc.

In cutting these animals, note legs are short, joints in back legs are visible, and upper part of leg slants back. Muzzle is short and blunt, body longer than wide. Follow method of cutting developed in Book I, Page 33.

BOOK II, PAGE 27—ABRAHAM LINCOLN

Character Objective: Honesty

Spiritual Objective: To cause children to realize that honest work is most pleasing to God and always acceptable to Him as another form of prayer.

Art Objective: To develop manual skill through construction of cabin, as well as tearing and cutting of trees.

Supplies: Images of trees, thin paper for tearing, green and brown construction paper, crayons

Procedure: Tell the story of Abraham Lincoln's boyhood, during the week of February 12th.

After showing several pictures of trees, have children try tearing the shape of one of the models in the panel at the bottom of the page. Use thin pad paper for tearing and be careful that paper has the same proportion as tree. Then demonstrate to class that, beginning with the trunk of the tree at the bottom of the paper, tearing must be continuous until the tree is completed as large as paper. The space left in the sheet should show a perfect tree. Clean tearing should always be emphasized. The technique of tearing should only be used when model has an uneven or irregular contour.

Lesson 2: Try folding paper and cutting three tree shapes alike for pasting to make "stand up" trees for forest on sand table if desired. Use green construction paper or green crayon, for color.

Lesson 3: Follow directions for making log cabin, using either brown construction paper or gray bogus paper that has been colored with crayons.

Assemble parts as shown in illustration and paste. Small scraps of paper pasted to base of trees will fasten them firmly. Crayon the ground green and background blue.

BOOK II, PAGE 29—THE WEDDING

Character Objective: Obedience

Spiritual Objective: To acquaint children with Christ's first public miracle, which emphasizes the outstanding example of obedience to parents and to all other authority which He has left to children.

Art Objective: To enrich the graphic vocabulary of the child through figure drawing and to inspire his creative expression through illustration.

Supplies: Crayons, paper, pictures of different sizes of jars, construction paper, scissors, image of Christ, paste

Procedure: Tell the story of the Miracle, calling on children to supply to your word picture from their imagination their ideas of the setting for the miracle. Copy stick figures in lower panel and dress them as guests at the wedding. Try drawing them from memory at the blackboard, adding necessary details to tell the story.

Lesson 2: Show several pictures of jars of different shapes before children attempt to cut them. Call for criticisms of shapes. Would they stand solidly if bases were too narrow? Crayons may be used to get pleasing colors if colored construction paper is not available.

Cut figure of Christ from white paper. Omit features, showing only the characteristic beard. Have children observe one of their own number to discover that when head is turned the contour may not show features. Notice head contours of background figures. Nimbus should be cut separately and pasted. Windows or doors may be shown by pasting light shapes on the dark wall.

Children are now ready to plan an individual illustration of the story, selecting any phase of it that they may wish. Initiative should be encouraged and commended. Always have an exhibition of work with children's criticisms immediately after the lesson. This develops critical judgment.

BOOK II, PAGE 31—LENT

Character Objective: Self Denial

Spiritual Objective: To teach children the reason for and value of Penance and the meaning of the Lenten Season.

Art Objective:

1—To teach symbolism of primary and binary colors.

2—To teach an orderly plan of arrangement for a book page and cover.

3—To simplify the child's creative expression through cut paper illustration which eliminates detail.

Supplies: Chalk and blackboard (optional), crayons, paper for booklets

Procedure: Develop spiritual objective, to create the need for the suggested problem, of a penance booklet.

Review meaning of primary colors learned in Book I. Add the symbolism of the binary colors.

Color	Symbol	Activity
Red	Love	Self sacrifice and sympathy
Yellow	Light and understanding	To study; obedience
Blue	Truth and honesty; "True Blue"	Truthfulness
Orange	Wealth of God's gifts	Generosity to missions
Green	Hope and faith	Prayer
Violet	Penance	Self denial
White	Purity	Beautiful Thoughts

Plan booklet following model used in Book I.

Plan title. Use the term Penance as a virtue. Suggest on the blackboard other arrangements for cover, ex., border lines above and below letters with no other decoration. Plan to emphasize one color with its suggestions, for each week, etc.

It is not advisable to require too much letter cutting for the problem, the page title is sufficient; sub-titles may be added with crayon. Be careful that title on cover is more important than decoration and placed **above** the center. Teach children to plan a page with plenty of marginal space and more space at **bottom** than at **top**.

Discuss illustration in book. Why have buildings been suggested? Do they look like our buildings? Are the buildings near the crosses? How do we know? Which cross suggests Christ? Why? Lead children to see that simple shapes of objects tell an interesting story when no details are shown, also that a picture must not be crowded.

BOOK II, PAGE 33—BE CAREFUL

Character Objective: Good Judgment

Spiritual Objective: Appreciation of God's great gift of Reason and our duty to develop it by using it to protect our bodies.

Art Objective: To continue development of a sense of fine page arrangement of letters and pictures as well as fitness of cover design.

Supplies: Pictures of items listed below, paste, chalk and blackboard (optional)

Procedure: Ask children to find pictures of houses, automobiles, etc., to paste on the blank page to enrich graphic vocabulary.

Discuss dangerous habits, while developing spiritual objective and have children formulate a number of safety rules. Book may be made as a classroom project, using best illustrations for rules to be emphasized. Review points taught in previous lesson which are repeated in text. Keep illustrations simple and praise each new idea as it appears. Always have as much blackboard work as possible before lesson, to familiarize children with an adequate vocabulary.

BOOK II, PAGE 35—SOMETHING ABOUT MASS

Character Objective: Faith

Spiritual Objective: To give children a knowledge of the Mass and help them to realize the wonderful gift of the Holy Eucharist. The cutouts in the lower panel are given to help impress on the child's mind the essential things to be remembered. Develop the lesson to correspond with *Course in Religion,* for the grade.

Art Objective: To develop craftsmanship and reasoning powers through making a booklet and arranging material in it.

Supplies: Paper, scissors, paste, pencil, string

Procedure: Discuss with the children their impressions while assisting at Mass. This gives an opportunity to correct many erroneous ideas formed outside.

The method of procedure is clearly given on plate. Book and contents being definitely religious will not permit much change. Emphasize nice space relations of each page.

BOOK II, PAGE 37—TO MAKE AN ALTAR

Character Objective: Reverence

Spiritual Objective: To acquaint children with the use of the Altar, and emphasize the meaning of its essential parts; what the Altar Stone is and why it is necessary; what the Tabernacle holds. The Mass for Children, by Father Kelly, is an excellent supplementary book on the subject.

Art Objective: Constructive design and development of skills in folding, cutting, and pasting an altar.

Supplies: Construction paper, bogus paper, paste, scissors

Procedure: Use construction or gray bogus paper about 6 x 9. Follow steps in construction shown on plate. Be careful that folding of edge to edge is done accurately. Make creases **flat**, with thumb-nail. When finished add Altar cloth and flowers for decoration.

BOOK II, PAGE 39—THE LITTLE HOUSE OF GOD

The color photograph of the beautiful altar on this page is planned as a subject for appreciation. Read the text for the children as a basis for general discussion. Why is the altar bare of external things? What must be placed there before the priest begins Mass? How does this altar compare with the altar in your church? What colors do we find in the lovely decoration?

In the Greek alphabet the letter A is called Alpha; it is the beginning letter of the alphabet and is placed there to tell us that God is the beginning of all things. The other letter is the last letter in the Greek alphabet, and is called Omega and tells us that God is the end of all things. God had no beginning and will have no end!

BOOK II, PAGE 41—MOTHER'S DAY

Character Objective: Parental Love

Spiritual Objective: To awaken in the minds of children a keen realization of the precious gift God bestows on them each time they receive Him in Holy Communion. The gift for Mother's Day is a step toward habit formation of presenting this beautiful tribute during life.

Art Objective: To develop in children their innate powers of original creative design through cutting decorative flower shapes for a basket of flowers.

Supplies: Images of baskets and flowers, scissors, paste, colored paper, crayons

Procedure: Show pictures of baskets and ask children to find pictures of baskets and flowers to paste on the blank page. Have children cut basket shape shown in book and then try cutting modified forms.

Lesson 2: Study simple flower shape counting number of petals, then fold and cut half that number. Try modifications of cuts. Add centers with tiny scraps of contrasting color.

Scraps of paper from many lessons may be interestingly used during this lesson. Symbolism of color may be reviewed and woven into the lesson. Have children develop neatness in pasting in order to keep gift very beautiful.

BOOK II, PAGE 43—BERNADETTE

Character Objective: Devotion.

Spiritual Objective: To kindle in the minds of children devotion to, and love for our Blessed Mother.

Art Objective: To develop discrimination in color selection, and recognition of tints of colors. To develop imagination through illustration.

Supplies: Chalk and blackboard (optional), scissors, crayons or paints and brushes, paper, landscape images, paste

Procedure: Tell the story of Bernadette, emphasizing the fact that she was a little girl whose daily actions were pleasing to God and His Blessed Mother. Have children suggest the many ways they may daily please God.

Precede the lesson with blackboard work, showing Bernadette in many positions based on stick figures. Practice drawing and cutting figure of Our Lady.

It is advisable to plan a paper-cutting lesson for harmonious color results and elimination of detail. Follow directions given in text for green hills in background and possibly a blue sky. Using crayola or brush and color, color small sheets of paper blue, purple, and lighter tints of each color, and after tearing them into smaller pieces, paste them to background to form the grotto for the Blessed Virgin. Costume for child may be cut in separate pieces or cut in silhouette and colored. Find landscape pictures with fine color to paste on the blank page.

BOOK II, PAGES 45 AND 47—THE ROSARY

A pageant planned to be given, preferably outdoors, in either May or October, in honor of our Blessed Lady.

Character Objective: Reverence

General Objective: To direct all Catholics toward a real appreciation of the exquisite beauty of the devotion of the Rosary and counteract the usual mechanical method of reciting it.

General Suggestions: About eighty children may take part in the pageant, but the number forming the cross may vary. A tall girl from an upper grade may represent our Blessed Mother. She may be the chosen May Queen.

If children are placed close together the making of the Chains suggested will be superfluous. The formation of the Rosary may be planned in many ways, ex., by decades led by boy representing the Pater Noster who will say his lines as Rosary is formed, or the entire Rosary may be formed before any lines are spoken.

Open the ceremony with a hymn to Our Lady. After the lines spoken by each of the Pater Nosters, explaining the Joyful Mysteries, the Aves or roses of his decade will sing two lines of Adeste Fidelis, preferably the English, "Come All Ye Faithful."

At the end of the Joyful Mysteries, the entire Rosary will sing the last stanza. After the lines spoken for each decade of the Sorrowful Mysteries, the individual decades will sing two lines of Stabat Mater in English, and at the end the entire Rosary will sing the closing stanzas. After lines explaining decades of Glorious Mysteries, individual decades sing two lines of "Holy God," and at the end the entire Rosary will sing the second stanza of "Holy God."

Finish the pageant with selected hymns to Our Lady.

Two heralds may announce **the days** on which Rosary is to be said.

Supplies: Crepe paper: pink, green, dark red; scissors

Costumes: The directions for costumes are clearly illustrated on page 45. Two rolls of pink crepe paper and one roll of green will make two costumes for the Aves. One roll of dark red will make one costume for the Pater Noster. Each child should plan to make his own costume, but the lesson may be very much simplified by having several skillful children who have been coached previously circulate among the other children helping them over difficult places.

Finish one complete costume before the lesson, to determine time necessary for making, etc. Make **depth** of petals from **width** of paper.

WORDS FOR DRAMATIZATION OF THE ROSARY

R—Is for Roses to make Mary's crown.

O—Is this Offering to spread her renown.

S—Is her Service and Songs of praise, too.

A—All good Acts that her children should do.

R—Is for Red which means love strong and deep.

Y—Is for You and the Faith you must keep.

And now all united to sing Mary's praise
You will hear her beads' message for different days.

JOYFUL MYSTERIES—Monday—Thursday

R—Rustling wings announce Gabriel fair
  With "Hail full of Grace" to the Maid who knelt there.
O—Over hills to her cousin she went
  On a visit to tell her of this strange event.
S—For her Son, tiny Jesus so sweet
  At His birth came the Wise Men to kneel at His feet.
A—Is for Altar where they gave Him His name
  Which we honor and praise but must never defame.
R—For the Rabbis the Boy Jesus taught
  In the temple they found Him when for three days they sought.
Y—Is for You and the joyous beads tell
  Of our Queen's happy days with the Babe she loved well.

SORROWFUL MYSTERIES—Tuesday—Friday

R—For the Rest His disciples must take
  Leaving Christ all alone with His suffering, awake!
O—For the Orders that from Pilate came
  They tied Him and whipped Him and scoffed at His Name.
S—For the Sorrow that pierced Mary's breast
  When she saw the sharp thorns on His loving head pressed.
A—For the Awful trip up Calvary's road
  While He carried His cross, falling thrice 'neath His load.
R—The Result of the sins of all time—
  A Crucified God's reparation, sublime!
Y—Is for You and the sorrow beads tell
  Of our Lady's deep grief at these things which befell.

GLORIOUS MYSTERIES—Wednesday—Saturday

R—Resurrection, when three days were o'er
With wonder and joy they beheld Him once more.
O—For Mount Olivet where at the end
In wonder they watched Him to heaven ascend.
S—The Surprise of apostles at sight
Of the Holy Ghost coming as strange tongues of light.
A—The Assumption of Mary above,
God wished her in heaven surrounded with love.
R—Rings of angels bright, dazzling her gown,
The heavens resounded when God placed her crown.
Y—Is for You and the glorious beads tell
Of our Queen's place near God, where some day we may dwell.
We should love our dear Mother and ask for her aid
To help us live right and meet God unafraid.
If we think of the story of each little bead
While we ask her to send us the help we may need,
We are sure our petition to God she will take
He may grant our request for His dear Mother's sake.

CORRELATED WORK

1. ENGLISH:

   1. Recognition of new words in memorizing the lines of the poem.
   2. Reproduction in writing of required lines to test knowledge in placing of capital letters.
      a. Beginning sentences.
      b. Beginning lines of poetry.
      c. Proper names.
   3. Free speech encouraged during making of costumes to develop a good speaking voice.
   4. Development of correct enunciation.

2. ARITHMETIC:

Counting children or roses by twos, three, and fives to 60. Learning tables 2 and 5. Understanding of signs, **plus, minus,** and **equal** in number of beads. The term decade means 10. How many children are missing from decade on the left? On right?

Quick problems in addition and subtraction while observing the picture. Other things will suggest themselves.

3. NATURE STUDY—The Rose:

Its characteristics, its symbolism, its care in the garden.

4. RECOGNITION:

Of new words in lines of pageant.

5. COLOR AND DESIGN:

Recognition of the tints of red used in costuming.

6. COSTUME STUDY:

Developed in construction of costume, as a form of Nature Study.

7. CREATIVE WORK:

Is being developed during the entire working out of the plans for the pageant.

8. SOUVENIR:

Mount the colored picture carefully on gray, light blue, or white paper as a souvenir gift for Mother, when she comes to see the pageant.

Always have children cut pictures at least ½ inch from binding.

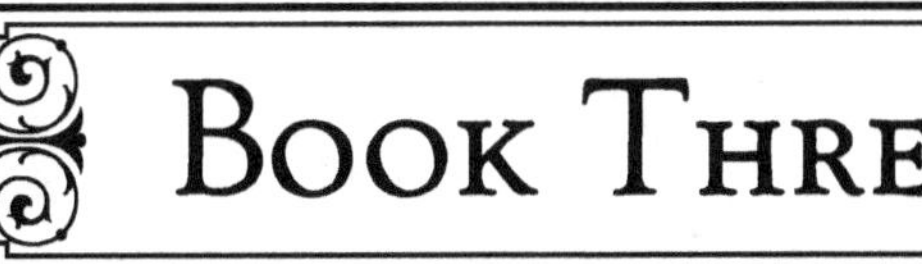

Book Three

BOOK III, COVER

See page 3 of this manual.

BOOK III—END PAPER

Character Objective: Happiness

Spiritual Objective: To have children understand their similarity to the "Happy Trees." They have been "wrought by the Master's Hand." Their souls made beautiful to "grow in the Master's Garden." During their stay in the world they are being "cut and chipped and hewn" by His Law, as the Great Artist continues to make them more perfect for Eternity.

Art Objective: To increase the graphic vocabulary of the child through having him learn essential forms necessary for illustration.

Supplies: Crayons, images of houses, paste, blank paper

Procedure: Have children memorize the verse after discussing the imaginary pictures called up by its lines. Turn to the end paper at back of book for a study of houses and trees. Have children memorize shapes separately and when they have become familiar with essential construction of various models, ask them to illustrate stories in which these can be used. Have children bring pictures of houses to paste on the blank page. Discuss characteristics of houses in the neighborhood. Suggest that they try to draw from memory the shape of the house in which they live.

BOOK III, PAGE 1—BOY AND ANGEL

Character Objective: Sensitivity

Spiritual Objective: To make children aware of the value of conscience as a sentinel or safeguard against sin. Just as the unseen voice of the radio comes to their physical ears when they have a receiving set, so the voice of Conscience will speak with a spiritual voice, so long as the grace of the Sacraments keeps the receiving set of Conscience in good condition.

Art Objective: To develop in children appreciation of pictures through the appeal to human interest, imagination, and effect on the senses.

Teacher's Preparation: As a preparation for your teaching, study the picture and analyze its appeal to yourself.

Does its message to you have an emotional quality that makes you a participator in that intimate communion of innocent childhood with the Creator, the psychological moment of which has been so deftly caught and held fast by the artist?

Are your senses captivated by the fine color, radiant rich harmonies of green and gold, intriguing your imagination to delve deep within its mysterious depths? Notice that the richest and most beautiful effects emphasize the **center of interest** in the picture.

Perhaps its fine composition may have a strong appeal to your natural sense of order. Notice how the artist has built up his center of interest which is the inspired face of the boy.

Notice the fine balance of the large dark masses of wings and ground at the top and bottom and the contrasting small light masses of sky, right and left, which combine to frame in the central figures.

Notice the lovely oval shape formed as the eye travels from the face of the boy following down the line of the arms and back again to the face, and see how the shape has been repeated in the flowing sleeve of the angel, smaller again in the head of the angel, and again echoed in the golden nimbus above his head. But now the attention travels back to the eyes of the boy, by way of the subtle rhythmic curves of the drapery. The artist emphasizes, through contrast, the powerful strength of the Angel, held in abeyance by his gentleness, with the strength of desire, shown in the immature boy.

The artist, Abbot Thayer, was an American artist of our own day, having died in 1921. He painted in the modern manner, eliminating details and laying in the picture simply, in broad vigorous brush work of rich color. He is represented in all the great galleries of the United States.

Procedure: Allow the children to open their books and enjoy the picture undisturbed for a few minutes in order that the beauty of the picture may make its own appeal. Call on children to give their impressions, as a basis for discussion. What do you think the angel is saying? Is he telling a story? What is the boy seeing? Does the angel look powerful enough to help the boy if necessary? Why is the boy not looking at the angel? Why do you think the angel is protecting the boy? From what may he be protecting him? Does he know the angel is with him? Is the boy wealthy? Can you tell where the boy is standing? What season of the year is it? Does the place look real or like a dream garden? Do you think the boy will follow the voice of his conscience? What colors do you recognize? Notice that a yellow tone enters into all the colors. Do you remember what yellow means? (light, wisdom, the Holy Ghost). Continue the discussion as long as children are interested. Questions should be planned to develop **thoughtful** observation and **individual** answers.

After the picture has been enjoyed by the class, have the page cut about half inch from the binding to keep binding firm.

Put picture away to preserve it until ready to send it home as a Christmas gift, nicely mounted on strong paper of a neutral tone.

For additional picture study, see page xxx.

BOOK III, PAGE 3—NATURE

Character Objective: Alertness

Spiritual Objective: To help children to see the reflection of God's love in the miracle of growth in fruit and vegetables. Through this habitual association they will become acutely conscious of His existence.

Art Objective:

1—To develop visualization through study of the form and color of fruits and vegetables.

2—To develop manual skill through mastery of color technique.

Supplies: Pumpkin (if possible), crayons, blank paper, images of fruits and vegetables, paste, chalk and blackboard (optional)

Procedure: Always work from a real model to get full value from the lesson. As a rule some pupil in the class may be depended upon to bring to school the model needed.

This will assure original interpretation of color and form on the part of the child. Have pupils note proportion and characteristics of object under observation. Note that division marks on the pumpkin meet at center of **top** and **bottom**.

Since pictures may help them to recognize similar aspects of color and form ask the children to bring pictures of fruits and vegetables cut from food advertisements in magazines. Paste these on the blank page for additional color study and vocabulary enrichment. The pasting should be a lesson in arrangement.

As a preceding lesson have children work on the blackboard, using their books to learn the method of drawing the form with chalk. Teach the new term Radiation by showing how the lines radiate from the center of top. Notice that the curvature of the lines follows the direction of the contour or outline. Note also the flatness and darkness of the cast shadow.

BOOK III, PAGE 5—MOSES

Character Objective: Obedience

Spiritual Objective: To teach children the meaning and origin of the Commandments.

Art Objective: To develop skill, judgment, and visualization through cutting the forms necessary for illustrating the finding of Moses.

Supplies: Scissors, paste, images of baby and basket, crayons, colored paper or gray bogus paper

Procedure: Tell the story of the Jews in Egypt and the events leading up to the placing of the infant Moses in the bulrushes. Tell them of the great future that God had planned for Moses as the deliverer of his people, and how God preserved his life and placed him in the household of the king. The two tablets have been arranged to review or teach Roman Notation. In order that children may not be confused, the Roman figures are shown separately.

The problem suggested in the text requires the children to cut the tablets and place on one the **three** Commandments relating to God and on the other the **seven** Commandments relating to man.

The basket and baby may be cut separately. The figures may be pasted. The figures may represent the princess and her attendants or the mother of Moses and his sister. The number is optional, but emphasis should be placed on action. Discourage copying the arrangement shown on the plate.

Make a lesson of the tablets and do not include them in the illustration lesson. As much as possible has been shown in the plate, as suggestions for child's vocabulary, to enable him to give his own expression to the story. Illustrate other Bible stories in the same way. When colored papers are not available, gray bogus paper may be colored with crayola.

BOOK III, PAGE 7—LETTERS TO DRAW

Character Objective: Accuracy and Neatness

Spiritual Objective: To help children to understand that just as the perfect letters are developed by the aid of the helpful squares, so God has given each of them a special place in their families and the perfect pattern He wishes their lives to be is made possible through His helpful Grace found in the Sacraments, and obedience to those in authority at home.

Art Objective:

1—To develop accuracy of vision through study of letter forms while learning to draw letters and figures.

2—To learn the use of squared paper in design.

Supplies: Squared paper or lined/unlined paper, rulers, crayons, chalk and blackboard (optional), scissors, magazines, paste, blank paper

Procedure: If squared paper is not available, have children square ruled or unruled paper as an exercise in measuring ¼ inches. Use paper rulers with ¼ and ½-inch measurement only. These can be made easily from strips of oaktag or heavy construction paper. Teach children to measure on **both** sides of paper in order to have two points through which to draw straight lines.

Keep crayola sharp and have children aim to **fill** the blocks but not allow crayola to go outside the lines. Praise work showing **clean** edges to letters. Plan a "memory" lesson at the blackboard, using side of chalk.

Have children cut examples of **similar** letters from advertisements to paste on the blank page.

BOOK III, PAGE 9—THE COLOR KNIGHTS

Character Objective: Purity

Spiritual Objective: To help children to visualize purity and understand what happens to the soul as God sees it, when sin soils it.

Art Objective:

1—To teach the recognition and mixing of six intermediate colors.

2—To teach children the necessity of keeping colors clean.

Supplies: Colored paper, paints and brushes, water

Procedure: The color page has been planned as source material to be used all through the year.

Read the text and have children dramatize the story of the Color Knights to make them familiar with the new colors.

A game can be played in which each failure to recognize a color penalizes the Knight by eliminating him as a protector. Large sheets of colored paper may be used for shields and banners.

If paints are used for color work, teach children to clean paints carefully at the end of the lesson by dipping brush in water and lightly brushing it over the paint. Then pinch brush dry and lift off surplus water. Always dip brush in water when changing from one color to another in order to show the purity and brilliance of the colors.

Brown may be made by touching the brush to red, yellow, and blue in succession, then a final touch of the color desired to predominate in the brown.

Failure to keep colors clean will result in smudgy tones lacking in brilliancy. Children quickly get the suggestion of the Dragon of Carelessness and it helps to make them form good habits in painting. Since children can see the ruinous results in color caused by this Dragon of Carelessness, it is an easy matter to have them visualize a similar result when the dragon of Sin is substituted. Read color text in Book 1, page 9 and review it with children. Intermediate colors are formed by adding to the binary, more of the primary color used as the adjective, ex., green is yellow plus blue, yellow-green has additional yellow added to the green.

Suggested Problems:

1—Faint balloons showing the intermediate colors.

2—Make soldier hats on a national holiday and assign intermediate colors for different rows after they are made from gray bogus paper.

3—Using six glasses of colored water (three with primary and three with binary colors) have children demonstrate making the intermediate colors by the addition of a primary to a binary.

BOOK III, PAGE 11—HEALTH

Character Objective: Responsibility

Spiritual Objective: To help children to become aware of the marvelous, automatic mechanism of their bodies. Planned by God to produce continuous comfort provided they cooperate with the laws of health.

Art Objective: To awaken interest in beauty of surroundings, a discriminating taste in color, and an appreciation of a neatly kept bedroom.

Supplies: Crayons, scissors, paste, gray bogus paper or soft-toned construction paper

Procedure: The picture has been planned for the application of color to illustrate the color theory discussed on the color page.

In the interest of health the lesson is planned for projection into the home when finished.

After reading and discussing the text, demonstrate the method of handling crayola, that is holding it as chalk is held under the hand, while rubbing lightly with the beveled side for the larger spaces and putting pressure on the point, for the small brilliant spots.

Discuss with the children, the furnishing of the rooms in which they sleep. Emphasize **cleanliness** and **order**. Direct attention to beautiful color arrangements possible in curtains, walls, beds, etc. When color lesson is finished cut picture about half inch from binding in order to keep binding firm. Mount on gray bogus or soft toned construction paper. Keep bottom margins widest, and side margins narrowest. The picture, **placed on the wall at home,** will be a constant reminder of the lesson.

SUGGESTED LESSON

Supplies: Colored paper scraps, scissors, crayons, chalk and blackboard (optional)

Window Drapery: Using scraps of colored papers allow children to select harmonious colors to drape toy house windows. Frames may be drawn or cut. Show several varieties on the blackboard.

BOOK III, PAGE 13—ANIMALS

Character Objective: Courage

Spiritual Objective: To lead children to understand what is meant by Courage, both physical and moral and to create in them a desire to express it and keep it in evidence in classroom contacts. This will help to make **outside reactions** to similar circumstances more probable.

Art Objective: To develop keen observation while teaching children to see and draw animals.

Supplies: Gray bogus paper, crayons, chalk and blackboard (optional)

Procedure: Tell the story of St. George and the Dragon, Beowulf, or a similar story to create an immediate need for these animals in the illustration vocabulary. Compare the proportions of lion and camel. The lion would fit into an oblong while the camel would fit more comfortably into a square. Compare necks, heads, tails, legs. Notice similarity of structure of back legs, the upper part slants back and lower part slants front in both animals.

Have children review method of drawing camel, learned in books 1 and 2. Have them practice on blackboard the construction of lion on the double square. Demonstrate on board characteristic shape of muzzle of lion, dog, wolf, etc., with placing of eye and mouth. Emphasize shape and direction of legs.

Encourage children to make original illustrations of stories frequently, while reviewing points to be emphasized under "Illustration" in the General Notes and in Book 2. Use gray bogus paper and crayola.

BOOK III, PAGE 15—A CHRISTMAS GIFT

Character Objective: Patience and Perseverance

Spiritual Objective: To infuse children with a personal love of the Divine Infant as the paramount thought of the Christmas season in order to subordinate the pagan practice of Santa Claus so prevalent in their homes.

Art Objective:

1—To teach accuracy through basing construction of mantel on ½-inch measurement.

2—To develop visualization through free paper cutting of Christmas symbols such as stockings, candles, holly wreaths, etc.

3—To develop creative construction of furniture based on any forms previously taught.

4—To develop creative design and a feeling for good spacing in the planning of the Indian rug borders.

5—To develop skill in the folding of a five pointed star.

6—To develop creative imagination in the construction and decoration of a Christmas tree.

7—To develop a sense of good proportion and judgment in the assembling of the completed problem.

Supplies: Rulers, red construction paper, scissors, white chalk, pasteboard box or gray bogus paper

Procedure: Consider each objective in the problem as a separate lesson. If possible have children use flat rulers marked with ½-inch measurements only. Use red construction paper 6 x 9 for mantel. Measure carefully as shown on plate.

Note: Do not fold on horizontal dotted lines 2 ½ inches from top. **Do not fold** on **vertical** dotted lines **above** horizontal line to be cut. Finished model shows result of folding lower vertical lines. Bricks are made effective by using white chalk and may be made with or without measuring. Notice how bricks are "laid."

Folding heavy paper is simplified by scoring lightly with a pin and ruler before folding.

When mantel is finished it should be laid aside until needed to complete the problem.

Ask children to cut from magazines pictures of anything they may find that is related to the problem, to be pasted on the blank page.

Have children precede cutting lesson by memorizing shapes of Christmas symbols at blackboard.

Review methods already learned for furniture construction. Discuss room to be furnished and kinds of furniture suitable for it. The box form as a base of construction can be readily adapted, or paper scraps may be utilized through using the hollow square construction method.

Discuss types of decoration found on rugs, borders, all-over designs, and panels. Allow pupils to decide on type desired. If Indian symbols are used, review design arrangements previously used: Repetition, Alternation, Radiation. Test their recognition of Alternation shown in rug borders and Radiation shown in the star.

Follow directions on plate and use star as part of tree decoration to symbolize the Star of Bethlehem.

Review method of tree construction used in books 1 and 2, and decorate with cutouts of toys and colored strings.

If pasteboard box has been provided for a room, a color scheme may be planned for walls and floor, curtains for windows, etc. For pupils without boxes a large sheet of gray bogus paper may be used for floor and back wall. Add support for back.

BOOK III, PAGE 17—A STORY BOOK

Character Objective: Perseverance

Spiritual Objective: An appreciation of the great gift of Faith which God has given children and the great need of their prayers for the Missionaries who are bringing that Faith to persons who do not have it.

Art Objectives:

1—To develop visualization and imagination through illustration of the story of St. Boniface.

2—To develop a keen sense of proportion and order through planning the proper size of container for Christmas trees.

3—To develop skill and initiative by cutting several figures at once when properly folded.

4—To develop a fine arrangement of lettering and decoration suitable for a book cover, and a fine page arrangement inside the book.

Supplies: Scissors and paper, crayons

Procedure: Read to the children the beautiful story of St. Boniface as told by Dr. Henry Van Dyke in "The First Christmas Tree." The story may be reproduced orally as an English lesson and then illustrated.

THE FIRST CHRISTMAS TREE

By Dr. Henry Van Dyke

To be used as an English correlation through reproduction.

It was the day before Christmas in the year of our Lord 722. Winifrid of England, whose name in the Roman tongue was Boniface, and whom man called the apostle of Germany, a great preacher, a wonderful scholar, a daring traveler, a venturesome pilgrim, a holy priest of God, had left his home and fair estate in Wessex to go out into the wilderness to preach to the heathen.

Through forests and along the borders of Saxony he had wandered for years with a handful of companions, sleeping under the trees, crossing mountains and marshes, always in love with hardships and danger.

What a man he was! Fair and slight, but as straight as a spear and as strong as an oaken staff. His face was still young, but bronzed by wind and sun. His gray eyes, clear and kind, flashed like fire when he spoke of his adventures and of the evil deeds of the false priests with whom he had contended.

Boniface today with his little band of pilgrims, less than a score of men, was traveling slowly northward through the wide forest that rolled over the hills of central Germany. At the head of the band marched Boniface, clad in a tunic of fur, his hunter's boots each crusted with snow; drops of ice sparkled like jewels along the thongs that bound his legs. There were no other ornaments on his dress except the bishop's cross hanging on his breast and the silver clasp that fastened his cloak about his neck. He carried a strong, tall staff in his hand, fashioned at the top in the form of a cross.

The weird woodland, somber and illimitable, covered hill and vale, tableland and mountainpeak. There were wide moors where the wolves hunted in packs as if the devil drove them, and tangled thickets where wild bears made their lairs. Fierce animals lurked among the rocky passes. The gloomy excesses of the forests gave shelter also to outlaws, sturdy robbers, mad wolves, and bands of wandering pilgrims.

The steps of the pilgrims were noiseless. The sun went down and darkness followed swiftly. This was Christmas eve in the forest. The pilgrims still pressed forward and presently the moon came up. Then Boniface spoke and said, "Courage, my brothers, and forward yet a little. We have work to do before we feast tonight, for this is Yuletide, and the heathen people of the forest are gathered at the Thunder Oak of Geismar to worship their god, Thor. But we are sent to lighten their darkness; and we will teach them to keep a Christmas with us, such as this woodland has never known."

After a while, the wood began to open out a little. There were spaces of meadowland; rude houses of hewn logs appeared in these openings. All the houses were silent and unlighted. The travelers passed the houses and plunged again into the forest, but they had not gone far when they emerged suddenly upon a glade, round forest, and level except at the northern side where a little hillock was crowned with a giant oak tree. It was an immense tree, larger than any of the others that the pilgrims had seen in the forest. "Here," cried Boniface as his eyes flashed and his hands lifted his heavy staff, "here is the thunder oak and here the cross of Christ shall break the hammer of the false god "Thor."

Withered leaves still clung to the branches of the oak, the bright crimson of autumn had long since disappeared, but tonight the leaves were red again for the immense fire had been kindled in front of the tree and its red flames lit everything around. Boniface and his companions could not see the fire from a distance for a great throng of people were gathered around it in a half circle, their backs to the open glade, their faces toward the oak. Boniface and his companions advanced unnoticed for all of the pagans were looking intently toward the fire at the foot of the oak. Then Boniface's voice rang out, "Hail, ye sons of the forest! A stranger claims the warmth of your fires tonight!" Swiftly they turned and looked at the speaker, then silently the circle opened and Boniface and his companions stepped in and the circle closed again. Then Hunrad, the old pagan priest, spoke, "Who are you, hence come you, and what seek you?"

"I come from England," answered Boniface, "to bring you good tidings and a message from the All-Father, Whose servant I am."

"Welcome, then," said Hunrad, "welcome and be silent, for what we are going to do is too high to wait and must be done before the moon crosses the high heaven. This night the great god Thor, the god of thunder and war, to whom this oak is sacred, is grieved and angry with his people because they have not worshipped him as they should have done. It is a long time since we fed the roots of his tree with blood; therefore, its leaves are withered and dead. This night the son of the chief must give his blood for the roots of the tree. Here is the son of the chief, the darling of the people!"

"Hearken, Bernard," for that was the little prince's name, "wilt thou go and carry the message to Thor, wilt thou give thy blood to feed the roots of thunder oak?" "Naught fear I," said the boy, "for I am Gundhar's son and the defender of my fold." Then the old man stooped to lift a black hammer from the ground—the sacred hammer of the false god Thor. He raised it high with all the strength of his withered arms above the little boy's head; it poised in the air and was about to fall when Boniface thrust upward with his staff and lo! Instead of crashing down upon the head of the innocent boy, the pagan priest seemed forced by an unseen power to swing his stroke in an opposite direction and it crashed down on the altar instead, breaking it to pieces. The pagans were astonished and terrified at their priest's act for they felt in some way he was responsible. The altar stone lay broken! Then Gundhar, the chief, spoke for he was glad that his son should not die, and said, "Let this stranger speak and tell us why he has done this thing."

Then Boniface lifted himself upon the broken altar stone and drew a roll of parchment from his bosom and began to read, "A letter from the great Bishop of Rome, who sits on a golden throne, to the people of the forest." The letter told them what Boniface was sent to do, to teach them the only true faith, to baptize them, and to lead them to God. It told them to worship not the false gods, to offer no more bloody sacrifices, but to do as Bishop Boniface commanded them. It told them to build a house for him, and a church where they might offer their prayers to the true God.

The pagans were quieted as they heard some beautiful music, and then Gundhar said, "Tell us, Boniface, what first shall we do?" Boniface beckoned to Gregory, one of his strongest companions of the forest, "Bring the axes, one for thee and one for me 1 The king of the forest shall fall at once or all is lost!"

Firmly they clasped the axe-helves and swung the shining blades. Clang! Clang! The strokes beat time upon the hard ringing wood. In a few moments the huge trunk quivered, there was a shuddering in the branches, then a mighty rushing noise sounded overhead, a strong whirling wind passed over the tree-tops, it gripped the oak by its branches and tore it from the roots, and backward it fell like a ruined tower groaning and crashing as it split asunder in four great pieces.

Then Boniface let his axe drop and turned to the people. "Here is the timber all ready felled and split for your new building. On this spot shall rise a chapel to the true God and his servant, St. Peter, and here," he said, as his eyes fell on a young fir tree standing straight and green, with its top pointing toward the stars, "is the living tree of the Christ Child. Take it up and carry it to the chieftain's hall. You shall go no more to the thunder oak to keep feast with dark deeds of crime. The thunder oak has fallen and from henceforth in every home in Germany the people shall gather around a little green fir tree to rejoice in the birth night of Christ."

So they took the little fir tree from its place and carried it in joyous procession to the hall of Gundhar and set it in the midst of it. They kindled lights among the branches until it seemed to be tangled full of fireflies. They loaded it with jewels and beautiful things. Then Boniface stood beside the tree and told the story of Bethlehem, of the Babe in the manger, of the shepherds on the hills, of the host of angels and their midnight song. All the people listened, charmed into stillness. And ever since that time evergreen trees have been taken up from their places in the forest, set in homes, and covered with dazzling lights and beautiful gifts as a sign of the Christ Child come amongst us on earth, for the evergreen tree is the tree of the Christ Child.

Cut trees suggested by the story. Plan type of trees to be used as cover decoration. Why is the Christmas tree suitable? Recall previous lessons on book covers, as to decoration and lettering, placing of title, etc. Notice how container may be made to harmonize with shape of tree and how tree shape may be elaborated, by additional cutting.

Look closely and notice how paper is folded into an M shape so that two children may cut at once. Be sure that paper will fold into oblong of correct proportion for figure required. Notice shoulder and foot do not extend beyond **middle** and arm occupies other half of paper. Finish the booklet as directed.

Christmas Gift: As a Christmas gift for parents, the beautiful picture of the Boy and Angel may be artistically mounted on brown, gray, or very dull green paper, and sent home.

BOOK III, PAGE 19—AN OFFERING

Character Objective: Gratitude

Spiritual Objective: To bring children into a sweet intimacy with the Divine Infant and His Blessed Mother through teaching the meaning of the Presentation.

Art Objective: To develop judgment in estimating spaces and skill in cutting and pasting the doves offered by our Blessed Mother.

Supplies: Crayons and paper, scissors, paste, blank paper

Procedure: Read the text as a basis for discussion. Through well directed questions lead up to the reasons why gratitude should cause each child to wish to make an offering of love to God. Using books, have pupils practice drawing dove at blackboard until form and proportion are very familiar. Then try cutting paper from the visualized form without drawing. Fold paper to cut cage. Be careful that paper given to children is the proper proportion to make full-sized cutting desired.

Find pictures of birds to paste on the blank page.

BOOK III, PAGE 21—THE CARPENTER SHOP

Character Objective: Industry

Spiritual Objective: To cause children to consider St. Joseph as a loving and powerful patron because of his nearness to and his care for the Divine Infant.

Art Objective: To develop accuracy in measuring and skill in manipulating materials through the construction of a carpenter shop.

Supplies: Chalk and blackboard (optional), various images from advertisements, heavy paper

Procedure: Develop the story of the life of the Holy Child with St. Joseph and our Blessed Mother. His work as a Carpenter with St. Joseph, etc. Discuss the usefulness of carpenters today and the honor of the profession. Lead children to appreciate carpentry work in their homes. Discuss tools, their shape, and use.

Develop drawing on blackboard from collected pictures found in advertisements. Shop may be made from heavy paper. Always construct model before attempting to teach it.

Follow directions on plate. A similar model may be made later for a picnic project as an amusement stand.

BOOK III, PAGE 23—LEARNING ABOUT GOD'S HOUSE

Character Objective: Reverence.

Spiritual Objective: To impress on the minds of children the meaning of the most essential parts of the Altar and its use during the most important ceremony of their Faith.

Art Objective: To develop craftsmanship in making a well constructed piece of work.

Supplies: Containers (to hold flowers), flowers of various heights

Procedure: Develop the lesson along religious lines while the construction of the problem is carried along. Review lessons on altar in Book II for symbolism. In this type of lesson planned particularly to motivate the religious lesson, there is not much opportunity for individual variations. Design of altar may be varied but symbolism must be followed. The design of the containers to hold the flowers for the altar offers an excellent lesson in creative expression and judgment. Fold paper for cutting bowl and vase shapes, remembering that **short-stemmed small flowers** look best in **broad low containers** and **long-stemmed flowers** look well in **tall slender vases.**

This problem may be taken as a separate lesson in appreciation of beauty in the home and reviewed for use on the altar.

Ask children to find lovely container shapes for the blank page.

BOOK III, PAGE 25—A COLOR LESSON

Character Objective: Understanding.

Spiritual Objective: To teach children the meaning of the common symbols used in church architecture, in order that they may understand the messages about God to be found in His House.

Art Objective:

1—To make children sensitive to beautiful color in its many combinations through the experience of making a stained glass window.

2—To continue the development of a sense of fine arrangement through making a booklet of Gothic symbols.

Supplies: Chalk and blackboard (optional), paper, scissors, paste, paint and brushes

Procedure: Discuss with the children why God's House should show man's most beautiful work. Draw symbols on the blackboard, giving their meaning. The **circle** symbolizes Eternity because it has no beginning and no end.

The **square** symbolizes the world and life and the **square within a circle,** life eternal. The tiny **crockets** found on the arches are suggestive of the top of a shepherd's crook to remind us that God is the Great Shepherd, and the Pastor of the church takes His place as the shepherd of his parish.

Ask children to notice windows in church, whether **pointed**, called Gothic, or **round**, called Roman. Follow directions in painting, cutting, and pasting the window in order of steps shown in the book.

Make a booklet and draw the symbols, placing name and meaning under each with crayola. Children plan color and page arrangement. Notice the relationship of letters to illustration on each page and emphasize correct margins.

Review lesson on cover design given on page 17 and have children suggest various arrangements for decoration of title. Show several types on blackboard, ex., borders of symbols repeated or alternated. Radial arrangement or Radiation as shown on plate.

BOOK III, PAGE 27—LEARNING TO SEE

Character Objective: Initiative

Spiritual Objective: To develop appreciation of God's wonderful gift of sight by training children to see truthfully.

Art Objective:

1—To develop observation and coordination through drawing pail or other circular container with handle.

2—To develop alertness and originality through the game of changing the appearance of a basic shape quickly.

Supplies: Chalk and blackboard (optional), paints and brushes

Procedure: Read text and follow directions for coloring outside of pails. This simplifies the problem for the children by massing the spaces showing **inside** and **outside** of pail. Call for criticisms of relative proportions, proportions of handle to pail; how far up may it go? How far down?

Close books. Continue work at blackboard, using a real model similar in shape and large enough to be seen by all the children. Arrange handle, allow children to look **once** and draw from memory.

Failure causes loss of place at board and if the work is being used as a game, opposing sides take vacated places. Children at seats are quickly aware of errors, as they are comparing **drawing** with **real object.** At this stage accuracy of **drawing** is unimportant as compared with accuracy of **placing handle** and **fair proportions.** This tests true vision. Children are still in the play period of childhood and this instinct should be used to add interest so vital in making deep and lasting impressions.

Continuing with the game of "Seeing" shown in the lower part of the plate, ask children to notice objects outside or at home, based on the shape of the half sphere or hemisphere. Then follow directions suggested for game, using either blackboard or paper. Ask children to find pictures based on hemisphere to paste on the blank page to help them know shapes for future games.

BOOK III, PAGE 29—FOR OUR PATRIOTIC PARTY

Character Objective: Patriotism

Spiritual Objective: To teach children that love of God and love of country go hand in hand, and the victory for both is achieved through following God's laws.

Art Objective: To teach recognition of basic shapes used in construction and design.

Supplies: Chalk and blackboard (optional), crayons, colored paper

Procedure: The problem is planned for Feb. 12th or 22nd.

Read the text and follow instructions for coloring, after shapes with their names have been placed on the blackboard and compared.

Have children note points of similarity as a help for future recognition.

The game of finding the shapes on the soldier by similarity of color used offers a test of a child's ability to recognize form.

When ready to make original soldier, vary the shapes by adding the circle and half circle and then continue in the same way. Colored paper may be used for original figure. The addition of a support will adapt this lesson to place cards for a real party.

Shapes to be learned are square, (having four sides equal and four square corners) right triangle, (having one square corner) oblong or rectangle, (having two long and two short sides and four square corners). The other shapes are combinations or modifications of these.

BOOK III, PAGE 31—CLAY PICTURES

Character Objective: Love and Sympathy

Spiritual Objectives:

1—To give children an acute realization of the story of Calvary through their building in miniature its details.

2—To review the meaning of the Rosary through constructing it from clay.

Art Objective: To teach construction of a clay tile keeping it of uniform thickness.

Supplies: Clay, wire or wood, crayons

General Suggestions: The problems on page 31 are planned for various seasons throughout the year to emphasize the work in religion. The Calvary should be made as a classroom project. The crosses in the picture have no inside support, but it is more satisfactory if wire or wood is used to support the clay. An incident will illustrate the effect this work has on the child mind: A member of a group at work on the story, in a settlement school, inquired how the hillside should be made. Before the teacher could reply, another boy had answered "Make it rough—didn't He fall going up!" Again a child inquired abruptly while making the Rosary, "Does our Blessed Mother know we are making this now?"

The new step in clay modeling to be mastered in this grade is keeping uniform thickness in the making of a tile. Read directions for handling clay under General Notes and Books 1 and 2, subject matter. Then follow directions given in text below the plate.

Notice how the difficulty of weight has been eliminated by the addition of the pedestal in making of the rooster.

At the end of the lesson the clay is always put back into the bag. Save only a couple of the best models. When dry they may be colored with crayola.

BOOK III, PAGE 33—ON THE FARM

Character Objective: Truthfulness

Spiritual Objective: To teach children that real bravery results from the strong growth of courage in little acts of every day.

Art Objectives:

1—To teach a knowledge of form through observation, and to increase graphic vocabulary.

2—To teach the adaptation of **natural** forms to design.

Supplies: Chalk and blackboard (optional), paper, scissors, paste, crayons

Procedure: Tell the story of St. Peter's denial of Christ and his subsequent repentance as a basis for the religious objective. Explain why the cock is the symbol of the **vigilance** of the Church because always the dawn finds him alert to announce its approach. So the church is the alert guardian of her children, ready to warn them of the dangers of sin.

Have children follow the method of drawing shown on the plate, at seats, and then have them work from memory on the blackboard, as soon as forms are sufficiently familiar, in any suggested action through adjustment of ovals; suggest illustrations for "Little Half Chick," "The Little Red Hen," etc.

Lesson 2: As an English lesson reproduce the story of St. Peter's Denial in booklet form and decorate cover with cut out rooster and suitable lettering which is to be drawn instead of pasted.

BOOK III, PAGE 35—HEALING THE SICK

Character Objective: Charity

Spiritual Objective: To acquaint children with the Divine Power shown on earth by our Lord during His ministry to the poor who followed Him daily. Aim to build within them a supreme faith in His loving tenderness. Show how they too may help the sick by kindness.

Art Objective: To teach children the essentials of landscape composition.

Supplies: Scissors, magazines, paste, blank paper, crayons

Procedure: Read the text and discuss it with the children after telling the story of Christ healing the sick. As in other picture study, by well directed questions, stimulate the imagination of the children to visualize other settings for the story. Could the group be placed in a setting under the palm trees across the river? Could they be placed near the buildings across the river? If so, what changes would have to be made in the composition or picture?

Points to be learned by children for future work are:

1—Objects in **distance** are placed **higher** in picture and vice versa.

2—Objects in distance are **smaller**.

3—Objects in distance are **lighter in color.**

Have children cut pictures of modern figures from magazines and use them as models for cutting action figures, for Parables and other stories.

Show pupils as many pictures of figures costumed in Biblical costumes as possible. Discuss the costumes as compared with clothing of today. Paste these on blank page.

Have children recognize familiar points in composition, in numerous pictures.

BOOK III, PAGE 37—AN EASTER CARD

Character Objective: Thoughtfulness

Spiritual Objective: To teach children the meaning of the Resurrection and the symbols relating to it.

Art Objective: To teach children that good design must harmonize with the object decorated, both in feeling and subject matter.

Scissors: Paper, crayons, paste, blank paper, bigger piece of paper for envelope

Procedure: Create in the pupils a desire to show their thoughtfulness of parents by remembering them on Easter with an Easter card sent to bring them the gladness of the Blessed Day.

Read the text and discuss it with the children, making clear the type of decoration suitable for the problem. Have children make suggestions of things they think would be suitable for the card. Plate shows two variations of the same theme, which will suggest others. A variation of the stained glass window used in the booklet with appropriate lettering might be used. Ask children to bring Easter cards of other years. Discuss and paste only those appropriate to the season, on the blank page. After the card has been finished, estimate the size of the envelope by making the paper more than twice the depth of card in order that upper and lower flaps will overlap for pasting.

BOOK III, PAGE 39—DAYS WE MUST KNOW

Character Objective: Responsiveness to Beauty

Spiritual Objective: To develop in children an appreciation of the beauty of the Catholic religion and to give them a knowledge of, and reason for, observing the laws of the Church.

Art Objective: To make children more observant of, and sensitive to the beautiful colors in nature through the experience gained in attempting to interpret them.

Supplies: Paints and brushes, crayons, construction paper, paste

Procedure: Read the text, emphasizing to children that Sundays are Holydays of Obligation as well as the special Feast Days named on the color circle. Study the landscape pictures, suggesting how color helps to give the sensations felt during the seasons. Demonstrate to children how landscape forms shown in each picture may be rearranged to make a new and original composition. Use the pictures shown on plate as models for color and rendering with either brush or crayola.

The four pictures may be put in booklet form if desired, to impress the facts on memory. As a help in memorizing the special Feast Days have children associate the color symbolism with the season during which the Feast occurs. Blue, yellow, green, and orange reflect the color of Nature's face during the advance of the seasons; purple symbolizes the penetential season of Advent and red symbolizes the love of the Divine Infant.

As this page has been planned as an informational lesson to be projected into the home, it will perform its most effective service there, if **sent home** artistically mounted on strong construction paper of a dark neutral tone, **at the time the lesson is finished** or as a gift.

BOOK III, PAGE 41—SPRING FLOWERS

Character Objective: Conservation

Spiritual Objective: To cause children to associate the beauty of goodness with the beauty of Spring flowers.

Art Objective: To develop in children an appreciation of the beautiful color and lovely shape of a tulip or other Spring flower.

Supplies: Tulip (if possible), crayon, colored paper, scissors, paste, blank paper

Procedure: Read the text and practice with crayon the method of drawing the tulip shown in the plate.

Follow the practice lesson with a lesson using a real tulip as a model. Place flower on paper harmonizing in shape with the flower. Have the stem of the flower extend below the paper, preferably not cutting the lower edge in the middle. Do not allow the flower to cut diagonally across the paper. Have the flower shape a little above center. Notice that background spaces made by flower and leaves are not monotonously alike. Allow the children to discuss the flower and leaves as to colors, growth, proportion, placing, shape. Recalling method of rendering already made familiar, have children interpret what the flower means to them.

Emphasize clean pure color, encouraging children to work vigorously, directly and intelligently. At the end of the lesson have quick exhibit for criticism.

Find flowers or other Spring growths to paste on the blank page.

BOOK III, PAGE 43 —A MAY ALTAR

Character Objective: Reverence, Devotion

Spiritual Objective: To create in children a sense of nearness and devotion to the Queen of Heaven.

Art Objective: To develop skill and neatness through construction of a shrine for our Blessed Mother.

Supplies: Construction paper or bogus paper, flower containers, flowers (if possible), paste, crayons, printed pictures of our Blessed Mother, blank paper

Procedure: Have children develop as much initiative as possible through helping to make a classroom May Altar. This may be expressed in decorated covers for flower pots; arrangement of flowers in suitable containers, etc. While interest is high read the text and allow them to discuss the method of construction.

Use colored construction or gray bogus paper. Follow directions shown on plate, being careful to paste the top squares one over the other.

Decorate with flowers cut from small scraps of colored paper or gray paper colored with crayola. Notice carefully the detail shown on page for method of obtaining small folds shown on unfolded model. If a sufficient number of printed pictures of our Blessed Mother are available, they will make the tiny shrine interesting. Find spring flowers to paste on the blank page.

BOOK III, PAGES 45 AND 47—A SCHOOL ROOM PLAY FOR OCTOBER

Character Objective: Cooperation

Spiritual Objective: To implant in the hearts of children a desire to help others to love God and to have children know something of the many visible manifestations of His approval of their work, that God has permitted to his followers.

Art Objective:

1—To develop creative imagination and skill in craftsmanship through play production.

2—To awaken interest in a native American art through Indian symbolism learned, and to teach its adaptations.

Supplies: Large sheets of bogus paper or tough wrapping paper, clay beads, cloth, chalk, paint and brushes

THE MISSIONARY

A legend of Father Junípero Serra from authentic memoirs of Archbishop Lamy, the first Bishop of Santa Fe, for whom the station of Lamy, N. M., has been named. Bishop Lamy has been immortalized by Miss Willa Cather in her superb story, "Death Comes for the Archbishop" (Alfred Knopf, New York), from which this story is taken.

"One night Father Latour (Bishop Lamy) was entertained by a priest from one of the western missions, who told him a story of the beloved Father Junípero Serra, which had come down in his own monastery from the old times.

Father Junípero, with a single companion, had once arrived at this monastery on foot, without provisions. The Brothers welcomed the two in astonishment, believing it impossible that men could have crossed so great a stretch of desert in this manner.

The Superior questioned them as to whence they had come and said the mission should not have allowed them to set off without a guide and without food. He marveled how they could have come through alive. But Father Junípero replied that they had fared very well and had been most agreeably entertained by a poor Mexican family on the way. At this a muleteer who was bringing in wood for the Brothers, began to laugh and said there was no house for twelve leagues, nor anyone at all living in the sandy waste through which they had come; and the Brothers confirmed him.

Then Father Junípero and his companion related fully their adventure.

They had set out with bread and water for one day, but on the second day they had been traveling since dawn across a cactus desert and near sunset had begun to lose heart, when they espied in the distance three great cottonwood trees, very tall in the declining light. Toward these trees they hastened. As they approached the trees, which were large and green and were shedding cotton freely, they observed an ass tied to a dead trunk which stuck up out of the sand. Looking about for the owner of the ass they came upon a little Mexican house with an oven by the door, and strings of red peppers hanging on the wall. When they called aloud, a venerable Mexican, clad in sheepskins, came out and greeted them kindly, asking them to stay the night. Going in with him they observed that all was neat and comely, and the wife, a young woman of beautiful countenance, was stirring porridge by the fire. Her child, scarcely more than an infant, and with no garment but his little shirt, was on the floor beside her playing with a pet lamb.

They found these people gentle, pious, and well spoken. The husband said they were shepherds. The priests sat at their table and shared their supper and afterward read the evening prayers. They had wished to question the host about the country and about his mode of life and where he found pasture for his flock, but they were overcome by a great and sweet weariness, and taking each a sheepskin provided him, they lay down upon the floor and sank into deep sleep.

When they awoke in the morning they found all as before, and food set upon the table, but the family were absent, even to the pet lamb—having gone, the Fathers supposed, to care for their flocks.

When the Brothers at the Monastery heard this they were amazed, declaring that there were indeed three cottonwood trees growing together in the desert, a well known landmark, but that if a settler had come he must have come very lately. So Father Junipero and Father Andrea his companion, with some of the Brothers and the scoffing muleteer, went back into the wilderness to prove the matter. The three tall trees they found shedding their cotton, and the dead trunk to which the ass was tied, but the ass was not there, nor any house, nor the oven by the door. Then the two Fathers sank down upon their knees in that blessed spot and kissed the earth, for they perceived what Family it was that had entertained them there.

Father Junipero confessed to the Brothers how from the moment he entered the house he had been strangely drawn to the Child and desired to take Him in his arms, but that He kept near His mother. When the priest was reading the evening prayers, the Child sat upon the floor against His mother's knee with the lamb in His lap and the Father found it hard to keep his eyes upon his breviary.

After prayers, when he bade his hosts good-night, he did indeed stoop over the Little Boy in blessing and the Child had lifted His hand and with His tiny finger made the cross upon Father Junipero's forehead."

This story of Father Junipero's Holy Family made a strong impression upon the Bishop when it was told him by the fire of that great hacienda where he was a guest for the night. He had such an affection for that story that he allowed himself to repeat it on but two occasions, once to the nuns in Mother Philomene's convent in Riom, and once at a dinner given by the Cardinal Mazzucchi in Rome.

There is always something charming in the idea of greatness returning to simplicity—the queen making hay among the country girls—but how much more endearing is the belief that They, after so many centuries of history and glory, should return to play Their first parts in the persons of a humble Mexican family, the lowliest of the lowly, the poorest of the poor, in a wilderness at the end of the world, where the angels could scarcely find Them!

General Suggestions: The selection of one of their own number as a Director for the play adds interest and arouses a sense of responsibility in each member of the group. Help the Director to organize groups with definite assignments for various parts of the completed unit of work, such as library references, costume making, blackboard illustration, wigwam decorating, pottery making, etc.

If the play is given for the school all the children in the class may be included in the characters. If given in classroom, half the room should be kept as audience and the play repeated to allow all children to have an active part. If repeated, the story may be changed to the incidents in the life of "Tagewatha" which may be found in the Catholic Encyclopedia. Remember that simplicity is the keynote of success and children's imagination will be found valuable in supplying deficiencies.

Costumes: Costumes may be made from large sheets of bogus paper or large sheets of tough wrapping paper. Clay beads made in previous lessons and colored may be used for decoration. If it is necessary to paint a design on cloth, apply design first with chalk and then add color.

The Story: The dialogue of the play should be planned as an **English** correlation and should grow out of the children's efforts to reproduce the story in their own way. This will give it new life each time it is repeated. It is a good plan **to make an outline of events** to be incorporated before beginning, in order to help children to develop logical thought.

Read directions given for sets in Book I and Book IV. The same general scheme may be followed for location, curtain, etc. The action of the play begins **outside** the curtain showing the two priests lost on the desert. Have the dialogue include a description of the desert from pictures previously seen and descriptions heard. Copies of geographical magazines are excellent and can be had at a library. The scene will end as they start for the three cottonwood trees.

The second scene is shown when the curtain is pulled aside to show an Indian village which was the objective of the Missionaries when they become lost.

The Missionary and his companion tell to the Indians the story of their wonderful visitation. They tell also of their stopping at the monastery. The rest of the play should develop around the mode of living and customs of the Indians, and the dangers risked by the Missionaries to bring to them a knowledge of the loving God.

Religion: Elaborate on work of Missionaries, today and long ago. Essential need remains same. Opportunity is presented here for teaching form for **emergency Baptism** if an American trapper or scout is added to the company to perform it before the Missionary arrives.

English:

1—Have entire class repeat complete an oral reproduction of the story by having each pupil give three or four well constructed, coherent sentences.

2—Have story briefly reproduced in written form in paragraphs of three or four well constructed, coherent sentences. Emphasize the habit of indenting paragraphs and keeping left hand margin, as well as capitals previously learned.

Arithmetic: Problems about distance traveled by Missionaries; numbers of persons helped by Missionaries in a stated time; amount of paper required for costumes; many other problems will suggest themselves, suiting the degree of attainment required in course.

Nature Study: Study of desert growths as cactus and animals familiar to Indians. Teach care and kindness to animals.

Geography: Home and environment of Indians, occupations, etc.

History: Work done by early Missionaries in the development of the country, in every State of the Union.

Word Study: Recognition of new words and their meaning.

Music: Learning an Indian song and a simple dance to be given around campfire.

Color Design: Comparison of strong colors used by Indians with subdued colors used in homes of today. Colors did not appear too strong as they were used in the open spaces. Use of Symbols in their design.

Costume: Compare costumes of Indians, Missionaries, and Trappers or scouts. Allow children to discover that there is usually a reason behind a particular style of dress.

Creative Expression: Is developed as a vital necessity in all related work.

Book Four

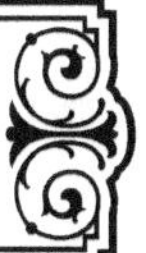

BOOK IV—COVER

See page 3 of this manual.

BOOK IV—END PAPER

Character Objective: Prayerfulness

Spiritual Objective: To teach children the meaning of a Vocation, as exemplified in the story of Martha and Mary.

Art Objective:

1—To teach the use of the bird in design as shown in an all-over pattern.

2—To develop appreciation of a fine arrangement of lettering and decoration.

Supplies: Paint and brushes, crayons

Procedure: Read the poem, explaining the meaning of the lines. Call on the imagination of the children to describe the setting of the little home. Make it clear that birds used in the design have been selected because the parrot shapes fitted into an interesting design and presented a contrast to the singing birds. The notes are symbols of music and are designed to lead the eye from one group of birds to the next. Notice the fine contrast of dark and light and the interesting smaller designs shown on the birds' wings. A nice effect may be obtained by painting a light wash of color over the birds with a contrasting tint on the notes, for example, tints of violet and green.

Have pupils try original bird designs in an all-over pattern and use one on the cover of a booklet about birds.

BOOK IV, PAGE 1—ST. JOHN THE BAPTIST

Character Objective: Courage

Spiritual Objective: To teach children that as St. John the Baptist went out as a messenger of God, "a voice crying in the wilderness," so they also have a responsibility as "messengers" to go through this world spreading a love of God by showing a fine example of love and service to all with whom they may come in contact.

Art Objective: To develop in children an increased appreciation of pictures through their understanding of the principle of dominance in a composition.

Teacher's Preparation: As a preparation for your teaching, study the picture and analyze its appeal to yourself.

Is its strongest appeal for your appreciation in the strong young body with its clear, fearless eyes of youthful certainty? Radiating health and vigor, the artist has shown us a perfect specimen of the Creator's work. Possibly added to this you may have felt its religious appeal because of the rich background of events surrounding this best beloved of the Disciples. Were you first conscious of the warm rich wave of color that seems to envelop the whole picture like a burst of beautiful music which continues in its still lovelier echoes until they gradually die away?

Notice the gorgeous red with its symbolic meaning, caught in rhythmic folds of the cloak over his left arm, a little more orange as it swings around the right hand, emphasizing the rich golden tones of the body accented again by the red and orange tones of the curly hair. The rich colors of the mysterious background give hints of a wealth of buried brilliance, deftly subdued by the "faultless painter," Andrea del Sarto. The picture shows superb modeling of the boyish figure and faultless design in the composition. The figure placed slightly to the left of the center is perfectly balanced by the red robe. The light paper in his hand is balanced by the knot on his shoulder.

Notice the rich transparent shadow behind the cross which emphasizes it without making it too important. Notice the fine textural quality shown in the painting of each piece of material.

Andrea del Sarto always achieved a calm majesty in his figures whether used singly or in groups and the rich brilliancy of his colors has not been surpassed.

He painted in Florence, Italy, in the early part of the 16th Century and was a friend of Raphael and Michael Angelo.

Procedure: Have pupils open books and enjoy the picture for a few minutes, undisturbed. The beauty of the picture should be allowed to make its own appeal. Call on pupils to give their impressions as a basis for continued study.

Develop the fact that the artist in planning his composition planned carefully every tiny detail and any change would detract from its beauty.

How has the artist made St. John the **dominant interest?** Has he made use of the **principle of contrast?** Notice the rich transparent shadow behind the cross which emphasizes it without making it too important. What principle of composition does this illustrate? How has it helped the artist?

How many tones of orange has the artist used? Why does the boy's face compel your attention (effect of portraiture achieved by artist)? Has the artist shown the character of the boy? How? What features are most expressive? In what other picture did we find St. John as a child? Does the figure show action? Why?

Continue the discussion as long as interest continues keen. When finished, cut the picture about half inch from the binding and preserve it until Christmas when it will make a beautiful gift artistically mounted.

For additional picture study, see page xxx.

BOOK IV, PAGE 3—NATURE

Character Objective: Love of Beauty

Spiritual Objective: To open the eyes of children to the wondrous beauty and miracles of nature and at the same time open their **spiritual** eyes to the Beauty that is God. As leaves need water to give them life and perfect growth so that they may reach their final beauty under Autumn sunlight, **so the soul must receive life** from the Sacraments to achieve final beauty for God.

Art Objective: To develop a discriminating color sense through color experience and skill in interpreting color observed.

Supplies: Paints and brushes, crayon, colorful leaves

Procedure: Using books, have children read text carefully and experiment with both methods of rendering leaves.

Ask each pupil to find a beautifully colored leaf if possible so that each pupil will have his own specimen. Have each pupil discuss structure and color of his individual leaf. Brush and color is more satisfactory than crayola, as pupil sees effects of color combinations. Green, orange, and pure fresh red are added for the brilliant colors, while the shadow colors, purple and blue, are added and allowed to blend with the brighter colors as indicated in the real leaf. If crayon is used as shown in the upper picture, **stronger** pressure will give **more brilliant** color.

Examples of flowers showing Radiation may also be pasted on the blank page. Children may exchange leaves for continued study.

BOOK IV, PAGE 5—VEGETABLES

Character Objective: Alertness

Spiritual Objective: To cause children to visualize the effect of sin on the soul through seeing the result of the **lack of cleanliness** in using paint, as suggested in Book III, Page 9. The highlight shows the reflection of the light on the pepper and when its shape is kept free of paint, it makes the pepper shine; the soul shows the bright reflection of God after Baptism and must be carefully guarded from evil to keep the soul shining and bright.

Art Objective: To teach skill in the technique of water color and keen observation in characteristics of nature forms.

Supplies: Paints and brushes, paper

Procedure: Have children read text carefully and then experiment by following directions on plate. After trying the pepper try the other forms in the panel at the bottom of the page. Test children's knowledge of vegetable color by having them make their own selections of color.

Emphasize the use of pure color and direct painting in all nature work. Touch brush to water and then to each primary needed to make the binary and allow colors to mix on the paper. Brush must be made clean after each time it is used on the paper to be sure that colors are kept pure and brilliant. Follow the practice lesson from the book with a lesson from any real vegetable. This is the test of the pupil's real ability to interpret what he sees. The method of rendering will be the same. Discuss texture, proportion, use, etc., carrying on a lively discussion before the painting lesson begins.

BOOK IV, PAGE 7—FREEHAND LETTERING

Character Objective: Neatness and Order

Spiritual Objective: To help children to see that just as devices and guide lines help them to make letters true and beautiful, so God gives them His priests and Sisters and their parents to guide them in making the patterns of their lives beautiful. He also gives them a way to test themselves through the practice of obedience.

Art Objective: To develop skill in lettering a simple alphabet quickly and well.

Supplies: Rulers, ruled paper, crayons or pencils

Procedure: Read the text carefully. The children should be aware of the essentials of good lettering which are:

1—Uniform size.
2—Uniform thickness.
3—Uniform slant
4—Apparently uniform spacing.

Have children use ruled paper and begin practice in making a series of vertical strokes, an essential part of most letters. After making a number, test accuracy, as shown in illustration, by using a card or envelope with one edge on the line to see whether letter stroke is parallel with the other edge of the card. Continue vertical strokes making them in pairs spaced as shown and turn them into the letter H by adding the horizontal stroke above the middle. Using this letter as the measure of size for all the other letters, turn the vertical strokes into as many letters as possible, by curving the corners. Finish with the slant letters, keeping the same width and height as H. When pupils have gained sufficient skill in lettering with guide lines have them try placing two straight edges of paper as shown in the illustration to keep letters uniform. Changing the width of the space changes the size of letters and when finished there are no lines to be erased. This plan is convenient for maps and is an excellent way to impress the spelling of new words in English.

BOOK IV, PAGE 9—THE COLOR STORY CONTINUES

Character Objective: Purity

Spiritual Objective: Through association, to create in the child's mind a keen realization of the powerful assistance God has placed in their possession by means of the Sacraments of Penance and Holy Communion, which form **a magic curtain of safety** for the soul, protecting it from the ugly dragon of Sin.

Art Objective: To develop a discriminating color sense in children which will make them conscious of color combinations in their environment, rejecting those not pleasing.

Supplies: Glasses of water, paint or ink, magazine clippings, paste, blank paper

Procedure: Have children read the text discussing how the magic curtain has changed the color on each of the colored knights as well as changing the white knight and the black knight. The transparent curtain has three bands, light gray, middle gray, and dark gray. If time permits the color pages may be dramatized into a color **pageant**, elaborating on the story of the knights in Books III and IV.

The values of gray shown on the curtain at the top of the page and a similar scale shown on the blocks at the bottom of the page are called **neutral** values, because no color can be discerned in them. They are made by combining varying amounts of black and white. An equal amount of black and white produces **middle gray;** an equal amount of black with middle gray produces **dark gray.** Black is the absence of all light. White is the absence of all black.

White added to any color makes that color a **lighter** color value or a **tint** of the color. Black added to any color gives that color a **darker** value or a **shade** of the color. A color in its pure state is called **normal** and when we add black or white to it we change its **value**.

Demonstrate the effect of the addition of black and white to color by using two glasses partly filled with colored water, both showing a primary color, as red—to one slowly add white and note result, to the other slowly add black and note the change. Pupils should experiment with the other colors in the same way. Note which normal colors are on the **light** side of the value scale shown on the curtain and which are on the **dark** side. Have children find **neutral** values and **color** values in their clothing, in objects in the class room, etc. Have them bring to class magazine clippings illustrating points discussed in the lesson. Paste neatly on the blank page with appropriate lettering to explain.

BOOK IV, PAGE 11—COLOR VALUES

Character Objective: Carefulness

Spiritual Objective: To help children appreciate the wonderful scheme of nutrition, planned by God to keep them well and strong to love and serve Him. Show what an important part teeth play in carrying on the work. As a thorough brushing of teeth daily removes dangerous particles of decayed food from the teeth, so frequent Confession and a thorough **brushing** or **examination** of Conscience will remove dangerous blemishes from the soul.

Art Objective: To teach children the necessity of keeping a center of interest in any composition they may wish to create.

Supplies: Pictures of bathrooms or other details, paste, blank paper, water, paints and brushes, white paper, heavy paper/construction paper

Procedure: This poster has been prepared to test the pupils in their understanding of the color theory presented as well as the design principle of dominance.

Read and discuss the text, developing the health lesson and the religious lesson through well directed questions.

As a second lesson discuss the furnishing and color of bath rooms as compared with other rooms at home. Is the color scheme of the bath room usually planned with light or dark values of color? Find pictures of bath rooms or other details related to the lesson. Paste them on the blank page to create a **dominant interest** on the page. The third lesson may be the color application. Each pupil plans his own color scheme. What color should the mirror be? As it reflects the light it should have the same color as light shown in window. Emphasize the use of very light values of color for everything in the background. One way to emphasize the center of interest is to keep colors **flat**, that is all parts the same value. Colors on posters are usually painted this way.

Place two or three brushfuls of water in lid of color box and add one brushful of color desired; paint carefully within space planned for color. Colors used on the boy's costume may be **stronger** to **emphasize the interest,** and a tiny touch of pure color on the **back** and handle of the brush will also emphasize the message of the poster. Flesh tones may be made by placing a brushful of water in the box lid and touching the tip of the brush **lightly** to red and to the yellow. Try the color before painting the face, and if too strong, add more water. The white paper helps to make the light values. The addition of black or other dark color to trousers or hair helps to emphasize the **center of interest** through **contrast**.

The lettering may be emphasized through contrast by making panel dark and letters light, or vice versa.

After the poster has been carefully painted, cut it about half inch from binding, mount it artistically on heavy paper and send it home as a daily reminder of health, both physical and spiritual.

Review this lesson by requiring pupils to make an original poster much more simple, when a school occasion such as "Thrift," "Punctuality," or other campaign requires it. At this stage **figures are too difficult for posters.** Keep decoration very simple, as toothbrush and glass, only, for this type of health poster. Special attention is directed at this time to fine arrangement of good lettering.

BOOK IV, PAGE 13—CHARITY

Character Objective: Charity

Spiritual Objective: To help children to realize that the Holy Souls were once living people just like themselves. Just as the man driving an automobile will make mistakes if he fails to watch the sign posts, lose time getting to the end of his journey, and have to depend on other motorists to help him get there, so the Souls in Purgatory when alive sometimes failed to see the signposts of God's love and grace and carelessly offended Him. Now we want to help them reach the end of their journey.

Art Objective: To develop an appreciation of fine spacing through a study of suitable cover design and fine page arrangement.

Procedure: Read the text and develop the religious objective. Review previous lessons on marginal spaces as fine margins always give distinction to a page. Notice that two pages are shown as a **single unit** which conforms to rules already given.

Have children suggest other plans for the decoration of the cover. Which should be made **dominant**, the letters or the decoration?

In what other ways could they show **contrast of values?** Why are **neutral** values best for this problem? What symbols could be used with the offerings instead of the figures to show the number? Creative original work is always secured through specific questions planned to start **thinking**. Follow the lessons on this page with another similar lesson for fruit, trees, etc.

BOOK IV, PAGE 15—DESIGN

Character Objective: Initiative

Spiritual Objective: To teach children that each day they are making a design of their lives. Their acts and thoughts are like the design blocks they are making. Some combinations are beautiful and please God, others are not pleasing and must be remedied. The impression is made and long after we have forgotten, God still keeps the pattern to show to us when we return to Him. Emphasize the difficulty in removing impressions made by the blocks when they are incorrect.

Art Objective: To teach children to create orderly design by stick printing.

Supplies: Paints and brushes, cardboard, scissors, paste, pins, pencil, paper

Procedure: Have children read the text carefully, discussing new terms and their meaning. It is easy for children to acquire a necessary vocabulary of technical names if they are made familiar with them through constant use. Follow the method shown clearly on Page 15. Use any of the media suggested for making design block. For the problem use colors contrasting in dark and light. Use this page as suggestions for practice work, then later apply method to a real problem.

A simple pin holder may be made by covering one side each of two cardboard squares, folding edges to inside. Paste unfinished sides of squares together and stick the pins around the edges of squares. Decorate the squares with an original block, either all-over or border. A pencil holder may be made from oblong the length of a pencil, covered on both sides and with an additional piece of paper added to the lower half to form an envelope for the pencils.

Decorate with stick printing.

BOOK IV, PAGE 17—A CHRISTMAS GIFT

Character Objective: Thoughtfulness for Others

Spiritual Objective: To give children a deeper appreciation of the "Great Christmas Gift" when God gave Himself to them, and following that example cause them to desire to give their best efforts to show their love for somebody. The snapshot book may also be paralleled with the book of Deeds, good and bad, which fill the "picture book" God keeps to record their lives.

Art Objective: To teach good craftsmanship through mastering the essentials of elementary book making.

Supplies: Magazines, paste, newspapers

Procedure: Read the text and make sure that pupils understand the meaning of all words used in the directions. Suggestions for simple design may be found as decorations on the advertising pages of any magazine.

When pasting paper it is wise to cover the desk with a newspaper and **allow paste to go over the edge** of the cover paper onto the newspaper. Apply paste evenly with three fingers, **keeping thumb and forefinger clean.** The best results are obtained by covering the entire paper with paste, but when economy makes this not advisable, the paste may be applied to edges only.

BOOK IV, PAGE 19—THE PRESENTATION

Character Objective: Fortitude

Spiritual Objective: To help children to understand that God sends pain and suffering to those He loves as another form of Grace, when these are accepted without protest. Just as a little dark in a pattern makes it more beautiful because it emphasizes the light, so suffering emphasizes happiness.

Art Objective: To teach simple proportions of the human body through folding paper.

Supplies: Paper, scissors, magazines

Procedure: Read the text as a basis for the religious development. Note characteristics shown in silhouette figures to denote different ages. Have children find magazine figures showing different ages and compare them.

Be careful that pupil uses a piece of paper for his cutting which has the same proportions desired for figure. Then cut to folds as shown on the plate. The cutting of Simeon shows him holding the Infant. This figure might also represent St. Joseph. Using these figures as part of their vocabulary have children create a new setting for the story instead of copying the one shown.

The picture shown on the plate is always intended as a fine standard of work and a suggestion for the pupils' own creative expression. **Originality develops through its stimulation and exercise.**

BOOK IV, PAGE 21—EGYPTIAN DESIGN

Character Objective: Faith

Spiritual Objective: The story of Nile River with the resultant sacred symbol, the Lotus, which meant so much to the pagan Egyptians, will suggest the effects of the cleansing grace of Confession and the purity of the soul when it receives the All Pure in Holy Communion.

Art Objective:

1—To teach Egyptian Symbolism as an aid to appreciation of Architecture and Museum study.

2—To teach something about another form of picture writing.

Supplies: Charcoal, white chalk, gray bogus paper, paper, paste, crayons or pencils, scissors, newspapers

Procedure: Read the text and develop the picture along similar lines as suggested on Page 1 in each book of the series. The illustration on the plate was made with charcoal and white chalk on gray bogus paper.

The panel at the bottom of the page shows some significant Egyptian motifs commonly used in design today.

Egyptian ornament, because of its source in the legendary days of antiquity, can be made to arouse the keen interest of a class of this grade for its obvious relationship with the childhood days of Christ, the story of the Children of Israel, or the story of Joseph.

Tell the origin and use of a pyramid as the grave of the king or Pharaoh. To give an idea of size, compare it with something familiar, for example, a side of a pyramid 250 yards long could be compared with the distance of a 100 yard dash repeated.

These pyramids were built about 6,000 years ago, or three times as long ago as the birth of Christ. These pagans worshipped the sun because they knew it gave them life so the pyramids were on the left side of the Nile facing the setting sun. Only one person as a rule was buried in this great tomb. They believed the soul would be reunited with the body after doing penance, and therefore they prepared the dead to keep forever. We call them mummies. All the information we have about these people we have learned from the hieroglyphics. The finding of a stone on which a certain law was written in three languages, one being hieroglyphics, gave a key to this strange language. This stone is called the Rosetta Stone, and is now in the British Museum. The Sphinx is near the Great Pyramids and is even older. The head is of a human being, the portrait of the reigning king. The body is that of a lion, combining the highest type of intellectuality with the greatest strength and agility. As the king was supposed to be a relative of the gods, the Sphinx was an object of worship and a small temple for religious purposes was built directly in front of the body. The Sphinx is carved from solid rock and is 70 feet high and 150 feet long. The lotus flower, sacred because it sprang up in the rich mud after the annual overflow of the Nile river, was their popular design motif. We find it shown on either side of the panel at the bottom of the page. Completely opened, it is much like our water lily. The picture in the book shows the two leaf forms as well, planned as a decoration. The narrow panel with the curved lines shows the symbol the Egyptians used to show the sacred River Nile. It is the wave scroll. The center panel shows the winged globe, commonly used today, in modified form. The circle means the sun (creation), the wings protection, and the snake or royal asp on either side of the sun means the power to distribute blessings, as the asp was the emblem of the king. Notice the asp on the headdress of the king in the picture.

In making their statues or pictures, they made the king the center of interest by making him larger than other people.

Ask pupils to make a booklet about some of the Biblical stories related, and decorate it with some Egyptian motifs or make a booklet of motifs with explanations neatly lettered. Encourage trips to the Museum if you are near one, and have children find other symbols and characteristics. The newspapers are often filled with colored pictures of early Egyptian excavations.

BOOK IV, PAGE 23—SHADOW PICTURES

Character Objective: Cheerfulness

Spiritual Objective: To have children feel that just as the shadow pictures on the page tell what each child is doing, so each thought and action of their lives will leave a picture which does not disappear, as does the shadow, but remains to show God how much we love Him or how little.

Art Objective: To teach children essential proportions for sketching children in **action**.

Supplies: Rulers, magazines or newspapers, yardstick

Procedure: The step in figure drawing to be stressed in this is action with fairly good proportions.

Have a pupil stand before the class. With a long ruler show the meaning of the proportion or skeleton lines shown at the top of the page by placing the ruler on his back, legs, arms, etc. As he bends, have children observe that the ruler changes direction as shown on body, arms, or legs. Copying the pictures on the plate helps them to estimate thickness and details of clothing. Have them find silhouettes of children in magazines and newspapers for observation and comparison. Tell a story involving dramatic action as the story of St. George and the Dragon, allowing another boy to impersonate the dragon, and having a dramatization of the duel with St. George, by using a yard stick for his sword.

While the interest is high, call for an illustration of the story, starting with the best action of St. George held for a few minutes as a posed figure. The story of Beowulf is full of dramatic action. At the end of the lesson have children criticize the results of the lesson from the standpoint of action, but with incidental criticisms of proportion.

BOOK IV, PAGE 25—ST. FRANCIS

Character Objective: Love

Spiritual Objective: As St. Francis spread a love of God by his example of showing love for his neighbor, so children can show by good example to others, how they are trying to serve God through everything that contributes to make up their days. Help them to know that **service is prayer.**

Art Objective: To develop an appreciation of good composition through a knowledge of the principle of **Dominance**.

Supplies: Scissors, paper

Procedure: Tell the story of St. Francis, explain that the cord worn by all the members of the Franciscan Order, both Monks and Nuns, symbolizes the subjection of the body to the spirit and the coarse brown habit symbolizes penance.

Review what was learned about Dominance on page 11. What has the artist done to make St. Francis the **center of interest?** By using dark paper he has given the saint **strong contrast** against the **light background**. The circular movement of the birds on the left leads the eye from his head to his feet and on the right the tree trunks serve the same purpose. The dark foreground and vertical figure give strength to the composition.

Ask children to illustrate other incidents in the life of St. Francis. A class room community border could be planned, having different groups illustrate various incidents. A project of this type is most effectively carried out with cut paper.

BOOK IV, PAGE 27—LEARNING TO SEE

Character Objective: Alertness

Spiritual Objective: To develop a keener appreciation of God's priceless gift of sight with a sense of responsibility for using it correctly and in God's service.

Art Objective: To teach children to correctly observe and interpret what they see.

Supplies: Chalk and blackboard (optional), paints and brushes, gray bogus paper, white chalk

Procedure: Read the text and follow the directions. The **three** circles on one pencil allows children to see at once the result shown in the picture. The text directs them to use one circle seeing the effect as it changes position. As the circle is slowly raised, the colored **diameter** grows **shorter** and **shorter**. When it has entirely disappeared, ask children to **bring it toward them,** when they will discover for themselves that it touches the eyes, proving that when on the eye level only the edge can be seen as **a straight line.**

Have children work on the blackboard with swinging free arm movement and then observe how many common objects illustrate the ellipse in various positions. Follow this lesson with tests on quick sketches of familiar circular objects in classroom. Objects having color will be found much more interesting than those without. A Japanese lantern lesson is always a source of joy. The wooden bands, top and bottom, serve to test the level of ability of the pupils. The lesson is effective with brush and color on gray bogus paper, using white chalk for highlights.

BOOK IV, PAGE 29—OUR FLAG

Character Objective: Patriotism.

Spiritual Objective: To associate in the minds of children the close relationship existing between true love of Country and love of God. To teach children that the ideals on which this country were founded are pleasing in God's sight and that serving them, is serving Him.

Art Objective: To teach accuracy of measurement and symbolism through the making of the American flag.

Supplies: Rulers

Procedure: Using your classroom flag, which should not be left out continuously to be soiled, discuss with the children what they have previously learned about the flag. Teach the symbolism of the colors—Red, love and sacrifice; white, purity; blue, truth and loyalty.

The flag shown on the plate was carefully made to Government scale for correct proportions. If stripes are planned for ½ inch width the oblong for the flag would be 11 x 7½ inches with the blue field 3½ x 4½. The banners at the foot of the page are suggestions for other forms of patriotic decorations such as place cards for a Washington Birthday party, or other use that might suggest itself.

BOOK IV, PAGE 31—AT NIGHT

Character Objective: Reverence

Spiritual Objective: To help children to become conscious of the magnitude of God's power and to reverence the marvels of His creations, and realize by contrast how wonderful is His close intimacy with little children in Holy Communion, and His pleasure in receiving their love.

Art Objective: To direct attention to nature as a source of design.

Supplies: Scissors, thin paper, paste, colored construction paper

Procedure: Read and discuss the text, calling for stories about the stars to help fix some of the major planets and constellations. Get stories from the library about the sun and the moon and correlate with nature study. Experiment with cutting star shapes from thin folded paper, and pasting to a contrasting color as design units.

Observe shapes of baskets and cut original shape to be filled with decorative star flowers to show an interesting arrangement of light and dark colors on a background of neutral value. Have children suggest many possible types of design suitable for cover. Praise those showing much originality.

The booklet is planned as an illustrated nature study lesson.

BOOK IV, PAGE 33—A PARABLE

Character Objective: Thrift

Spiritual Objective: To teach children to exercise their reasoning powers and ability to draw conclusions as Christ intended they should, in understanding His parables, in order that their service of Him may be intelligent and loving.

Art Objective: To develop appreciation of fine composition through understanding the principle of dominance and to develop skill in cutting and pasting.

Supplies: Paper, crayons or pencils

Procedure: Tell the parable of the Lost Coin and interest pupils in reading and orally reproducing the other parables. In the illustration place well directed individual questions to develop the fact that the woman has been emphasized as the **center of interest** by placing her near the center, by making her dark in contrast to the background; by causing the dark door to lead the eye toward her; by causing the dark broom to lead the eye toward the lamp and thence to her arm. The attention is directed to the coin because of its **contrast** with the floor and the pointing finger of the woman. Dramatic interest is held because its hiding place has been found. The picture shows the type of home as compared with homes of today. Have children make an entirely different illustration, very much more simple than the plate, which should be considered as a fine standard.

If a standing figure sweeping is used, have a pupil dramatize the action before children attempt to illustrate. The lights in the picture are planned to give contrast and avoid monotony.

BOOK IV, PAGE 35—A CLAY TILE

Character Objective: Thoroughness

Spiritual Objective: To cause children to realize the immediate obedience Jesus rendered to His mother's wish and the relationship of the great miracle manifested then to the still greater miracle of the Holy Eucharist today.

Spiritual Objective: To cause an appreciation of sculpture through decorating a tile and learning the process of incising the lines.

Supplies: Clay, pencil, thin paper, candle

Procedure: Read the directions for presenting a clay lesson given on page xx and also review lessons previously presented in Book 2, Page 17 and Book 3, page 31. The pictures show clearly how the problem is carried on after the original drawing or design has been made with pencil on thin paper. Be sure to place margin line around picture and dimension lines on paper to show where surplus clay is to be cut off. Notice how the smooth finished line catches the light in the photograph. Notice the interesting spaces caused in the background by having the figure break the top, side, and bottom. The lettering would not be so legible if it touched the left margin line. The candlesticks would make an interesting lesson to be used to decorate the May Altar. Make stem and base separately and then weld them carefully together. Use a candle to make the opening.

BOOK IV, PAGE 37—TO MAKE A STENCIL

Character Objective: Judgment

Spiritual Objective: To develop in children an appreciation of what the **first** Easter meant to our Blessed Mother, and the others of Christ's followers. She alone was sure of His return, hence we do not find her at the tomb. Consider the joy of having dead loved ones suddenly return to life. Have children realize that God planned to come to them in the Blessed Eucharist that they too might share the joy of the Resurrection.

Art Objective: To teach children the use of a stencil in creating an original design for an Easter card.

Supplies: Chalk and blackboard (optional), scissors, paste, paints and brushes or crayons

Procedure: Read the text and review the previous lessons concerning the relationship lettering should have to decoration. Decide which is to show dominance. Have children suggest as you place them on the blackboard, the many symbols that would be appropriate for an Easter card.

Having decided on the subject matter, follow directions shown to add the bridges holding the design firm after background has been cut away. The arrangement of these little holders adds beauty to the design when carefully placed. Making the lines parallel to the enclosing shape insures a **likeness** or **harmony of shape** that is interesting. Care must be taken to avoid cutting the background into monotonous spaces.

Ask pupils to find cards showing fine simple lettering to paste on the blank page for reference.

Have children use colors showing contrast in light and dark. Call attention to the use of yellow, violet, and green as colors, symbolic colors for Easter—joy victorious over sorrow, light victorious over darkness. Refer to Book III, page 37 for construction of envelope.

BOOK IV, PAGE 39—THE MASS VESTMENTS

Character Objective: Reverence

Spiritual Objective: To develop in children a knowledge and appreciation of the liturgy and symbolism related to the Mass.

Art Objective: To arouse in children a responsiveness to beauty as shown in beautiful textiles and craftsmanship of articles used in the ceremony of the Mass.

Supplies: Gray bogus paper, scissors, paste, paints or crayons

Procedure: This page has been planned as source material for information and appreciation of articles related to the Holy Sacrifice of the Mass. The page should be cut one half inch from the binding to keep the binding secure. A booklet of desired size should be made, and as each article is explained it should be pasted and explanatory lettering placed beneath it to make a well designed page. When the book is finished, send it home to project this information into the home, where adult members will be found glad to receive it. Teach the colors of the vestments with their symbolical meaning and Church season in which each is worn.

The Alb: Originally a garment of every day worn by Romans in the first Centuries of the Church. It is now a white linen vestment with close fitting sleeves reaching nearly to the ground. It must be white, signifying purity. The priest puts it on with this prayer: "Purify me O Lord and make me clean of heart, that washed in the blood of the Lamb I may possess eternal joy."

The colored border shown at the bottom of the Alb in the photograph is called "Apparels." This dates back to the 13th Century as a form of decoration.

Maniple: A small strip of cloth, uniform in material with the Stole and Chasuble, embroidered with a triple cross, one in the middle and one at each of its extremities.

Its original use was as a towel or handkerchief to absorb the perspiration of the wearer and dry the hands to prevent soiling the vestments. It is assumed after the Cincture and before the Stole. It signifies:

1—The chains which bound Christ to the pillar.

2—The tears of penance and the labors and fruits of a good life. When he assumes it the priest says: "May I deserve, O Lord, to bear the Maniple of weeping and sorrow in order that I may reap joyfully the reward of my labors."

The Amice: A rectangular piece of linen with a string at two of its upper corners by which to fasten to the shoulders of the wearer. There is a cross on the middle of the upper edge which the priest kisses when vesting. It cannot be seen in the picture, being under the Alb. It comes from the words "to cover," originally, the head. It is part of the armor of a soldier of Christ and reminds him that life is a warfare in which he must strive for victory.

The priest says: "Place upon my head, O Lord, the helmet of salvation for repelling the attacks of the evil one."

Cincture: A heavy cord usually white, used to tie the vestments closely at the waist and terminating with two large tassels of same color.

Mass Stole: A band of cloth of same material as Maniple and Chasuble, worn around neck of priest, crossed on his breast and held in place by the Cincture. It is a symbol of spiritual power and jurisdiction. Its original use is questionable, possibly to wipe the face; it is symbolic of the ministry of the Lord carried out by the priest.

Chasuble: Outer vestment assumed last. Color prescribed by rule or rubrics. It was originally a storm cloak worn exclusively by slaves and peasants. It has changed its form many times.

The two forms shown on the plate are the common forms worn today. The set of vestments on the left are called Gothic and date back to the fourth Century. The vestments on the right are called Roman and are more commonly worn and known.

The Chasuble: It is the emblem of Charity which clothes the soul as the vestment envelops the body.

The priest says: "My Yoke is sweet and my burden light, grant I may carry it to merit Thy grace." The white and gold vestments belonged to the late Archbishop J. F. Regis Canevin of Pittsburgh, Pennsylvania.

Chalice: The Chalice is the Eucharistic cup in which the wine is consecrated in the Mass. Its cup at least should be solid gold, or if silver is used, the inside must be plated with gold. It must be consecrated before use. The Chalice may be touched only by a priest.

Paten: A small metal dish shaped like a saucer covering the Chalice, on which the bread to be consecrated in the Mass is placed, at the Offertory, and which shares with the corporal the privilege of carrying the Sacred Host. It means "shallow dish." It is gold, like the Chalice.

Ciborium: A sacred vessel shaped like a Chalice, only wider and shallower in the cup in which the smaller Hosts are reserved and placed in the Tabernacle for the sick and ordinary communicants. Name means receptacle for food (Food of Angels).

Material is gold or if not, cup must be plated. It has a tight fitting cover surmounted by a cross and a veil of precious texture embroidered in gold and silver, and white in color.

The veil is only used when particles of the Blessed Sacrament are in Ciborium.

This lesson should be carried out in many lessons so children will not be confused. Other details should be added.

Place lessons when completed in booklet form.

Make a suitable design for cover. Gray bogus paper is a good medium for the book.

BOOK IV, PAGE 41—PUSSY WILLOWS

Character Objective: Neatness

Spiritual Objective: As directions for painting can be carried to a successful finish only by the combined use of paper, paint, and brush, so a beautiful impression on the soul can only be recorded when children, after listening carefully to directions from God's representatives, cooperate by keeping a loving desire to please God, side by side with a strong will to do the right thing.

Art Objective: To arouse a keen appreciation of the beauties of early spring through the experience of painting the pussy willow.

Supplies: Pussy willow spray (if possible), paints and brushes, charcoal, water, pictures of spring, paste, blank paper

Procedure: Have a real spray of pussy willow for observation and discussion to get the full benefit of the lesson. Notice the position for brush holding. Neatness in painting depends very much on the emphasis placed on this point. When pupils hold the brush lower, fingers touch the paint and unpleasant fingermarks mar the result.

Insist on careful handling of materials and direct painting, without pencil drawing. The placing of the stem and location of the buds may be shown lightly with the tip of the brush or with charcoal, which disappears when the paint is added. Paint the lightest part of bud with water first and then a tiny touch of black to make light gray. When almost dry, add darker parts. Be sure proportion of paper harmonizes with shape of spray. Notice that allowing spray to cut the bottom of the paper gives it life and strength, as it appears to be still growing. Find pictures suggestive of spring to paste on the blank page.

BOOK IV, PAGE 43—BIRDS

Character Objective: Kindness

Spiritual Objective: Develop in children a reverence for all of the creations of God and, as He keeps watch over even "a sparrow's fall," how pleasing it must be to God to see His children caring for these helpless things while appreciating their beauty and music.

Art Objective:

1—To develop in children a responsiveness to beauty in birds through observation developed during the experience of painting a bird.

2—To teach the adaptation of nature forms to design.

Supplies: Colored images of birds, paints and brushes, water

Procedure: Develop the general proportions of the bird on the blackboard, following method shown in the book. Notice that the three strokes for the bird's bill all curve upward and are made **toward** the head. This insures a sharp point where they join.

Change the direction of the triangular form as though it were on a pivot, dropping the head to the ground to show feeding, etc. Use good colored pictures of birds as models for the painting lesson. These can be obtained from any Audubon Society or from the library. Use the robin or other familiar bird for the lesson. If robin is used, paint shape with yellow first. Touch the brush to pure red and paint the breast, orange and red orange. Touch the brush to red, yellow, blue, and red again, and paint the rest of the body brown, being careful to save the light circle for the eyes and bill. With dark purple or black add a few brush strokes for wings and legs and tail feathers. With point of brush gently paint circle for eye, being careful to save the highlight. Add dark touches to bill, allowing a little light color to show through for highlight. Notice size and flatness of feet.

Emphasize necessity of washing brush each time new color is used, to keep color bright and to avoid smudginess.

Lesson 2: An interesting project is a bird chart which can be planned to record the appearance of each new bird. An adaptation similar to that shown at bottom of page may be used to decorate the chart. Have a quick competitive test to see how many original bird forms may be produced, and select the best original motive for the chart. The chart may be prepared as a calendar and bird form with name drawn on date line.

BOOK IV, PAGE 47
A CHRISTMAS PLAY, "WHY THE CHIMES RANG"

Character Objective: Generosity and Self-Sacrifice

The story, "Why the Chimes Rang," may be found below. **Read the story to the children** in order that they may get its full beauty.

Skeleton Outline:

Location: Old cathedral town in Germany.

Characters: Two little boys, Pedro and Little Brother, who live outside the town, merchants, choir boys, old woman, king, nobles, etc.

Skeleton of Story: In the belfry of the old cathedral in the town are supposed to be wonderful chimes which will only be heard when a gift which is unusually pleasing to God is placed on the altar on Christmas eve.

The two boys have been looking forward to their visit to the great church and Pedro has saved his bright penny for an offering.

On the road to the town they find a poor old woman buried in the snow and Pedro stays to help her, sending Little Brother on alone, giving his bright penny for the Christ Child offering. He is heavy hearted and sad because he could not go.

Suddenly he hears the most beautiful music ever heard—the chimes are ringing—and when he turns his head there stands a beautiful angel in a dazzling light and back of her he sees an altar and in front all the gorgeous throng of worshippers. On the altar steps he sees the priceless gifts of the wealthy and crouching down in a dark shadow is Little Brother who has placed Pedro's penny when he thought that he was unseen. Smilingly the angel speaks to Pedro, telling him that God considered his gift finer than all the others because he had sacrificed himself to give it.

WHY THE CHIMES RANG

There was once, in a far-away country where few people have ever traveled, a wonderful church.

It stood on a high hill in the midst of a great city; and every Sunday, as well as on sacred days like Christmas, thousands of people climbed the hill to its great archways, looking like lines of ants all moving in the same direction.

When you came to the building itself, you found stone columns and dark passages, and a grand entrance leading to the main room of the church. This room was so long that one standing at the doorway could scarcely see to the other end, where the choir stood by the marble altar. In the farthest corner was the organ; and this organ was so loud that sometimes when it played, the people for miles around would close their shutters and prepare for a great thunderstorm. Altogether, no such church as this was ever seen before, especially when it was lighted up for some festival, and crowded with people, young and old.

But the strangest thing about the whole building was the wonderful chime of bells. At one corner of the church was a great gray tower, with ivy growing over it as far up as one could see. I say as far as one could see, because the tower was quite great enough to fit the great church, and it rose so far into the sky that it was only in very fair weather that any one claimed to be able to see the top. Even then one could not be certain that it was in sight. Up, and up and up climbed the stones and the ivy; and, as the men who built the church had been dead for hundreds of years, every one had forgotten how high the tower was supposed to be.

Now all the people knew that at the top of the tower was a chime of Christmas bells. They had hung there ever since the church had been built, and were the most beautiful bells in the world. Some thought it was because a great musician had cast them and arranged them in their place; others said it was because of the great height, which reached up where the air was clearest and purest: however that might be, no one who had ever heard the chimes denied that they were the sweetest in the world. Some described them as sounding like angels far up in the sky; others, as sounding like strange winds singing through the trees.

But the fact was that no one had heard them for years and years. There was an old man living not far from the church, who said that his mother had spoken of hearing them when she was a little girl, and he was the only one who was sure of as much as that. They were Christmas chimes, you see, and were not meant to be played by men or on common days. It was the custom on Christmas Eve for all the people to bring to the church their offerings to the Christ-child; and when the greatest and best offering was laid on the altar, there used to come sounding through the music of the choir the Christmas chimes far up in the tower. Some said that the wind rang them, and others that they were so high that the angels could set them swinging. But for many long years they had never been heard.

It was said that people had been growing less careful of their gifts for the Christ-child, and that no offering was brought, great enough to deserve the music of the chimes. Every Christmas Eve the rich people still crowded to the altar, each one trying to bring some better gift than any other, without giving anything that he wanted for himself, and the church was crowded with those who thought that perhaps the wonderful bells might be heard again. But although the service was splendid, and the offerings plenty, only the roar of the wind could be heard, far up in the stone tower.

Now, a number of miles from the city, in a little country village, where nothing could be seen of the great church but glimpses of the tower when the weather was fine, lived a boy named Pedro, and his little brother. They knew very little about the Christmas chimes, but they had heard of the service in the church on Christmas Eve, and had a secret plan, which they had often talked over when by themselves, to go to see the beautiful celebration.

"Nobody can guess, Little Brother," Pedro would say, "all the fine things there are to see and hear; and I have even heard it said that the Christ-child sometimes comes down to bless the service. What if we could see Him?"

The day before Christmas was bitterly cold, with a few lonely snow-flakes flying in the air, and a hard white crust on the ground. Sure enough, Pedro and Little Brother were able to slip quietly away early in the after-noon; and although the walking was hard in the frosty air, before nightfall they had trudged so far, hand in hand, that they saw the lights of the big city just ahead of them. Indeed, they were about to enter one of the great gates in the wall that surrounded it, when they saw something dark on the snow near their path, and stepped aside to look at it.

It was a poor woman, who had fallen just outside the city, too sick and tired to get in where she might have found shelter. The soft snow made of a drift a sort of pillow for her, and she would soon be so sound asleep, in the wintry air, that no one could ever waken her again. All this Pedro saw in a moment, and he knelt down beside her and tried to rouse her, even tugging at her arm a little, as though he would have tried to carry her away. He turned her face toward him, so that he could rub some of the snow on it, and when he had looked at her silently a moment he stood up again, and said:

"It's no use, Little Brother. You will have to go on alone."

"Alone?" cried Little Brother. "And you not see the Christmas festival?"

"No," said Pedro, and he could not keep back a bit of a choking sound in his throat. "See this poor woman. Her face looks like the Madonna in the chapel window, and she will freeze to death if nobody cares for her. Every one has gone to the church now, but when you come back you can bring some one to help her. I will rub her to keep her from freezing, and perhaps get her to eat the bun that is left in my pocket."

"But I can not bear to leave you, and go on alone," said Little Brother.

"Both of us need not miss the service," said Pedro, "and it had better be I than you. You can easily find your way to the church; and you must see and hear everything twice, Little Brother—once for you and once for me. I am sure the Christ-child must know how I should love to come with you and worship Him; and oh! if you get a chance, Little Brother, to slip up to the altar without getting in any one's way, take this little silver piece of mine, and lay it down for my offering, when no one is looking. Do not forget where you have left me, and forgive me for not going with you."

In this way he hurried Little Brother off to the city, and winked hard to keep back the tears, as he heard the crunching footsteps sounding farther and farther away in the twilight. It was pretty hard to lose the music and splendor of the Christmas celebration that he had been planning for so long, and spend the time instead in that lonely place in the snow.

The great church was a wonderful place that night. Every one said that it had never looked so bright and beautiful before. When the organ played and the thousands of people sang, the walls shook with the sound, and little Pedro, away outside the city wall, felt the earth tremble around him.

At the close of the service came the procession with the offerings to be laid on the altar. Rich men and great men marched proudly up to lay down their gifts to the Christ-child. Some brought wonderful jewels, some baskets of gold so heavy that they could scarcely carry them down the aisle. A great writer laid down a book that he had been making for years and years. And last of all walked the king of the country, hoping with all the rest to win for himself the chime of the Christmas bells. There went a great murmur through the church, as the people saw the king take from his head the royal crown, all set with precious stones, and lay it gleaming on the altar, as his offering to the holy Child. "Surely," every one said, "we shall hear the bells now, for nothing like this has ever happened before."

But still only the cold old wind was heard in the tower, and the people shook their heads; and some of them said, as they had before, that they never really believed the story of the chimes, and doubted if they ever rang at all.

The procession was over, and the choir began the closing hymn. Suddenly the organist stopped playing as though he had been shot, and every one looked at the old minister, who was standing by the altar, holding up his hand for silence. Not a sound could be heard from any one in the church, but as all the people strained their ears to listen, there came softly, but distinctly, swinging through the air, the sound of the chimes in the tower. So far away, and yet so dear the music seemed—so much sweeter were the notes than anything that had been heard before, rising and falling away up there in the sky, that the people in the church sat for a moment as still as though something held each of them by the shoulders. Then they all stood up together and stared straight at the altar, to see what great gift had awakened the long-silent bells.

But all that the nearest of them saw was the childish figure of Little Brother, who had crept softly down the aisle when no one was looking, and had laid Pedro's little piece of silver on the altar.

Directions: Follow all directions given in textbook. The corner of the room makes a convenient place for arranging curtains strung on picture wire. Old portieres or faded cretonne hangings are excellent when dyed a dark color.

Christmas hymns should be sung by altar boys and class.

Children plan the gifts to be presented by each of the notable people in church. The king gives his crown.

Angel appears outside curtain, before curtains part to show altar and church.

CORRELATED WORK

1. ENGLISH—Reproduction:
   (a) Pick out main thoughts in order.
   (b) Retell the story by topics.
   (c) Strengthen the "sentence sense."
   (d) Add to vocabulary and plan dialogue.
   (e) Learn to use dictionary.

2. RELIGION:
   (a) Furnishings of altar.
   (b) Arranging altar for Mass.
   (c) Vestments and their use.

3. GEOGRAPHY:

   Comparison of German customs with our own. Comparison of climate, government, language, etc.

4. EXPRESSION AND WORD STUDY:

   Originate conversation in short sentences about ordinary occurrences in daily life of Pedro and Little Brother; their pets, their work, their food, their method of sleeping, etc.

   Watch: clear enunciation and correct pronunciation. Have written exercises to obtain best sentences for final use in dialogue.

5. ARITHMETIC—Develop ability to:
   (a) Estimate size of window for church.
   (b) Number of pieces of colored glass to cover area.
   (c) Estimate amount of paper for choir boys' costumes, etc.

6. COSTUME STUDY:

   Compare German peasant costume with modern American costume. Advantages and disadvantages of wooden shoes.

   Effect of climate on costume.

7. COLOR AND DESIGN:

(a) Illustrations of the story in crayon and cut paper.
(b) Study of church windows.
(c) Knowledge concerning color purity.
(d) Co-operation needed in final plan.

8.CREATIVE DEVELOPMENT:

Creative work encouraged and stimulated in every line.

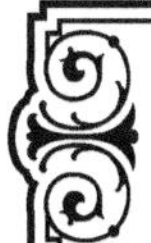

Book Five

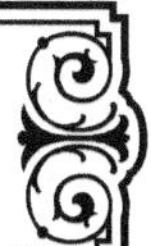

BOOK V—COVER

See page 3 of this manual.

BOOK V—END PAPER—OTHER CHRISTS

Character Objective: Thoughtfulness

Spiritual Objective: To develop in children a deep love and reverence for priests and nuns because of the sacrifice they have made for God, with an appreciation of what pupils gain because that sacrifice has been made. Also to think about what the future boys and girls would miss if nobody else would be found willing to make similar sacrifices.

Art Objective: To teach the use of a monogram as a motif of design for an all-over pattern.

Supplies: Scissors, paper, paints and brushes

Procedure: Read Father O'Donnell's beautiful verse as the nucleus for the religious discussion. Ask children to give their ideas first, making corrections later where meaning has not been understood. The complete poem was not used because of lack of space. After the lesson have pupils memorize the poem.

Lesson 1: See how many monograms pupils can recognize and interpret. This type of alphabet was used because this decorative form is usually used in ecclesiastical decoration. Do not have pupils try to imitate it. As a problem, have pupils select any two monograms and, following method shown on page 31, plan an all-over design, using simple block letters shown on page 13. Change shape and width as desired. The design might be planned as lining paper for a Christmas envelope, or greeting for any special Feast Day. Turn to end-paper on back cover and notice rhythmic repeats of large and small oval shapes and additional design units not monograms, introduced to give a vertical movement on the page.

Lesson 2: Have pupils plan a color scheme of closely related neutral color tints, to paint the design which decorates the poem. Mix these color washes in the box lid.

BOOK V, PAGE 1—THE IMMACULATE CONCEPTION

Character Objective: Purity

Spiritual Objective: To arouse in children a response to the beauty of purity, symbolized in the Immaculate Conception. To help them realize why God never permitted sin to touch His Blessed Mother. He wishes them to know how necessary is **purity** in every form if they wish to be truly God's children. (Discuss the meaning of Original Sin and benefit of Baptism. Read correlated "religion" under "Lourdes".)

Art Objective: To continue development of picture appreciation through additional power of recognizing design principles of **Dominance** and **Subordination**.

Teacher's Preparation: Study the picture and analyze the appeal it makes to you. Does it affect you spiritually, intellectually, or sensuously?

Murillo has shown in his painting a powerful penetration of this spiritual subject, with a loving tenderness in portraying exquisite beauty in his beloved Patroness.

We see her flooded with divine light, enveloped in flowing draperies, borne aloft, standing upon the clouds, while her longing eyes out-run her body in its heavenward ascent.

In this picture, as in all pictures of the Immaculate Conception, she is pictured as the woman in the Apocalypse "clothed with the sun, having the moon under her feet." Other artists have usually pictured her with a crown of twelve stars, and at her feet the head of the bruised and defeated dragon.

Bearing her up are four cherubs, each holding symbolic nature forms, the palm, the laurel, the lilies, and the roses.

It was when painting this type of subject that Murillo attained a glowing, overpowering expression of religious enthusiasm never equalled by any other painter.

Notice how the purity of her gown is emphasized by the contrast of the dark blue robe, which combines with her dark hair to form a frame for her and creates a beautiful large dark pattern silhouetted against a light background. Notice the subtle change from light to dark in the background, as the eye sweeps downward. Notice how the artist makes the cherubs (the subordinate elements of the picture) show a reverse contrast of light on a dark background, while emphasizing the dominance of the Virgin's figure. Notice how many times the oval of the face is repeated in other forms in the picture. We find it in the shape created by head, arms, and hands; in the oval swing around the cherubs from the Virgin's knee; in the bit of blue drapery at her feet; in the larger rhythmic shape of the mantle and finally in the burst of light behind her.

Notice how cleverly the cherub guard of honor has been introduced, now visible, now retreating into friendly depths of cloud, where they may continue to peer out in safety, but always creating interesting space relations.

Procedure: Open books and allow pupils to enjoy the picture undisturbed, for a few minutes. Call on individual pupils to give reactions. Discuss the meaning of the Immaculate Conception. How has the artist emphasized the purity of his subject? How has he emphasized her beauty? The vertical figure of the Virgin gives great dignity to composition, while the bent knee and raised arms add lovely graceful curves. The long curve of the body is repeated in the rhythmic folds of the dark blue robe. The arrangement of cherubs at her feet gives added length to the figure. The figure has been beautifully posed. The body is turned in one direction while the head is turned in another, thus escaping the center of the space and adding contrast.

Notice how pleasant background spaces are created on the left, by the blue robe; on the bottom by the cherubs; on the right by the palm and the dark mass; on the top by the angels' heads.

The artist has used many closely related colors. Name those you think closely related. The artist has used large masses of orange (gold) and blue for contrast. Why do these colors give contrast? Do you find other echoes, or gradations of orange and blue in the picture? How are the shadows on the white gown shown?

The artist Bartolomé Murillo painted in Spain in the 17th Century. The Spaniards called him "The Painter of Heaven".

For additional picture study, see page xxx.

BOOK V, PAGE 3—NATURE

Character Objective: Attention

Spiritual Objective: As the movable frame or "finder" aids in the selection and emphasis of the finest aspect of the flower growth **by covering parts not desired,** so the "finders" of Christian love and sympathy, possessed by every pupil, should be used on associates, to find their good qualities, instead of using the magnifying glass of criticism.

Art Objective: To teach children the use of finders in selecting a fine flower composition.

Supplies: Real goldenrod or other fall flower (if possible), paints and brushes, rag/blotter, paper,

Procedure: Use real model of goldenrod or other available fall flower. If a flower other than the goldenrod is used, have pupils practice lesson given in the book, to learn method of approach to the problem. Make a point on the brush by touching its side to a rag or blotter. Practice leaf forms, keeping brush nearly vertical and held at top of metal. Begin leaf with a very light pressure, then a heavier pressure to spread the brush at center, and again very light pressure, as the stroke is finished and brush lifted. Close attention to the placing of the pressure will quickly give skill in rendering any foliage. To paint the flower, a scribbling motion with the brush was used at figure 2 and the darker color touched lightly to the orange before it was dry.

Review rules for interesting spacing:

1—Avoid monotony of equal spaces.

2—Avoid an increasing sequence of spaces, as narrow, medium and wide, or 1-2-3.

3—Achieve an interesting arrangement by getting contrast, as narrow, wide, medium or 1-3-2.

Teach necessity of keeping the attention on all parts of the composition, or the finders will be of no use. To illustrate, have pupils number the width of background spaces caused by plant cutting side of frame on the plate. The right side would read 4-2-3-1; the bottom would read 1-3; the left side would read 3-1-4; the top shows no divisions. Have pupils use finders to make margin lines around flowers pasted on the blank page, to test their ability to produce good spacing.

BOOK V, PAGE 5—MARTYRS

Character Objective: Sacrifice

Spiritual Objective: To teach children that the many little sacrifices necessary in their daily lives are infinitely pleasing to God if offered to Him with the same spirit shown by the early martyrs. Discuss what these sacrifices may be.

Art Objectives:

1—To help children to appreciate the beauty of nature forms in silhouette, through rendering trees with brush and ink, or paint.

2—To teach adaptation of symbols to design units.

Supplies: Ink/black paint and brush, ruler, pencil, paper, pictures of trees, paste, scissors, stencil, crayon, sewing bag/doily (if desired)

Procedure: Study the picture and note relationship of background spaces. Use either ink or black paint with a number 7 brush. Follow directions given in text for painting.

Measure and draw a line one inch from long edge of paper on which tree is to be painted.

The sheet is to be folded on this line later. In this way several lessons finished at different times may be stitched together into a strong book. Show pictures of various trees for painting, also have pupils find trees to paste on the blank page.

The **crown** signifies victory, as does also the **palm**. The panel at the bottom of the page shows three different ways in which the artist has combined them to make design units, suitable to decorate anything related to the martyrs, such as a statue, altar or book cover. Try placing the symbols in shapes familiar to pupils, as square, circle, etc. and ask for original modifications of design units shown. Aim to have symbol fill the space being used.

Have pupils reproduce from memory the story of a martyr, previously heard, and possibly an original story of "A Martyr of Today." The booklet cover for these stories may be decorated with the design units already planned. Follow this lesson with design units made from any leaf shape, changing the form as many times as possible to create new units. Select the most interesting one for a stencil, as learned in Book IV, page 37.

By rubbing stencil with crayola, apply to a sewing bag or doily if desired, or use for any form of decoration.

BOOK V, PAGE 7—COMPOSITION

Character Objective: Ingenuity

Spiritual Objective: To teach children a reverence for the beautiful in nature, as a fine rendering of God's handiwork. Review "The Happy Trees" in Book III. As a fine strong straight tree is the result of good soil, enough water and tempered winds, so a strong character will be the result of good soil in the form of attention necessary to absorb the essential water of good instruction.

Art Objectives: To teach children to associate beautiful space arrangements found in nature with commercial adaptations used in manufactured materials for clothing.

Supplies: Pencil, cut paper, pictures of trees, scissors, 6 x 9 manila paper, paste, paints and brushes,

Procedure: Have children practice methods of sketching shown on plate and follow with original arrangement of tree trunks to show interesting spacing. After original plaid has been made, make a landscape adaptation of it, either with pencil or cut paper. Find tree forms to paste on the blank page for study.

Lesson 2: Review suggestions for interesting spacing given in an earlier lesson. Compare illustrations shown on page and then read and discuss the text.

After samples of plaid, contributed by pupils, have been exhibited and discussed, pass sheets of 6 x 9 manila drawing paper. Have pupils fold in half and cut or tear.

On first sheet have entire class follow the measurements of the most pleasing sample in the collection. This is done to show method of planning and painting. Follow color scheme of plaid being used, by painting all vertical stripes not touching. As these stripes must be allowed to dry before adjoining stripes are painted, the second sheet should now be used for an original arrangement of spaces.

Having pupils work on two sheets at the same time will give each ample time for drying and insure an original creation as the result of the lesson. When the vertical stripes on the demonstration sheet are dry, paint the horizontal stripes the full width of the paper. If complementary colors are used, pupils may observe the neutralizing effect of one complement upon another. Mount both results and have class criticism of space arrangements.

BOOK V, PAGE 9—COLOR

Character Objective: Cooperation

Spiritual Objective: To help children to understand that, as in every beautiful composition it is necessary to subordinate some colors so that others may be made more important, so in their daily lives they must learn to **subordinate**, for the good of others, their own desire to shine. This will defeat the two dragons of Conceit and Selfishness.

Art Objective: To teach children the meaning and use of complementary colors.

Supplies: Three glasses of water, paints or ink, pictures of viking ships, scissors, paste, cut paper

Procedure: This page has been planned as source material for a number of color lessons. Read and discuss the text. The top line shows the evolution of each pair of complements. The pictures of the ships show the neutralizing effects of one color over another, as suggested on page 11, which is a continuation of the text on page 9.

Complements are necessary to subdue or neutralize colors that are too brilliant, in order to keep them from attracting too much attention. When we do this we **subordinate** the color. Review what has been taught about Dominance and explain that Subordination is the opposite of Dominance, and is always a necessary principle to use in order to emphasize the dominance of **one** thing only in the composition.

1—Place one primary color as red in three glasses of water. Into the first glass pour a small amount of green and watch the result on the red; into the second glass pour a larger amount, and into the third glass a still greater amount. Compare the three results. Perform the same experiment with blue and with yellow, to see how they are affected by their complements, orange and purple.

2—Tell stories of Leif Ericsson and the Norsemen and ask pupils to find pictures of the Viking ships to paste on the blank page. Have them plan a ship with cut paper, using the paper they have painted while experimenting with complements. A similar lesson may be carried out in poster form for Columbus Day, showing effect of the color of water on reflections from one of the ships of Columbus. Other lessons will be suggested by some pertinent need of the school.

BOOK V, PAGE 11—EXPERIMENTS WITH COMPLEMENTS

Character Objective: Judgment

Spiritual Objective: Just as an application of a neutralizing color dulls the bright color and if a sufficient amount of the neutral is added will cause the bright color to completely disappear, so the brightness and strength of a child's love for God will become less when he allows his thoughts of God to be neutralized by selfishness and conceit, and other things displeasing to God.

Art Objectives:

1—To have children experiment with complementary colors and learn how to reduce intensity of a color.

2—To become familiar with the use of varying intensities of color as a means of creating movement, or rhythm.

Supplies: Manila paper, newspapers, paints and brushes, water, posterboard

Procedure Lesson 1: Read text and review page 9. Pass manila drawing paper 6 x 9 and have children tear it in half for experiments. After desk has been prepared in "painting order," moisten each cake of paint to make it ready for use when wanted. Use one of the primaries, as red, and paint evenly over the paper, the pure intense color. Be sure pupils understand that a **pure** color means color of full, **strong intensity** or strength.

Place two brushfuls of water in box lid and add two brushfuls of the complement, green. Then paint this color wash over the red. Children will see how the red is affected by being dulled or neutralized.

To paint the other half of the sheet, mix the color in box lid. Two brushes of water, two brushes of red, and 1 brush of green should produce a clear neutral red. Have children compare results of both methods. Have them try neutralizing other primary and binary colors, aiming to produce fresh clear neutral tones, instead of muddy colorless results.

Lesson 2: Ask children to find pictures of flowers either natural or adapted to design motives, as reference, to be pasted on the blank page.

Using these as suggestions, plan decorative flower shapes for a basket of flowers to be used on a poster, planned for use in a campaign to "Conserve the Flowers." Have pupils originate many plans for the poster "layout" of letters and decoration. Borders may be used, or a garden, or perhaps window boxes.

On borders shown in book notice the ways in which rhythm or movement is created: by diminishing size; by increasing or diminishing intensities of color; by the shape of one unit carrying the eye over to the following one, etc. The use of rhythm in a poster is to make the **eye travel** to the lettering or advertisement. Refer to page 37.

BOOK V, PAGE 13—LETTERING WITH INK

Character Objective: Carefulness

Spiritual Objective: Just as letters are like rubber to be changed in shape to conform to any space, so it is possible for children to make themselves fit cheerfully into any situation, even when it is uncomfortable, thereby keeping sweet dispositions modeled on the Holy Child.

Art Objectives:

1—To teach good spacing in lettering.

2—To teach technique of elementary ink lettering.

Supplies: Chalk and blackboard (optional), round nib pens

Procedure: Read text and have pupils practice letters on blackboard, using rules given for lettering in text. Place emphasis on necessity of leaving a wider space between two letters, each having vertical strokes. Call for quick lettering of such words HILL in which the spaces between letter I and adjoining letters are wide while the second L may almost touch the first one. The inability to sense good spacing is one of the most common weaknesses of pupils, when lettering. Call attention to the fact that an envelope with a well arranged address is much more easily read by the postal employees, who have to handle so many.

Lesson 2: If round nib pens are not available, wooden meat sticks may be filed down to a flat wedge shape, and make excellent substitutes. Hold flat part firmly down, so that strokes will have an even width with clean edges. Carefully notice position of pen or stick in illustration.

BOOK V, PAGE 15—BETHLEHEM

Character Objective: Reverence and Patience

Spiritual Objective: Just as the Jews, through all their trials and sorrows, kept faith in the Messiah who had been promised to them, until finally they were rewarded with the coming of the Christ Child, so children should not grow impatient when they must wait to have their wishes granted, but remember that patience is as pleasing to our Lord today, as it was to the dear Infant who rewarded the shepherds by sending the angel to them to announce that their wishes had been granted through His Birth.

Art Objective: To teach pupils good proportions in figure cutting and skill in cutting and pasting a Christmas illustration showing good composition.

Supplies: Christmas figures, scissors

Procedure: Have children find Christmas figures, as suggested in text, for costume study. Figures may be cut in silhouette with one cutting, or details of costume may be cut and assembled later. Have the story read before cutting is attempted, and have individual pupils suggest word pictures for ideas of grouping and details other than that shown on the plate. Have pupils pose in positions planned for the shepherds. Call attention to location of features, and change of direction of nose and chin, as the head is raised or lowered.

Cut lambs and sheep in many positions and aim for fine grouping.

Have children discuss the many things in the picture which are subordinated in order to keep the star the center of interest, or most dominant thing, in the picture.

BOOK V, PAGE 17—A CHRISTMAS GIFT

Character Objective: Generosity—Parental Love

Spiritual Objective: As the frame is made strong and beautiful to hold the picture, and yet must be kept subordinate to the picture, so the body, which is the frame for the soul, must be kept strong and healthy, beautifully neat and clean, but yet not made, through vanity, the center of interest, nor dominant over the soul which is the picture God wishes to see us keep beautiful.

Art Objective: To develop skill and good craftsmanship in making a picture frame.

Supplies: Paper, cardboard, scissors, paste

Procedure: This type of industrial problem is to be followed by the class, as a demonstration problem to teach the elements of all similar problems. After pupils have mastered the essentials of making this problem, other adaptations may be tried in other proportions.

The plate shows clearly each step in the process. Good workmanship should be encouraged and praised. Original designs will give the finished problem variety. One of the pictures planned for the grade should be used in the frame. The use of cellophane will protect the picture in place of glass.

BOOK V, PAGE 19—THE UNSEEN PRESENCE

Character Objective: Piety and Service

Spiritual Objective: To make children conscious of the watchful care at all times of our Lord and especially to have them know that the attitude of prayer is not essential to piety, but that every act well done each day may be made into the most pleasing type of prayer that may be offered to God, if done in His honor.

Art Objectives:

1—To review the principle of dominance in illustrative composition.

2—To develop a sense of proportion of the human form.

Supplies: Pictures of children, paste, blank paper, scissors

Procedure: Discuss the picture in order to discover what means the artist used to show the important design principles of Dominance and Subordination. Christ is emphasized as the Center of interest by contrast of values; by having all figures looking toward Him; by the dark figures on both sides framing Him; by the curve of the hillside leading toward Him. Notice the interesting variety of spaces between the trees as also when comparing trees with each other. Notice the interesting pattern of blacks and grays which have been kept subordinate to the beautiful figure of Christ. Ask why the panel of babies was placed at the top, instead of at the bottom of the page. If this had been done the picture would have been overpowered by black at the bottom. By distributing the dark masses, another means of dominance was given to the figure of Christ.

Lesson 2: Have lesson on page 29 precede this lesson in order to fix as firmly as possible essential proportions of children with simple methods of showing action. Using pictures pasted on blank page as reference, cut many figures of children. Have children pose for special poses to keep eyes alert to see changes that may occur through movement.

Notice the indefinite features of the baby faces and the more pronounced features of the older children. Notice that the dent for the eye and the top of the nose is shown half way between the chin and the top of the head.

An additional lesson on simple costume may be given in connection with this lesson as suggested in the picture, by planning and placing collars, cuffs, and band trimming.

BOOK V, PAGE 21—LEARNING TO SEE

Character Objective: Judgment

Spiritual Objective: As eyes learn to see truthfully, pupils understand that it is impossible to have two objects occupy the same space at the same time, as all experiments on this page prove, so also they must know that in the soul there is room for but **One Master,** the Creator who gave it life.

Art Objective: To help children to estimate distances, while training their eyes to see correctly.

Supplies: 9 x 12 bogus paper, ruler, chalk and blackboard (optional), colored pencils, red crayon, circular objects from advertisements, paste, scissors, crayons or charcoal

Procedure: To make larger paper model, fold sheet of 9 x 12 bogus paper lengthwise and pull it quickly over edge of ruler to make the surface curved. If one folded end is placed **inside** opposite end, pins will not be needed. To make smaller model, fold a 9 x 12 sheet of bogus paper into thirds, lengthwise, and place one end **inside** the other to hold it firm. This gives two models in good proportion to each other.

Have pupils arrange them on desk until able to see a duplicate of the first arrangement in panel at the bottom of the page. After all four arrangements have been tried successfully, continue to sketch other arrangements on the blackboard, watching carefully to see whether models are moved in the proper direction. As a test, make a sketch showing small model in **front** of large model and **higher up** than base of large model. Note whether pupils **lift** to get result. Then emphasize the fact that to allow both models to rest on ground, the one in **front** will always be **lower** than one **back** and vice versa.

Follow game of quick placing, by passing paper and dictating about four positions for placing and sketching. Correct and return for comparisons.

Lesson 2: Have pupils prepare circles with colored diameters as a review of lesson taught in Book IV, Page 27.

Hold circles at levels to correspond to the ellipses illustrated in group of three circular forms shown on plate. Explain to pupils that the imaginary ellipse, dropped to ground level in this group, helps them to be sure that each one of the models has been allowed sufficient room. The same result would be shown on the ground if the models were actually turned **upside down,** since one form occupies the same space from top to bottom. The danger to be avoided is that of allowing enough room at bottom, and forgetting that the top needs **more** room than has been estimated.

As a test problem, have pupils find circular objects in advertisements, paste them on the blank page and then test the ellipses visible and invisible, with red crayon, similar to the test shown in the book.

Lesson 3: Arrange about six simple groups with not more than two objects in each, and have children make large sketches. Direct their attention to **points of contact** between the two objects as a help in correct placing.

Sketches may be made with crayola or charcoal on gray bogus paper.

BOOK V, PAGE 23—WHEN BEAUTY INSPIRED THE WORLD

Character Objective: Response to Beauty

Spiritual Objective: As pupils wish to absorb worldly culture through becoming familiar with what the world accepts as the masterpieces of art, so continuous effort to become familiar with what God accepts as necessary to complete His Masterpiece, the Soul, will produce soul culture, through God's grace.

Supplies: Books on Greek mythology

Art Objective: To teach children to appreciate their heritage of beauty from the ancients, and through it achieve a finer appreciation of the art products of today.

Procedure: Have the children bring from the library as many books as possible, with legends of the early Greeks, their victories and their heroes, their gods and goddesses, their religion and their games. Suggested books: "Four Old Greeks"—Hall; Stories of Old Greeks—Firth. When the whole atmosphere is electrified with interest about these early pagans, and after an exhibit of as many pictures as possible to be readily obtained from the library have been placed on the bulletin board, pass the books and have children read the text.

Tell the story of Athena the daughter of Zeus the father of all the gods, and the belief of the pagans that she sprang fully armed, from the head of Zeus to become the protectress of the city of Athens, bringing them victories in wars and defeating their enemies.

1—**The Parthenon.** To please the Goddess they planned to build the most beautiful temple in the world, of pure white marble, adorned by the greatest of Greek sculptors placing within it a colossal statue of Athena, 40 ft. high, in gold and ivory. The name Parthenon comes from Parthenos, virgin.

It remained a thing of beauty until 1876, when during a war with the Turks, while it was being used as a powder magazine, it was exploded and all that was left are the ruins we see in the picture. Today children will see buildings something like this in their streets, usually banks, because this was considered the most perfect building in the whole world. Although it looks so simple, it is the work of genius. Every tiny bit was carefully planned to the smallest detail. It was not an accident that the Parthenon had forty-six columns of that particular height and breadth; they knew these measurements would produce the best and most pleasing effects, as the Greeks knew more about the laws of proportion than any other nation.

Everything about the Parthenon was orderly, symmetrical, well-balanced and in perfect proportion. The columns are all of the same height and breadth and same distance from each other. (That is what is meant by symmetrical.) Its lines are horizontal and restful. The longer you look at it the more its quiet beauty will grow on you. It was decorated with a frieze (a horizontal band, running all around the building) just behind the top of the columns. They made it flat to get as much light as possible, and for the same reason decorated it with sculpture in very low relief, that is, not projecting more than an inch from the wall. The sculptors made the frieze tell the story of the procession of all Athens to honor Athena, at a great religious ceremony in her honor. It is wonderful and valuable not only as a beautiful work of art, but is also an important historical document.

The frieze shows more than a hundred figures with no two alike, full of life and vitality and represents every class of people. After the explosion, Lord Elgin, an Englishman, purchased a large part of this frieze and donated it to the British Museum in London, where its beauty may be seen by thousands. The triangular spaces, called pediments, at each end of the Parthenon, formed by the ends of the roof, held the finest sculptured statues of the gods, telling the story of Athena's birth. All these figures were adapted to their positions; those near the ends of the pediments where there was not much space, were made to lie down; those nearer the center were made sitting, and those in the center, Athena and Zeus, intended to be the center of interest, were made standing. Although the explosion took off all the heads of the figures, they are so beautifully modeled that each fold of the drapery tells its story.

2—The second picture at the top of the page shows the great sculptor, **Phidias**, favorite of the king, sculpturing part of the beautiful frieze, under the corner of the pediment. Notice the style of costume worn by Phidias; notice the type of scaffolding as compared with today. Notice that figures have not yet been placed in the pediment.

3—**The Slave.** Emphasize the dramatic moment caught by the sculptor and immortalized in marble. Have children write an original story about the slave. He is crouching, sharpening a knife; is he accidentally overhearing some political intrigue between his master and some friends? Is he overhearing a plot against his master's life? Is his head raised in answer to an indignant protest of his fellow slaves? Has he been captured from a home of wealth in an enemy country and held as a hostage? Here is rich material to be woven into creative English.

4—**The vase** will be of interest in this grade where racing cos-tests and trophies are always interesting and will give familiarity to the beautiful specimen of pottery, which is reproduced in every store they enter. This gives opportunity again for creative English. This time the vase will tell its own story of the days when it was new in ancient Athens. Refer to page 27 for analysis of its lovely curves.

5—**The head of Venus** should be instantly associated with the whole figure of Venus de Milo, which should be shown if possible. The detail of the head has been shown as the source of our Goddess of Liberty and the head of the woman on our silver dollar.

6—The next picture shows the United States Treasury building, the modern adaptation of the Parthenon, to give beauty and dignity to this great treasury. Possibly this is why nearly every city boasts a bank adapted to the same model. Ask pupils to find a similar picture of a local building to be used in their "Greek Book."

7—The lower left picture shows the marvelous statue of the **Victory of Samothrace,** made by some unknown genius lost in antiquity. The base of the statue has been made to show the prow of a ship and in every line of the wondrous drapery and extended wings, breathes the spirit of victory. One can almost feel the salt spray blowing steadily against the thin drapery, while the power of the spread wings gives surety and strength.This statue is one of the finest creations of beautiful rhythms ever known.

8—**The Horsemen frieze** is a picture of one of those Elgin marbles, showing the wonderful vitality and action of the horses in a procession, showing three or four abreast and with a relief of scarcely more than one inch! The horses seem alive and moving. When these marbles were being taken from Greece to England, a storm wrecked the ship and it sank to the bottom of the ocean. Here the marbles stayed until long after, when divers brought them to the surface and eventually to the British Museum in London.

The project of this page may be completed at once, or carried through the semester, reviewing it from time to time. Completed, it should make a very interesting book, with each page showing one picture and appropriate explanation. Have pupils plan a cover design suggestive of the project.

BOOK V, PAGE 25—APPRECIATION

Character Objective: Responsiveness

Spiritual Objective: To have children know that as the plastic clay changes easily under their fingers, with a result that may be either beautiful, commonplace or ugly, so we have in our possession a plastic soul, which we should continue to model on the pattern of our Savior, rather than allow it to become **commonplace through lack of service** or **ugly with sin.**

Art Objective: To encourage appreciation of architecture and sculpture through modeling in clay.

Supplies: Clay

Procedure: Review directions for caring for clay, given on page xx of the Manual.

The problems suggested on this page are best developed in connection with the project of **appreciation** planned on page 23.

The six problems of ornament shown on the lower part of the page may be distributed throughout the class, preferably by selection on the part of the pupil, after an explanation has been given for each.

1—**Scroll** will be recognized as an adaptation of the Egyptian wave scroll learned in Book IV. It is easily made by making tile shape first, then rolling a long coil and placing the S shape, scratching the edges to connect surfaces, and then **welding** smooth with finger. Notice shape has been **drawn** on tile **first**.

2—**Egg and Dart** is decoration resembling an egg, supposed to symbolize life, and an arrow or dart, supposed to symbolize death. It is always found on the Ionic pillar.

3—The **Fret** is one of a series of interlacing border patterns the Greeks delighted to use. Notice the **right** side of these patterns, where the pattern has not been completed, to see how it has been developed, by building on the parts of the design and then welding.

4—The three photographs in the middle of the page show the original designs contributed by the Greeks as decorations for their pillars or columns. A column consists of three parts, viz: A **Base** to stand on, a long body called the **Shaft**, and a head or Capital. Sometimes the **Base** is lacking.

The Doric column is the commonest, short and sturdy, with no base. The column grows the least bit narrower toward the top, like a tree. The narrow channels or grooves, all around the column, are called "Flutings." The capital has a square slab on top, called the "Abacus," that rests on the column like a hat; the circular band that connects it to the column is called the **"Echinus."**

The Ionic column is slender and graceful and has a base and deeper flutings on the shaft. The capital looks a little like ram's horns, the part that curls over being called **Volutes**. Some say it was suggested by the figure of a woman and the curls are her hair. The front and back of the capital are alike, but the sides show only the appearance of a roll. Look for the Egg and Dart moulding on the capital.

The Corinthian is the third member of this Greek family of columns and it is the most ornamental. It has a base and fluting like the Ionic, but its capital has two parts, a leafy one below and a flat slab above. Its origin is explained thus: A young girl in Corinth had died and all her keepsakes had been placed in a basket on her grave and covered with a stone. The root of an Acanthus (the Greek thistle), growing up under it, pressed down by the weight, was forced to curve out around the angles of the tile. A famous sculptor saw it in passing and decided that this basket, with its delicate foliage, would make an original capital for a column.

If pupils have now gleaned the characteristics of the three orders of columns, have them find pictures of them to include in their Greek booklet. Every porch they pass on the way to school will greet them with a familiar decoration, the beauty of which will be appreciated through this newly awakened sense of architecture. Every teacher should begin a collection of pictures related to Greek art and mount them as a permanent classroom collection.

BOOK V, PAGE 27—HOLY COMMUNION

Character Objective: Reverence

Spiritual Objective: To teach children the meaning of and necessary preparation for the **Sacrament** of **Extreme Unction.**

Art Objective: To teach the meaning and recognition of curves on which beautiful design is based.

Supplies: Paper, scissors, paints and brushes, paste

Procedure: Discuss the upper picture, giving explanations for each article found on the table and reason for this arrangement, as convenience for the priest.

To impress the lesson on the memory of pupils, have them construct a paper table (Book 2, Page 13) and make a small model for the sake of arrangement. In order to project this very necessary information correctly into the home, have the picture cut out and artistically mounted for home, or have a booklet made containing the picture and necessary information.

Lesson 2: Teach pupils that a knowledge of the essential elements of beauty is necessary in order to train the eye for their recognition. Nature is the source of all beautiful line composition, constantly demonstrating the beautiful flow of one line into another in a **tangential** union, as in joining of limbs and tree trunks, the veining of leaves, the features of the face, or the contours of the body. The most important forms of curvature found in design, are:

1—**The Spiral,** found in shells, curled leaves, and tendrils; it is constantly diminishing or increasing, no two parts ever alike. It is known as the **infinite curve.**

2—**The Curve of Force,** a curve expressing life and strength, showing constant variation from a straight line just as the sky rocket is being constantly pulled to earth by the force of gravity. It is more beautiful because it also shows a gradation in **thickness**. It may be studied in a sky-rocket, the goldenrod, fountains, and many other places.

3—**The Reversed Curve or Curve of Grace i**s the combination of two curves from the oval, having an interesting relationship, and is the basic curve of most beautiful objects. The oval is commonly found in most vegetable and animal forms; the Curve of Grace is found in the contour and veining of leaves, in flowers, fruits, birds, etc.

If the teacher is constantly on the alert for beauty in everything, she will impart the same alertness to her pupils and unless pupils are trained to see beauty, it will be impossible for them to express it in their original creations, for all beauty is in the perception or the imagination of the individual. It is very necessary that children get practice at the blackboard in drawing these beautiful curves freely, in order to impress them on the memory. Turn these curves into some of the many objects in which they are found.

Fold paper and cut beautiful curves then follow lesson suggested in text book.

Ask pupils to find pictures showing an example of each kind of curve taught and have them pasted on the blank page with notations.

Lesson 3: Have pupils fold thin paper and cut one side of a beautiful original vase form.

Use thin paper pattern to draw or cut vase form on colored construction paper. Plan a border decoration to be either painted or pasted on vase form made. Use neutralized colors, closely related, in color scheme.

Have children realize that expense is not necessary to beauty and that a cheap vase, beautiful in line and color, is often lovelier than one more expensive.

BOOK V, PAGE 29—FIGURES IN ACTION

Character Objective: Poise

Spiritual Objective: As emphasis in this lesson is placed on **action**, with its interesting effects on direction and position of the body, so children may be made to realize the effects on the soul of an **active** love of God, through frequent visits to the Sacraments, where they will obtain a storage of grace that will make them morally strong to perform many types of service for schoolmates and others with whom they come in contact. Discuss these types of service.

Art Objective: To develop in children the power of adding life interest to figure sketching, through a study of action.

Supplies: Chalk and blackboard (optional), cardboard, scissors, pins, pictures of action poses, paste, blank paper

Procedure: Read the text and have pupils make tests for proportion on themselves. Work on the blackboard with books until proportions are memorized, then work without books. Turn the figure in many positions, noticing change in shoulder.

Make movable cardboard figures, fastening parts together with bent pins.

Have dramatized stories in classroom for quick action poses.

Find pictures for the blank page to show many action figures. Notice that detailed features have been eliminated. Combine this lesson with story illustration where possible.

BOOK V, PAGE 31—HOW TO MAKE A MONOGRAM

Character Objective: Ingenuity

Spiritual Objective: To develop in children devotion and love for our Blessed Mother through a knowledge of the meaning of her various Feast days. As a pupil's monogram is a sign by which he may be known, so also his example of his Faith which should edify his neighbors, will be a sign to them either good or bad.

Art Objective:

1—To teach fine arrangement in designing letters to make a monogram.

2—To continue the teaching of fine page arrangement.

Supplies: Scissors, paper, paints and brushes, crayons, pencil, ink

Procedure: This lesson may be continued throughout the year if so desired, and finally made into a book form when completed. Illustrations may be cut paper or paint; lettering, pencil, crayola, or stick printing. Monograms are effective when done in ink. Call attention to fine marginal spacing shown on cover and pages, as well as simple decoration used to balance the lines of lettering in order that they may conform to the space.

Lesson 2: As legibility is of no importance, since a monogram is very personal, notice that letters may be reversed in making combinations. Notice that enclosing shape shown at 1 on the plate was discarded at 3 after it had served its purpose of suggesting the shape.

Make a large envelope of strong paper, large enough to hold materials left over when problems have not been completed. Have pupil decorate with his own monogram and a simple border.

BOOK V, PAGE 33—ILLUSTRATION

Character Objective: Initiative

Spiritual Objective: To arouse in pupils a reverent thoughtfulness about the Passion and an appreciation of what the Resurrection should mean to them.

Art Objective: To teach the value of the principle of Subordination through illustration in cut paper.

Supplies: Pictures depicting silhouettes of various emotions, paste, blank paper, brushes and ink, cut paper, crayons

Procedure: Use as many pictures as possible, preceding the lesson, to give pupils an opportunity to study the costume effects. Discuss the setting of the story in order to get a number of word pictures, other than the one shown on the plate. Ask pupils to find silhouette pictures showing other types of emotion such as surprise, joy, etc. Paste these on the blank page as reference for graphic vocabulary when other illustrations are called for.

Use brush and ink, or cut paper for first illustration and colored crayola for the lower subject.

BOOK V, PAGE 35—GOOD FRIDAY

Character Objective: Forgiveness

Spiritual Objective: As Christ died with a prayer for forgiveness for His enemies, so pupils can show their appreciation of His great Sacrifice by showing a forgiving spirit to those who offend them.

Art Objective: To continue the study of orderly arrangement and adaptation of decoration to subject matter.

Supplies: Red crayon, construction paper, paste, scissors

Procedure: Have the story of the Passion read slowly, so that pupils may note the many objects that are mentioned in connection with the Passion, practically something for each hour of the twenty-four, preceding His death. Notice that the light and dark blocks shown on the plate suggest an orderly rhythmic repetition giving contrast of light and dark. The symbols shown, nails, crown, scourge, spear, sponge, and dice, are subordinated to the center of interest, the cross and the lettering.

Notice there are **four** figures to be outlined in **red**, suggestive of His Agony borne for love.

Encourage as many variations of the theme as possible. The problem is planned to cause children to pause and re-live a part of the Passion. Emphasize beautiful Roman figures and well planned lettering.

BOOK V, PAGE 37—RHYTHM

Character Objective: Service

Spiritual Objective: As regular or consistent movement will produce rhythm in design creating a path for the eye, so regular and consistent reception of the Sacraments of Confession and Holy Communion will store up grace in the soul that will create a sure pathway to God's love and service.

Art Objective: To make pupils conscious of the principle of Rhythm through experiments with line, form, and color.

Supplies: Pictures of various rhythmic designs; paints and brushes, cardstock

Procedure: Read and discuss the text. Have pupils find pictures to illustrate rhythmic lines (veining of leaves, fold lines in curtains, etc.) rhythmic shapes (leaves on a stem growing smaller toward top, etc.) rhythmic color, (gradations of color shown on anything).

Use previously prepared mounted reference material in explaining the types of rhythm in design (including pictures). Have pupils paint a rhythm of color as suggested in first space at bottom of plate by adding a tiny bit more color to each new panel **downward**. Panel may be cut and used for card, or card may be painted direct as suggested on plate. Purple, yellow, and green are suggestive colors for Easter. Why?

Make the bookmark greeting as shown on plate and, after it has been completed, permit pupils to originate new variations. Encourage and praise initiative where shown.

BOOK V, PAGE 39—AT BENEDICTION

Character Objective: Respect and Reverence

Spiritual Objective: To teach children the meaning of the Benediction ceremony and intelligent recognition of vestments used in it.

Art Objective: To develop appreciation of fine craftsmanship in textiles and metal work.

Supplies: Vestments (if possible), scissors, paper, paints and brushes or crayons, paste

Procedure: If possible, borrow real vestments while the lesson is in progress. Describe the ceremony briefly: The Sacred Host is exposed in an ostensorium and is incensed during the singing of hymns, which may vary in different localities, but must always include the "Tantum Ergo." After chanting a versicle and prayer, the priest wearing a humeral veil, makes the sign of the cross over the people with the ostensorium. This blessing is given in silence, but it is customary to have the sanctuary bell rung three times. Wax candles, to the number of ten at least, must be used and the incensing may not be omitted.

This devotion is of rather modern origin and is the result of processions in honor of the Feast of Corpus Christi in 1246. Later, England and France had evening devotions which concluded with the exposition of the Blessed Sacrament and naturally a blessing with the Sacred Host. Thus the beautiful ceremony of Benediction developed into its present form.

Emphasize the profound reverence necessary, since Christ Himself is giving the blessing.

Have children plan a well arranged page for each of the vestments and vessels, with brief notes of explanation. When finished, plan an appropriate decoration for a cover. This plate, photographed in color, has been especially planned for projection into the home and will be much more effective if sent home as a special gift when completed, than if held over till the end of the year. When cutting the page be sure to cut at least a half inch away from the binding, that the rest of the pages may not be loosened. If pages are completed as separate problems, they may be bound together by following model suggested in Manual notes for Book IV, Page 39.

1—**The Cope or Pluviale** (rain coat) is an expansive vestment of silk or other rich material, reaching nearly to the feet and fastened with a brooch. It has a small triangular or semicircular cape at the back, the survival of its primitive hood as the cope or "cape" was originally worn outdoors as a protection against rain, or as an overcoat in draughty churches. It has been used as a vestment since the 9th century.

2—**The Humeral Veil** is worn on the shoulders of the priest at Benediction of the Blessed Sacrament when he holds the Sacred Host for the blessing of the people, and also when he carries the Blessed Sacrament in procession. It is used to show the great respect which we should have for the sacred vessels and especially for the adorable Body of our Saviour, which is not to be carried when possible, with bare hands.

3—**The Ostensorium,** coming from a Latin word meaning to show, is a large vessel used to expose in a more visible manner, the Blessed Sacrament to the adoration of the faithful. It is also called the Monstrance. It has a stem like a chalice and in its center an aperture in which the **Lunula,** a small circular case of metal and glass, holding the Blessed Sacrament, is placed.

It originated with the institution of the Feast of Corpus Christi by Pope Urban IV in 1264. The conventional form is that of a disc with encompassing sunbeams set upon a pedestal with surmounting cross, which is of obligation, as is also the hollow center for the Lunula. Laymen are not permitted to touch the sacred vessels.

4—**The Censer** is a small vessel hung upon chains, in order that it may swing when burning incense, before the Blessed Sacrament.

5—**The Incense Boat** is a little vessel of metal which contains the incense to be burned in the Censer. The incense offered to God represents, according to St. John in the Apocalypse, the prayers of the faithful which mount up to the throne of the Almighty; offered to the ministers of the Altar and to the faithful, it reminds them that they should bear always about them the sweet odor of Jesus Christ.

Review the symbolism found on the pictured vestments. Explain that vestments are worn by the priests as an external help to assist people to fix attention on sacred things.

Uniforms are worn in many fields of service for two reasons, that others may respect and obey those who wear them, and that they may respect themselves and be more conscious of duties and more attentive to them. The vestments are sacramentals, set apart and blessed by the Church, to excite good thoughts and to increase devotion in those who see, and in those who use them.

BOOK V, PAGE 41—OUR HOMES

Character Objective: Love of Home

Spiritual Objective: To help children to realize that just as their homes are made more pleasant places in which to live, when each thing within them conforms to the whole, and disagreeable things are removed, so will children be more pleasant to live with when they try to conform their wishes to the pleasure of others, and get rid of the disagreeable vices of Selfishness and Jealousy.

Art Objective: To develop in pupils a discriminating taste in color and arrangement, in relation to the home.

Supplies: Wallpaper samples, newspaper clippings of wall arrangements, paste, blank paper, crayons or paints and brushes

Procedure: All of God's creations express perfect fitness to purpose and the home can only be satisfactory when each room perfectly expresses its use. Nature expresses the greatest simplicity consistent with use. We should follow nature. Order is the most constant law of the universe. Our homes should be **orderly.** Our furniture and the pictures on our walls should be an orderly composition. Let us test our knowledge of **dominance** and **subordination** when we plan the color scheme for the room shown on the plate.

Suggestions:

Floors and Woodwork. Floors darker than walls or ceiling, not highly polished, but grayed with neutral stains. Woodwork related to walls, and other furniture. Ceiling should be lighter than floors or wall following nature's light sky.

Walls are backgrounds for pictures, furniture, and people, and should not be flashy or spotty, but subdued, plain, beautiful, and restful. On a quiet background our pictures may be enjoyed. Use vertical stripes in paper or hangings to make low rooms appear higher. Use horizontal lines and space divisions in a high room. For the sake of economy use wall papers that reflect light, as light values with combinations of yellow, instead of papers that absorb light, as the many varieties of reds and dark blues.

Use light colors on dark rooms and warm colors on rooms having a cold north light; use cool colors on the southerly side of the house.

Nature's colors over large surfaces are always grayed and restful, while strong colors are used sparingly, as in flowers. Use soft greens, grays, browns, etc. for walls and backgrounds, with strong yellows, purples, etc. used as **tiny jewels** for covers, vases, etc.

Pictures: should be reproductions of really great things and selected because they are lovable. The frames should be quiet and neat, rather than gaudy ones that attract attention from the pictures. The middle tone of a picture is a guide for the frame color. Hang pictures to fit in appropriate spaces comfortably, by two straight wires from a moulding, instead of over one hook which makes an unpleasant triangle above it and causes it to be constantly crooked.

Having discussed with the pupils these few items of practical use in the home, ask them to bring samples of wall paper. These sample books are easily obtained in any wall paper store at the end of the season. Plan a classroom book by having each pupil make one page, as suggested in panel at bottom of the page. Each page is a challenge to fine arrangement of lettering and illustration. If desired, individual books may be made at the same time. Have pupils bring pictures clipped from magazines showing a lovely wall arrangement and paste it on the blank page.

Emphasize the harmony of vertical lines shown in curtains, window pictures, mantle, and table. **Order is always restful.**

BOOK V, PAGE 43—PENCIL SKETCHING

Character Objective: Cheerfulness

Spiritual Objective: To have the pencil make a fine bold clear line, it is necessary to keep it flat and smooth by rubbing it on sandpaper and then keeping a firm, even pressure on the paper. So the everyday contacts of pupils should leave behind them beautiful, clear impressions of good will, when irritable dispositions have been rubbed smooth with a **cheerful** "Morning Offering" and shaped with a firm pressure to please God.

Art Objective: To teach children the technique of pencil sketching.

Supplies: Pencils, pencil sharpener, paper, pictures of trees

Procedure: Read the text and follow directions for sharpening pencil. Practice strokes shown at left of lower panel. Emphasize necessity of keeping pencil flat and pressed firmly to the paper, in order to keep the line an even width and color. An uneven pressure makes the line narrower in places and apparently lighter. Complete the method shown on the plate for the making of the tree. Follow this with an original attempt to make a tree in pencil, using as a model a picture of a tree, either a photograph or colored picture. Have children draw many trees from pictures. Encourage them to draw real trees outside, but remember that trees are very difficult to draw and good pencil technique will make the problem of interpretation from nature not too difficult in the following grade. Call attention to the rhythm of shapes in the "blocked in tree" shown in the first picture on the plate.

BOOK V, PAGE 45—STAGE PROPERTIES

General Suggestions: Read text carefully on pages 45 and 47 for directions. The corner of the room will be an excellent location for the setting.

Read suggestions for curtain given for Book I, Page 49. A curtain suspended on picture wire moves very easily, but cord will answer.

Use as many incidents of the story as you may see fit. As a preceding English lesson, list topics on blackboard and have pupils reproduce stories about each one. The dialogue of the play is to be **created by the pupils,** as natural conversation instead of being the result of memorized lines.

Always keep in mind that it is a **classroom** play.

Supplies: Chalk and blackboard (optional), curtain, picture wire or cord

Blackboard topics: Bernadette's home; family; work; amusement; friends; visions; troubles; later life.

Characters in the play might include:

Bernadette, a French shepherdess.
Tonette } her little sisters.
Jeanne }
Francois Soubirous, her father.
Louise Soubirous, her mother.
Curé of Lourdes, the priest.
Monsieur Jacomet, Supt. of Police } *(who tried to drive the people away)*
Monsieur Dutour, a policeman }
Peasants of town of Lourdes.
(These may include tradesmen whose conversation would explain their different trades, etc).

Act 1: The play opens **outside curtain**, in the very poor home of Bernadette, with the family seated around the breakfast table (the teacher's desk may be used if no other table is available).

Grace is said by father, and then conversation centers around the food, black bread, and milk; lack of work at the mill to keep the miller busy; smaller children begging to go with Bernadette in order that they may help with the sheep and bring home firewood. **Courtesy** at table is emphasized. All go off to work.

Curtain is drawn aside to show mountain side as shown in picture with grotto **covered**. Bernadette tells the story of the green sheep and the pet lamb. Companions respond appropriately and continue to discuss the care and use of sheep. Sisters go to collect wood and Bernadette kneels at her shrine before following. The vision appears —no word is spoken at this meeting. Bernadette shows bewilderment. The children return and hear the story.

Curtain.

Act 2: Bernadette, accompanied by parents and neighbors, returns to the grotto. Conversation includes what has happened in the meanwhile. Bernadette sees the Lady and talks to her and asks her name. The Lady answers by telling her to go to the rock and find the spring, then go to the priest, tell him to build a church, as a shrine, there. Bernadette answers many questions asked by the surprised crowd, about the water flowing from the rock.

Curtain.

Act 3: (**Outside curtain.**) Bernadette visits priest and is told she must find the Lady's name. The priest doubts her and thinks it is her imagination. Curtain drawn aside shows:

Crowd led by Bernadette climbing mountain to the grotto; police try to interfere. All kneel and recite a decade of the rosary. The Lady appears as it ends. Bernadette again asks her name and receives the answer, which to her means nothing. The priest is with the kneeling crowd and shows excitement, saying, "The good God has blessed our Holy Father Pope Pius IX by having His Blessed Mother announce to the world that the Pope has not been mistaken." People praise Mary with hymns as they march away.

Curtain.

Finale: Alone, little Bernadette returns to the shrine four months later, and is heartbroken because it is barricaded. She kneels to pray, when suddenly the Lady appears for the last time. The Lady smiles and blesses her saying: "Pray and do penance for sinners. I do not promise you happiness in this world, but in the next." She smiles again and vanishes and curtain drops on the kneeling Bernadette.

CORRELATED WORK

1. RELIGION: Be sure to give pupils a clear understanding of the meaning of the Immaculate Conception, by illustrating Original sin as an **inherited loss** of God's friendship, just as they inherit the name and home of their worldly parents, when they come into the world. This has been the case since our **first** parents deliberately gave that **friendship** up, by offending God, and accordingly, could not **bequeath** it to their children, who can only regain it **individually** through **Baptism**.
2. ENGLISH: "To encourage the spontaneous impulse to speak, write, recite, debate, and declaim through both independent and directed practice."
   (a) To train pupils to talk "to the point" for a minute or two, using good enunciation and a natural tone, which is neither shouting nor mumbling.
   (b) To acquire an effective vocabulary for oral or written work through use of a dictionary.
   (c) To secure a coherent paragraph of four or five clear and complete sentences, properly capitalized and punctuated. *(English Course of Study—Pittsburgh Public Schools)*
3. GEOGRAPHY AND HISTORY: Give general information about France and the French people following work applicable to grade. Mountains, rivers, etc.
4. NATURE—Study and use of water in its various forms. (The water of Lourdes has no medicinal qualities.)
5. ARITHMETIC: Problems in measurements, for set, etc.
6. COSTUME: Have pupils visit the library and obtain illustrated books about French children and people. French fairy tales and French folklore in many forms. Study pictured costumes and compare with American.
7. MUSIC: Hymns to our Lady and English translation of Marseillaise.
8. Use of dictionary for new words.
9. Color and design in painting and making set.
10. Creative development in all work done.

BOOK V, PAGE 47—THE MIRACLE OF LOURDES

A school room play in honor of the Feast of the Immaculate Conception or for February 11th, the anniversary of the miracle.

Character Objective: Purity

Spiritual Objective: To teach children the meaning of the Feast of the Immaculate Conception as well as to arouse in them a loving devotion to our Blessed Mother under that title, as an aid in achieving her purity. They should know that The Immaculate Conception is the National Patron of the United States.

Art Objectives:

1—To develop creative skill and ingenuity through the making of an exterior set for a play.

2—To arouse interest in costume through the study of French peasant dress necessary in the play.

THE STORY

(From authentic notes left by Sister Bernard (Bernadette) and translated by her Superior.)

Bernadette Soubirous was the eldest daughter of a poor French miller, Francois, living in the heart of the Pyrénées mountains in France.

Seven younger sisters and brothers made it difficult for her parents to provide food and clothing, especially since the business at the mill continued to grow less and less.

When Bernadette was fourteen she was asked by her godmother to come to her house to help with the children and look after the sheep on the mountain side.

Up in the mountains not far from the little town of Lourdes, where Bernadette lived, was a cavern hollowed out by the hand of nature from the cliffs lying to the west of Lourdes. It was called Massabieille (ancient pile of rocks). Branches of shrubs intertwined to form a frame work, while the waters of the river Gave raced incessantly at their feet. Far in the background the great summits of the Pyrénées loom in impressive solitude; nearer at hand the green-clad hills form a lovely pattern against the horizon. "The mountains seem to crouch and kneel at the feet of some majestic and half divine presence. All the landscape seems folded in expectancy awaiting the fulfilment of the prophecy tradition has handed down that 'a mighty sign is to be manifested at the grotto of Massabieille.'"

Bernadette loved her sheep and when not busy with them, she gathered wildflowers and with loving hands wreathed garlands to place upon the rustic altar she built with scattered stones in honor of Mary, her Mother, and her Queen; but her most imperishable offering was her constant chaplet of Aves.

Bernadette played with her lambs, above all with the smallest, her special pet. "From time to time he would come and knock over the little shrine I had made for the Blessed Virgin, but I easily forgave him and instead of punishing him, gave him bread and salt which he loved. I loved him because he was so little and my heart goes out to all little ones."

"Once when my father found me very unhappy watching my sheep, he wanted to know what was the matter. 'Just look at my sheep; some of them have their backs all green.' He replied, laughing, 'All the grass they have eaten is coming out on their backs; I suppose it will kill them.' I burst into tears, when he comforted me and explained that the green mark was the brand of the dealer to whom they had been sold. I did not know what a lie was and I believed everything I was told."

On the 11th of February, 1858, Bernadette with two little girls, were out gathering firewood on the mountain side. Her friends had crossed the stream and Bernadette was removing her shoes to follow them when she heard a rush of wind and on turning her head toward the grotto, she saw a Lady in white who smiled and beckoned to her, raising the rosary she carried and blessing her with it; then she disappeared. Bernadette told her companions and as a result her parents forbade her to return to the grotto, thinking she was only the victim of her imagination. She pled so earnestly that finally she was permitted to return, when again she saw the beautiful Lady, who was invisible to the others with her. The Lady asked her to return every day for two weeks. This she did, each day being accompanied by great crowds, who knelt and prayed while Bernadette talked to the Lady. On One visit she told Bernadette to go to the priest and tell him to build a church on the spot. The priest refused to listen to Bernadette, telling her to ask the Lady her name. This she did, but instead of telling her name, the Lady told Bernadette to remove with her hands some dirt from a rock in the grotto. She did so and at once there gushed forth a spring which immediately cured a man who was blind. Finally, on her **sixteenth** visit, which was on March 25th, the Feast of the Annunciation, after Bernadette had urged her to tell her name, she raised her hands to her breast and with a look of unutterable sweetness answered, "I am the Immaculate Conception," and disappeared. To Bernadette these words meant nothing, but she kept repeating them over and over until she reached the priest who understood their full import. For eighteen hundred years the dispute had been waged endlessly around this question of Mary's immaculate birth.

Finally, had not the saintly Pope Pius IX in 1854, just four years previously, pronounced it, at last, an Article of Faith? And now had come the gracious Queen of Heaven to vindicate his pronouncement and settle for all time the faintest doubt.

Two more visits were permitted to this little favorite of Mary, the last one being on the Feast of Mount Carmel, July 25th. But this time Bernadette had to see her heavenly Visitor from afar, as the Government had boarded up the grotto and forbidden the people to go there to pray or bathe in its water. The Lady saluted her, smiled and vanished, leaving Bernadette only her image and her name. But the fame of the curative waters had spread too far to allow this petty interference of the local police to continue and it was not long until the church Our Lady had requested, was built, and her Son came down to dwell upon its altar.

Bernadette grew up and became a Sister of Charity and until her death, her life was filled with noble work for God. In 1913 an investigation of her saintly life caused Pope Pius X to proclaim her title of Venerable, and who knows but that some day she may be called Saint.

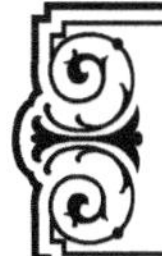

Book Six

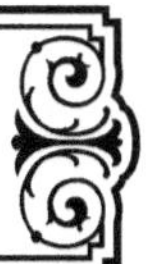

BOOK VI—COVER

See page 3 of this manual.

BOOK VI—END PAPER

Character Objective: Purity.

Spiritual Objective: To teach children that striving for an ideal makes for right thinking, and frequent Communion provides necessary grace to strengthen purpose.

Art Objective: To teach the adaptation of the cross as a motive in an all-over stencil design.

Supplies: Razor blade, paints and brushes, picture frame

Procedure: Read the verse and ask for reactions from class on meaning of lines.

Relate it to the story of Sir Galahad and his preparation for his quest of the Grail.

Have pupils memorize the poem.

Turn to end paper at back of book to analyze its design structure. Notice that the **white** design which so beautifully covers the page is the result of the "little bridges" added to hold the outline of the original cross motif. The black design is the part cut away. Notice how the monotony of the straight edge of the square unit has been avoided by curving the inside of each corner so that when four of them are repeated, a circle appears as a **subordinate interest** in the design.

Plan a design unit in a square. Add bridges to hold it in place while you cut out the background with a razor blade. Apply your stencil to make an all-over pattern for a book cover for your vestment book.

Plan a color scheme and paint the end paper in the front of the book. Use light tints of the colors. Frame it to hang on the wall.

BOOK VI, PAGE 1—SIR GALAHAD

Character Objective: Purity

Spiritual Objective: To awaken in children an appreciation of the ideals symbolized by Sir Galahad which the artist wished to express when he said he wanted to "suggest great thoughts that will appeal to the imagination and the heart and kindle all that is best and noblest in humanity."

Art Objective: To continue to develop appreciation of pictures through the additional recognition of balance as a principle of design.

Teacher's Preparation: Study the picture and analyze its special appeal to yourself.

What makes the strongest impression? Its story? Its composition? Its color? The artist has given us one of the most appealing pictures of this popular hero, that of manly purity and steadfastness.

Read the story of Sir Galahad given with the drama to explain the picture.

Notice how beautifully the knight has been posed to fill the space. Notice how weary he seems, yet not discouraged, how humble and how reverent, safe in the knowledge that the quest will be successful. "My strength is as the strength of ten, because my heart is pure." We know his rest is only for a moment because one foot is thrust forward, his head is up with his eyes mysteriously gazing ahead. His fatigue presents contrast to that shown in the weariness of the great strong horse with drooping head and tired eyes. What a beautiful curve the neck of the horse has introduced to lead the eye to Sir Galahad's face and again by its light value, affording a strong contrast to his dark figure.

Galahad is emphasized as the dominant interest through the strong dark and light arrangement. The dark at the left balances the two dark spots of the trees visible at the right. The white masses of the horse emphasize his dark form silhouetted against it. The red bands on the horse again center attention on his figure. The light sky at the top frames in his face.

The tangled vegetation at his feet suggests the difficulties of those who strive for perfection. Notice how the line of the sword, connecting with the clump of foliage singularly like a cross, almost creates the form of a processional cross.

Procedure: Have pupils observe the picture in silence for a few minutes; then call for reactions.

Tell the story of Sir Galahad briefly and see how many pupils observe in the picture significant facts related to it.

Note that the red of the horse and the green of the foliage gives a complementary color scheme which gives accent to the picture.

What lines in the picture have been planned to harmonize with the figure? Notice the rhythmic sequence of values shown by sky, horse, and armor. What other rhythms can you find? How does rhythm help the picture?

A lovely golden tone seems to envelop the whole picture dominating all the rest. This is called a **dominant color harmony.** The complementary scheme found in it is **subordinate** to this. What has the artist done to give balance to his picture?

The artist George Frederick Watts preferred to paint this type of picture. He belonged to the English school. His humility was very marked. When did he live?

For additional picture study, see page xxx.

BOOK VI, PAGE 3—FLOWERS IN DESIGN

Character Objective: Reverence

Spiritual Objective: Every morning this beautiful cup-like flower lifts its head and opens to receive the morning dew into its heart, as every morning finds priests all over the world lifting other Cups which receive for us life-giving Food for our souls. As the flower would lose its beauty and die without water, so will our souls lose beauty and die without the grace of the Blessed Sacrament, which the priest makes possible for us each morning at Mass.

Art Objective:

1—To teach the value of accented line in rendering flower forms.

2—To teach adaptation of flower forms to design.

3—To develop appreciation of manufactured textiles through experience in design created for them.

Supplies: Morning glories or other live flowers (if possible), pencils, pictures of textiles, paper

Procedure: Read the text and plan questions to test understanding of reviewed portions. Recall similar adaptation of flower form, Book V, Page 39.

Mount sprays of morning-glories or any other growths showing tendrils, on paper of contrasting color to emphasize pattern. Search the form for fine curves (Book V, Page 27). Emphasize rhythmic qualities when drawing. Review essentials of good composition, while referring to placing of real specimen and compare with plate. Remove from real specimen all unnecessary foliage or flowers in order to simplify drawing. Find **shadowed** edges needing **accent** and **delicate** edges to be drawn **lightly**. Finish lesson and have class criticism by comparison with original.

Lesson 2: Using flower shape just drawn, try making flower shape fit geometric shapes such as circle, square, triangle, etc., by arranging parts on diameter, diagonal, and radius. Aim for a nice balance of light and dark. Following method shown in book to make interesting units notice that it is necessary to **unite them** interestingly by using a smaller **subordinate** form which may be another part of flower or a contrasting bit of background.

The all-over pattern shows a repetition of shapes in a **horizontal** direction, while Page 9 shows a surface pattern developed by arranging the units in **vertical** rows and with the second row dropped below the first. This is called a "drop repeat" and is much used in textile patterns.

By repeating the unit through tracing, a surface pattern may be developed in neutral values to use in panel form. Use it to decorate the cover of a book of flower forms either printed or drawn, or as panel decoration for a campaign poster, "Flower Preservation." Ask pupils to find pictures of textiles that would suggest a use for this type of design.

BOOK VI, PAGE 5—THE EXALTATION OF THE HOLY CROSS

Character Objective: Loyalty

Spiritual Objective: To teach children the meaning and use of the **Sacramentals** of the Church.

Art Objective: To teach the use of the cross as a motive in design.

Supplies: Cut paper, paints and brushes

Procedure: Explain that sacramentals are used by the Church "to excite good thoughts and to increase devotion." Name some of the other sacramentals.

Read the text as a basis for the discussion of the cross. The Sign of the Cross is the most important sacramental of the Church, and is the one most frequently used, as no ceremony is performed without it.

By the Sign of the Cross we demonstrate the most important articles of our Faith: the Unity and Trinity of God, the Incarnation, Death, and Resurrection of our Saviour. Pupils must realize that since this sign advertises to others their active faith, they must be careful to honor it through not giving scandal in daily activities.

The central cross on the page is known as the **Latin Cross**. Explain the difference between cross and crucifix.

Although the cross in pagan times was an instrument of death, we find a most ancient cross in the form of the swastika, emblematic of the revolutions of the sun and hence a symbol of life.

The Maltese Cross was the badge of the military and religious order of the Knights of Malta.

The Greek Cross is so called because it was largely used in medieval Greek architecture. The Celtic Cross is a well known form found throughout Ireland on which the circle typifies eternity gained through the cross.

The Papal Cross has three cross bars in honor of the Blessed Trinity.

Candles: The use of candles originated with the idea of dispelling darkness, but their beautiful symbolism was quickly recognized by the writers of the early Church. Light is pure; it penetrates darkness; it moves with incredible speed; it nourishes life; it illumines all that comes under its influence. Therefore, it is a fitting symbol of God the All-Pure, the Source of all grace and enlightenment.

The wax, being spotless, represents Christ's most spotless Body; the wick enclosed in it is an image of His Soul, while the glowing flame typifies the Divine Nature united with the human in one Divine Person. Candles are made sacramentals by being blessed on the Feast of the Purification, or Candlemas Day, because in pagan times the Roman people had been accustomed to carry lights in procession in honor of one of their gods, so the Church turned this pagan festival into a Christian ceremony, honoring the Mother of God.

Candles are used at the administration of all the sacraments, except Penance. It is necessary that these candles be pure beeswax, because of symbolic meaning—The bee which gathers the honey and secretes the wax is virginal and an appropriate figure of the Virgin Mother, while the candle burning is the figure of the untainted Humanity of Christ.

The Paschal Candle is blessed on Holy Saturday and is lighted on the Gospel side of the Sanctuary. It burns until Ascension Day symbolizing the interim between the death of Jesus and His Ascension. During the blessing five grains of incense placed inside five little wax nails are fixed into its side, signifying the five wounds in our Saviour's glorified Body.

The Triple Candle signifying the Three Persons of the Blessed Trinity, is lighted on Holy Saturday from the new fire which has been blessed, to typify the Resurrection.

The St. Blaise Candle is especially blessed for use on the Feast of St. Blaise and used for the blessing of throats.

St. Blaise was a doctor who was martyred. While in prison awaiting execution he removed a fishbone from a boy's throat, saving his life. His intercession with God has since been invoked, for diseases of the throat.

This problem has been planned as a continued problem which, when finished, may be made into an interesting book to be taken home.

Illustrations may be used to develop careful technique in painting clean edges or to develop a sense of light and dark pattern through cut paper. An appropriate design may be worked out to decorate the booklet cover.

BOOK VI, PAGE 7—LETTERING

Character Objective: Helpful Service

Spiritual Objective: Capital or upper case letters attract attention by their size, while **lower** case letters are small and inconspicuous, but because they are so **necessary** they have been placed in the type box **close** to the hand of the typesetter.

We are all "typesetting" for God and the apparently unimportant small acts **close at hand** which are done in His honor make up the **necessary** record of our lives. **Don't wait to do the big thing** that will attract attention.

Art Objective: To have pupils learn a standard form of capital and small letters which they can use freely in class problems.

Supplies: Chalk and blackboard (optional), paper, colored construction paper, pencils

Procedure: Read the text and review rules of lettering learned in Book V, Page 13.

Have pupils work on the blackboard before working on paper, as corrections may be quickly and easily made and all work is visible during practice.

Follow blackboard lesson with a pencil lesson at desks, aiming to keep general proportions of letters as well as correct form. Give special attention to capital letters B, K, M, R, and S and to small letters a, g, k, m, n, r, and y. After sufficient practice, have pupils letter programs for a Hallowe'en party, with appropriate decoration of Jack-O-Lanterns. A short memory verse suitable for the month may be lettered. If colored construction paper is used, decoration may be added of a color complementary to the paper, which will help to neutralize it. Be careful not to ask pupils to letter **too much** subject matter. Emphasize the beauty obtained by making **the block** of **lettering conform** to **shape** of **paper**.

BOOK VI, PAGE 9—COLOR KNOWLEDGE

Character Objective: Poise

Spiritual Objective: To teach pupils that, as one strong color properly placed will counteract the attractive power of another strong color with a resulting emphasis on whatever is between them, so the naturally strong inclination to consider selfish interest first must be counteracted or balanced by a strong will to have consideration for others, with a resulting emphasis on pleasing God, which should be the most important business.

Art Objective: To teach the importance of the principle of **Balance** in color arrangement and its special application to the home.

Supplies: Neutral paper, black paper, paints and brushes, box or stiff paper and paste

Procedure: Review color complements and their use in neutralizing. Be quite sure that pupils know the difference between **color intensity** and **color value.**

Read and discuss the text. Test pupils' understanding of **attractive power** by having them illustrate with colored papers of different intensities (a package of assorted colored poster paper contains several intensities of each color). Compare the scales at the top of the page showing kinds of color balance, with two boys on a see-saw who must balance. Children have had experience with this kind of balance and know how uneven weights may be distributed correctly. Brilliant intense color, because of its strong attractive power, has the same effect on the eye as the heavy weight on the scales, and just as the weight must be equally distributed to keep the scales at rest, so the color must be equally distributed or balanced to keep the eye at rest. To be **beautiful** our homes must be **restful**.

The other term for unsymmetric balance is occult balance as it is **sensed** rather than seen.

Note that warm colors have stronger attractive power than cool colors, as illustrated by all-over patterns on the plate. Pleasing color harmonies are obtained by keeping strong colors neutralized when spread over large areas and of stronger intensity when used on small spots as accents.

Lesson 2: Use the all-over pattern designed on page 3, and plan a color scheme for it, using a pair of complementary colors on a neutral background which is a tint of one of the complements, as suggested on plate. To do this, paint the background and allow it to dry before painting the design. Try the same pattern again, using a black background and then compare the effects obtained. It will be found that black has intensified the colors.

In the arrangement of the room the large neutral area of gray wall balances the smaller masses of stronger blue-green in the chair and drapery; the large mass of green chair and curtain is balanced by the small mass of green curtain placed near the edge of picture; the red-orange shade and curtain fringe make a large mass near the center which is balanced by the tiny bit of red-orange fringe near the edge; on the table, the large mass of books near the center is balanced by the smaller bowl near the edge; the large mass of green in the room is carefully balanced by the smaller mass of the more attractive red-orange, which adds interest through accent.

The color harmony is made still more beautiful by having the table a dark value of red-orange to relate it to the shade, wall, and tapestry. The small spots of green on the table and the tint of green in the tapestry are relating or **harmonizing** links in the whole beautiful scheme of color.

Lesson 3: Plan a corner of a room by using a box or pasting three sheets of stiff paper. Cut furniture from magazines or catalogues and plan a good arrangement.

Plan color scheme for rug, walls, ceiling and draperies, and paint accordingly. Windows may be cut out and either textile or paper draperies used. While problem is in progress, community charts may be planned from excess samples brought to school, showing suggestive color harmonies for different rooms. If the classroom offers itself as a suitable problem, committees may be appointed to change arrangement of pictures, plan a center of interest, or make any other orderly changes where improvement is possible.

See Manual suggestions for Book V, Page 41.

BOOK VI, PAGE 11—COLOR LAWS

Character Objective: Cooperation

Spiritual Objective: To help pupils to understand that as the laws of color are given to guide them in beautifying their homes, so God has given them living guides to help them to know how to beautify their souls, which should be His home.

Their priests, Nuns, and parents help to do this, but the pupils' cooperation is necessary.

Art Objective: To teach the law of color areas and provide an experience in creating a beautiful color scheme of nicely balanced colors.

Supplies: Paints and brushes, paper

Procedure: Read the text and have pupils memorize the three rules for color balance, given in text page 11, when using intense and neutral colors. Pupils should plan their own color arrangement, but may ask advice on points not clear.

Emphasize necessity of a thoughtful plan. Try colors on practice paper and allow them to dry before deciding to use them. Use complementary colors in order to get contrast and remember the necessity of neutralizing them.

Paint quickly, without much water, to keep colors fresh and clear. Scrubbing over the color with the brush produces muddy effects.

Aim to paint clean edges. Read suggestions for Book V, page 11.

BOOK VI, PAGE 13—POSTERS

Character Objective: Sincerity

Spiritual Objective: A good poster must advertise well enough to "sell the goods." Pupils should be made to realize that **they** are "posters" for Catholicity as they go through life, and must be **good** advertisements of what they are. As a heavy black letter has **carrying power,** so frequent reception of the Sacraments will give **grace that has power to carry** them along the right path; if their **charity** will give the **color** to their poster while fine **daily acts** show its **design**, then both "color" and "design" will advertise **a desire to please God.**

Art Objective: To teach the essentials of a good poster.

Supplies: Posterboards or cardstock paper, crayons, paints and brushes, scissors, colored paper, paste

Procedure: Simplicity is the keynote of a good poster as well as of a good life. Read the text and discuss the Missions to get many, many slogans for individual posters.

The text is clear on essentials of a good poster. Aim to have block of lettering used conform to the space. The movable paper "layout" is valuable to aid pupils in getting a sense of balance which may be either bisymmetric or occult (review both terms). Have pupils identify flags at bottom of page by finding them in the dictionary. Any of these flags may be used in various arrangements, or something entirely different may be used. Be careful to **avoid** placing in direct center, as the "optical center" is a little above center. Have pupils notice the outside back covers of their books where the placing of the monogram adds interest.

Review the color **law of areas** when planning the color scheme for both background and decoration. Find examples of fine poster letters to paste on the blank page.

BOOK VI, PAGE 15—LEARNING TO SEE

Character Objective: Self-Control

Spiritual Objective: This lesson about handles impresses the fact that handles must be **firmly fastened** if they are to serve their purpose of carrying the weight of the vessel. Through it children may be made to see the necessity of daily practice of goodness in order that **strong habits** may be formed for "handles" that will **carry them safely through temptation.**

Art Objective: To develop truthful observation and graphic interpretation of circular objects involving spouts and handles.

Supplies: Chalk and blackboard (optional), stiff neutral paper, manila paper, pencils, gray bogus paper, crayons

Procedure: Read and discuss the text. Follow experiment suggested to show relative positions of spouts and handles of circular containers, in any position. Using text books, have pupils practice ellipses at blackboard turning them into objects suggested on the page. Pay careful attention to the **joining** of handles and spouts to the vessel. When they have become familiar with the forms have pupils discard books and draw a circular form on the board from memory. From **dictation** they should quickly add handles and spouts, placed in various positions. Call attention to the pencil **accents** shown in the rendering of the objects on the page.

Accented lines show **nearness** and, when used on the **under** part, denote **shadow**.

Plan at least four groups of two circular objects, one of which shows a spout and handle. Group should also show an interesting contrast of size and color. Have individual students arrange groups while class criticizes their placing. It is wise to have a group arranged for each two rows, on boards placed across the aisle from desk to desk. Place a large sheet of stiff neutral paper behind them to simplify the forms. Review points learned in Book V, Page 21, about **points of contact** as helps in correct drawing.

Manila drawing paper 9 x 12 may be used with a very soft pencil. Aim to make the drawing fill the paper while keeping true proportions. A similar lesson may be repeated later for review, using gray bogus paper and colored crayola.

BOOK VI, PAGE 17—MECHANICAL DRAWING

Character Objective: Accuracy

Spiritual Objective: All types of industry require **tools** as an aid in making things accurately so that parts will fit and results will be serviceable. God knows that children also need tools to help them fit their little difficulties of every day into a well made plan for God's service. These tools, which should be kept bright and sharp through use, are **prayer** and the **Sacraments** which supply grace that will keep strong an active love of God.

Art Objective: To teach the use of mechanical instruments.

Supplies: Chalk and blackboard (optional), string, compasses (if possible), paper, images of circular objects, scissors, paste, blank paper

Procedure: Read text and be sure that pupils understand that mechanical aids are to be used for **mechanical work only.**

Have problems solved on the blackboard, following the plan given in the book. Use a piece of string tied to chalk for a compass. **Length** of string makes the **radius**. Practice making circles and then continue with problems on page. Repeat from memory.

Practice at seats with metal compasses if they are available, following suggestions given in text. Make paper compasses as illustrated in book if no other kind may be had.

Find pictures of objects based on these forms to paste on the blank page.

BOOK VI, PAGE 19—A GIFT BOX

Character Objective: Thoughtfulness for Others

Spiritual Objective: As careful attention to all the small details of construction will produce a well made gift which we are proud to present to somebody, so should we be most careful of every detail that goes into the making of the gift of hearts to God.

Art Objective: To develop good craftsmanship in making a decorated gift box.

Supplies: Chalk and blackboard (optional), compasses, rulers, colored construction paper, scissors, crayons or paints and brushes, paraffin or shellac

Procedure: Practice making a hexagon at blackboard as in previous lesson to be sure children can solve the problem.

At desks, with compass and ruler, follow the directions given for construction of box. Other boxes may be originated later from geometric shapes learned on page 17. Trace shape of box lid and have pupils fold paper into as many parts as desired for the stencilled decoration. Cut leaf form or other motif from one section of paper previously folded. Decorate lid while it is flat before it is pasted. If crayola is used, rub lightly over opening in stencil. If paint is used trace shape with pencil and paint **inside** or outside the lines. Use colored construction paper for box. If paint is applied **over** the stencil, treat the edges of the cut paper with melted paraffin or shellac. This keeps edges firm.

BOOK VI, PAGE 21—GOOD TASTE

Character Objective: Good Manners

Spiritual Objective: To awaken in children a consciousness of the need of beautifying the Soul, the "house" to which God comes as a Guest. Refer to the poem "My House."

Art Objective:

1—To teach application of design principles to produce fine arrangements in the home.

2—To make a fine page arrangement of lettering and illustration.

The pages of pupils should include illustrations of anything that they may consider beautiful and also related to home or dress. Before selections are pasted they must have the approval of the class as measuring up to accepted standards of beauty and design.

(1) Fitness to purpose; utility.
(2) Pleasing in line and form.
(3) Harmonious in color.
(4) Show good proportions.
(5) Design adapted to material for which it is made.

Interest is added when a page may be arranged to show an illustration which is an example of violation of good taste, mounted beside a fine example of a similar subject. Appropriate criticism of each should be included. A loose-leaf booklet, similar to that on Book IV, Page 17 may be used since these individual pages are to be bound together.

Supplies: Pencils, paper, paste, loose-leaf paper, crayons, paints and brushes

Procedure: Read the text and after a lively discussion of what is appropriate in costume for those who would show good taste, as well as what is appropriate for home decoration, appoint committees to collect material for illustration of various points discussed. A class book may be made, or if preferred, each pupil may make his own book. Review lesson Book V, Page 41 to relate the problem to knowledge previously gained.

It will be found that **common sense** provides safe guidance for satisfying results in many things, as illustrated in the table arrangement and decoration at the top of the page.

BOOK VI, PAGE 23—WHEN LOVE OF POWER RULED THE WORLD

Character Objective: Judgment

Spiritual Objective: The ruins of the powerful Roman Empire will impress on pupils how lacking in judgment it is to fail to make use of the building material at hand every day, to build body and soul into "A living House of God" which will last through Eternity.

Art Objective: To interest pupils in architecture and arouse an intelligent appreciation of modern adaptations of the Roman style.

Supplies: Scissors or razor blade, crayons, paints and brushes, paper, colored construction paper, paste

Procedure: Read the text as a nucleus for a discussion of the Roman Empire. Any history will supply much interesting information concerning Roman life, customs, and religion. It will be of special interest as the background for the Birth of Christ. The Roman laws concerning the Jews explain the presence of Joseph and Mary in Bethlehem.

Review the fact that the Egyptians built temples and tombs, leaving a record of their **history and religion** and their art appealed to the **understanding**. The Greeks built **temples and theatres** to give joy to those who saw them because of beauty of form and color, so Greek art appealed to the **emotions.**

The Romans were warlike conquerors who were more interested in themselves than in anything else, so naturally we find their art centered in **things to benefit themselves** and so add to their **glory and power.**

We find theatres, baths, palaces, temples, aqueducts, triumphal arches, etc. We call their art **civic art** because it improved their cities. They did not originate beauty as did the Greeks, but took old forms and combined them to make new ones. We always associate with them the round arch, although it was used before them. But they did something **new with it,** by a combination of arches they produced the dome which has lasted ever since.

Before this time all buildings were only one story, but by building with the arches and pillars, the Romans were the first to erect buildings six and seven stories high. They copied the ideas of the Greeks but did not have the Greeks' artistic knowledge of how to use them, and so we find many of their buildings over-decorated; their art lacked the symbolism of the Egyptians and the refinement of the Greeks. It demanded admiration for its size and richness. If a pillar were removed from a Greek building it would fall, but if we remove a pillar from a Roman building it would not be missed. And that is the great difference between Greek and Roman art, and between all good architecture and that which is not so good. The Greeks took what was **necessary** to the building and **decorated it;** that is **Constructive**. The Romans used what **appeared to be structure,** as ornament only; that is **Decorative.**

The Colosseum: This building was a huge amphitheatre, much like our modern athletic stadiums. It meant double theatre with seats built around a circle and the stage or arena in the center. It was one of the largest buildings ever made, seating about eighty thousand people and permitting hundreds of gladiators to fight in its arena at the same time.

It was finished about thirty-five years after the death of Christ. Here the trained gladiators fought each other and fought wild animals, much as some countries today have bull fights and prize fights. But it was not long before Christians and slaves were condemned to go unarmed into the arena to fight hungry lions, "to make a Roman holiday." They were not afraid to die and gloried in their martyrdom.

The blood of some ten thousand martyrs soon had stained the arena floor. Today a large cross commemorates their memory.

The building was circular, 157 feet high, and we find three orders of columns used, the Doric on the first floor, the Ionic on the second floor, and the Corinthian on the third floor.

But these columns were only used as ornaments, as the weight of the walls rested on the arches. The artistic taste of the Greeks would not have allowed them to use so many kinds of columns. The building was constructed of little flat bricks and then completely covered with marble. Even today this imposing ruin shows what wonderful engineers these Romans were, because of the many intricate arrangements placed inside for the comfort of the people. It has furnished a model for modern theatres ever since. The picture on the upper right shows an American adaptation of the Colosseum for a civic building of beauty, although almost every city and town has a ball park or athletic stadium modeled on this great Roman building.

The Arch of Constantine: The Romans won many victories and their way of celebrating was to erect a triumphal arch much as we do today in many of our big cities. The Arch of Constantine was built in honor of a great Roman Emperor who was the first ruler to become a Christian. He is the Emperor who conquered the ancient city of Byzantium and renamed it for himself, Constantinople. It was his mother, Queen Helena, who found the True Cross.

This arch is in fine condition; the center panel at the top shows an inscription cut in the marble in beautiful Roman letters. The letters used in the text book are Roman letters.

Notice that the columns used between the arches have no other purpose than to **decorate** the walls. This type of arch often answered as a city gate with a center opening for horses and processions and side openings for people.

The Pantheon was at one time the entrance to one of the Roman Baths. Like the Colosseum it was round but was built without windows and its magnificent dome has never been surpassed in size. At the top there is a circular opening 23 feet across and this admits sufficient light for the interior. Shortly after it was built, another Emperor added the Greek pediment and pillars and changed it into a temple for **all the Gods**, hence its name, Pantheon. As in using other things borrowed from the Greeks, this combination of two such unlike parts as the portico and dome is not pleasing or harmonious. But the dome and interior of the building are so splendidly constructed and so simply decorated that it is considered the most magnificent of Roman temples. It became a Christian church later and many famous men are buried there, among them the artist Raphael.

The Roman Statue of Caligula has been used to show the typical Roman costume as well as to show characteristic Roman sculpture, which, like everything else, was planned to glorify the great men, and hence a portrait type of sculpture.

The Roman Chariot, the original of which is in the Vatican Museum, is one of the art treasures of the world because of the beautiful delicacy of the elaborate carving on the marble chariot and the lifelike portraiture of the horses, modeled life size. This was the type of chariot used in the great races and also driven by the Emperor in his wars.

The Leaning Tower of Pisa was built in Italy, hundreds of years later, under a new type of architecture, which was first cousin to the Roman and called Romanesque. When we look at it carefully we can see its relationship. It was purposely built to Jean at this dangerous looking angle, as an engineering feat to show perfect balance. There are many leaning towers in Italy, but this one is called one of the seven wonders of the world. It is called a Campanile, or bell-tower.

Have pupils go to the library and borrow large pictures of important Roman art treasures, and have them exhibited as the lesson progresses, to allow children to get a clear idea of details not clear on the small pictures.

"Quo Vadis" or "Ben Hur" will provide many interesting selections to be read concerning Roman life; lives of the martyrs are rich in the same subject matter and will have much more interest for pupils, after they have studied Roman art.

Cut page about a half inch from the binding to protect the other pages.

The lesson may be continued throughout the year if preferred, taking one picture at a time in connection with lettering to make a nice page arrangement. When completed, pages are to be bound into book form to be taken home.

BOOK VI, PAGE 25—APPRECIATION

Character Objective: Self Reliance

Spiritual Objective: Christ left the perfect example of the power of love when He left us the Eucharist and our appreciation may be shown by receiving the Blessed Sacrament frequently.

Art Objective: To develop manual skill and appreciation of architecture through modeling characteristics of Roman art.

Supplies: Clay, cardboard or stiff paper, ruler, postcard pictures of arches

Procedure: Read directions for care and handling of clay, page xx. Aim to have clay of proper consistency, neither too wet nor too dry, but about the consistency of soft putty or kneaded wall paper cleaner. Previous experience gained in Grades 3, 4 and 5, will leave nothing new in the rosettes but the form of the flower motif. These forms are commonly found on furniture, woodwork, stone trimmings, etc. Have pupils look for them.

The round arch and the triumphal arch afford a new problem, that of **modeling in the round.**

Have pupils cut off small pieces of clay and after pressing into shape, cut with cardboard or stiff paper or ruler. Build arch as suggested in book. Several arches placed together will show a barrel vault. Others made to intersect will readily show the development of the dome.

After making the simplified model of the famous **Arch of Titus** shown on the plate, ask pupils to find a postcard picture of a local arch in their town or nearby city. Notice how simply the decorations have been added in the modeled arch—sometimes by adding a small bit of clay and again by removing or hollowing out. The Tabernacle door offers a chance for original design and should center attention on its use or fitness to purpose. In the picture the Chalice has been **built up** and the space between the rays cut out. The artist always makes his model in clay, and then if he wishes he may have it cast in metal. Even when the metal work is done by hand he first models the design in clay. These pictures may be included in the Roman Book.

BOOK VI, PAGE 27—SILHOUETTES

Character Objectives: Honesty; Reliability

Spiritual Objective: Washington led his army to free the early Americans from unjust English laws, and Lincoln years later sent his army to free the United States from unjust slavery. As patriotic Americans, we love and honor both these presidents. How much more should we love and honor **Jesus who freed us from sin.**

Art Objective: To emphasize visualization and teach details of human proportions through cutting silhouettes of heads.

Supplies: Scissors, black or white paper, chalk and blackboard (optional)

Procedure: Read the text and illustrate by showing proportions of pupil standing before the class.

Procedure in text book is sufficiently clear to need no further comment. Be sure when making first fold of paper to chin, that enough paper is left **below** chin to form neck and shoulders. The lesson on Lincoln may be reviewed later in the similar lesson for Washington.

Do not draw before cutting, but characteristic features may be learned in blackboard practice while drawing from pictures.

Have pupils try cutting silhouettes of each other. Use black or white paper and mount on paper of contrasting value.

BOOK VI, PAGES 29-31—THE STATIONS

Character Objective: Compassion

Spiritual Objective: To help children to visualize the Passion of our Lord with its significant meaning for themselves.

Art Objective: Appreciation of the excellent interpretation and rendering of the human figure shown in these fine picture compositions by C. W. Chambers.

Supplies: Paper, scissors or razor blade, crayons, paints and brushes, colored construction paper, paste

Procedure: Read the beautiful poem by Father Blunt on Page 31. The title of this poem is "The Guilty One." The phrase "And nobody thinks of it" was suggested by a card bearing a similar phrase beneath every crucifix in a large convent, challenging every eye happening to fall upon them. This challenge to generous childhood may help to counteract thoughtlessness.

It is an erroneous belief that the **Stations of the Cross** are the **pictures** or **statuary** groups representing our Savior on His journey to Calvary. These are merely aids to devotion. The real Stations are the essential crosses which must be of wood, especially blessed and usually placed above each picture. The practice of the Stations originated with perilous journeys made by early Christians to the Holy Land to visit places sanctified by our Saviour's sufferings or as we call it the **Way of the Cross.**

When Jerusalem became a Mohammedan city this was impossible and the Church approved a similar devotion made in churches under the form of our present Stations. To perform this devotion it is not essential to say any special form of prayer though it is very commendable. The **two essential** points are the making of a journey as it were in company with our Blessed Lord from His trial to His tomb and the meditation on His sufferings while the journey is being made.

The Stations must be fourteen in number. Some of the scenes are described in the Gospels; others are transmitted to us by tradition. We have no Scriptural authority for the falls of Jesus under the Cross nor for the beautiful story of Veronica. They are based on pious beliefs probably handed down from the times of the Apostles.

Have children realize what a beautiful tribute this devotion will be when offered as assistance for the souls in Purgatory, who cannot make the journey themselves. Also how acceptable to God from themselves is this beautiful memory of His sacrifice. Cut the pages from the book about half inch from the binding in order to protect the rest of the pages.

Make the "Way of the Cross" booklet at the beginning of Lent, discussing each picture as it is made into a beautiful page arrangement. In discussing each picture call attention to the means employed to make the picture not only a fitting tribute of beauty to be offered by the artist to God, but also means used by the artist to deliver the particular message of the picture to the observers. Pupils should always be reminded of the necessity of **fitness to purpose.**

Suggestive phrases for the pictures which may be productive of thought:

I. Like a lamb He was led to be slaughtered.
II. He who would follow Me must take up his cross.
III. He carried our sins with His cross upon His Body.
IV. Let us also go with Him that we may die with Him.
V. He who does not take up his cross and follow Me is not worthy of Me.
VI. The Face of the Lord is against who do evil.
VII. I am a worm and no man the derision and outcast of the people.

VIII. Weep not for Me but for yourselves and your children.
IX. Who humbles himself shall be exalted.
X. Take off the old man with his works and put on the new.
XI. They have pierced My hands and My feet.
XII. Father unto Thy hands I commend My Spirit.
XIII. He who loses his life for My sake shall preserve it.
XIV. He who keeps My word shall not see death forever.

Compare XIII with the inscription on "The Seat Perilous" of Sir Galahad.

BOOK VI, PAGE 33—LEARNING TO SEE

Character Objective: Good Judgment

Spiritual Objective: The experiments planned to help us "to see" show us how easily our eyes may fool us. God knew our **spiritual eyes** would be fooled even more easily in selecting right and wrong, so He sent the Holy Ghost to us in Confirmation to help the eyes of our souls to see the difference between right and wrong.

Art Objective: To teach pupils to accurately estimate true proportions and contours of objects.

Supplies: 8 x 1 strips of stiff paper, chalk and blackboard (optional), pencils, paste

Procedure: Before the lesson give each pupil two strips of stiff paper about 8 x 1. Hold them vertically, edge to edge, on eye level and about eight inches away. Keeping one hand **still**, slowly move the other **directly forward,** keeping edges of two strips **apparently touching**. Pupils perceive instantly that the paper strip **farther away** has **apparently** become **much shorter,** demonstrating the fact that **distance** makes objects **appear smaller.**

This experiment emphasizes the necessity of keeping the **same distance** between eye and pencil, while estimating proportions. To do this **keep the arm perfectly straight.**

Draw vertical chalk line on blackboard and have pupils hold pencils to cover it. This shows how to "sight" the line. Using the width of a short piece of chalk, draw a line. Have children place pencils so that **top** of pencil which should be **flat** touches the **top** of the line and then keeping pencil **still** allow thumb nail to slide **down** the pencil until the **bottom** of **line** is reached when thumb stops and distance between thumb and pencil top measures the line. Be sure that thumb is always **kept above** the rest of the hand.

The pencil is held by the four fingers. When sure that every child has acquired a clear cut idea of what is to be done to **estimate** the length of one line, two lines should be drawn, on the board, short and long, and pupils required to measure the **short one** into the **longer one.**

Teacher proves accuracy by **actual** measurement of lines on blackboard. Pupils then find the proportions of different oblongs drawn on board and finally of oblong shapes found in the room. Enthusiasm waxes strong when scores are kept of correct estimates, for opposing sides of the room.

Lesson 2: Read the text, relating it to the pictures above it. Pupils will see the relationship of the pencil practice just finished, to the upper left illustration, in which the pitcher has been substituted for the lines they have been measuring. Notice that measurement is shown from the **middle of the bottom** line to the **middle of top,** as this shows the **nearest** or **largest** measurement.

The illustration upper left shows "blocking in" of object with addition of center line to test its correct **balance**. To avoid incorrect estimates based on poorly drawn ellipses, these are not added until measurements are finished. When several objects are grouped have student "block" the complete group to get correct estimate for placing it on the paper. Until now attention has been centered on training pupils to interpret as truthfully as possible what they observed. From now on, the emphasis is shifted to the **accuracy** of their drawings.

It is a good plan to allow pupils to sketch objects without measuring and then correct them after testing each dimension with a pencil.

Lesson 3: Have pupils observe that when looking **through** the window pane the objects outside fall into place **higher** and **lower** on the pane and if a piece of transparent paper were placed on the glass the picture could easily be drawn. This pane of glass is a simple illustration of what is known in perspective drawing as the "picture plane," or the area that falls within the vision of the eye. Throughout this Series perspective terms and rules are **not** presented in a technical way as is the usual procedure, but are being **taught through experiment with emphasis on accurate vision, correctly interpreted because understood through these experimental proofs.** After pupils have decided on simple outdoor subject to be rendered, have them sketch **quickly and lightly without measurement.** Test with pencil to verify proportions.

Test **direction** of edges by placing pencil **on edge** under observation and with picture directly in front of subject and resting on a **level** surface below it. Keep the wrist firm, while careful not to allow **direction** of pencil to **change while carrying** it to test the pictured edge. Practice in holding the pencil steady may be gained by using the pencil to carry the direction of contour lines of objects in the room **away from** and then **back** to the object. This shows whether the pencil is being **kept** in **true** position.

Encourage pupils to sketch outdoors. Have them find pictures to paste on the blank page to illustrate the effect of distance on size, color, and location in picture.

BOOK VI, PAGE 35—CIVIC BEAUTY

Character Objective: Good Citizenship

Spiritual Objective: As God has planned for the physical happiness of His children the beauties resulting from an unfolding seed, pupils may be led to visualize the great number of spiritual beauties they may cause to blossom for God, if the seeds of goodness, planted in their soul gardens, from day to day, are carefully remembered and made to grow strong.

Art Objective: To develop in pupils a sense of responsibility to create beauty wherever possible.

Supplies: Posterboard, crayons, scissors, colored paper, paints and brushes, images of civic improvement, paste, blank paper

Procedure: Have pupils read the text. While elaborating on the spiritual objective which should not only preface the lesson but be woven into its fabric, read the complete poem of Edgar Guest, mentioned in the text if it can be obtained, or other seed poem.

> These are seeds, but the plants and the blossoms are here
> With their petals of various hues;
> In these little pellets, so dry and so queer,
> There is power which no chemist can fuse.
> Here is one of God's miracles soon to unfold,
> Thus for ten cents an ounce is Divinity sold.
>
> —From "*A Package of Seeds.*"

Have children discuss citizenship and decide on several things essential to good citizenship. Refer to the civic pride of the Romans and their pride in all civic beauty. Discuss ways in which children can show good citizenship, viz: not littering the streets; not defacing property; obeying traffic laws; obeying fire laws; keeping orderly when in a crowd. Aim to have pupils plan to emphasize **one** point of good citizenship **each week.** Have good citizenship **begin in the classroom.**

Plan a poster for a **Civic Beauty** campaign. The design units in the lower panel, suggested by different arrangements of the tulip may be used with decorative effects as panels or borders on a poster, instead of houses or gardens. Stimulate originality by showing as many illustrations as possible having a relationship to the problem. Create enthusiasm in the project. Do not expect pupils to produce something new out of nothing. Originality is always founded on something already known. Old material must function in interpreting the new until finally, when self reliance has been made sufficiently strong through knowledge of the subject, we may expect varying degrees of pure invention. Review essential rules for poster making. **Do not** copy the picture in the book. Use it as a suggestion for some modified form. Find pictures suggestive of civic improvement to paste on the blank page.

BOOK VI, PAGE 37—FLOWER STUDY

Character Objective: Response to Beauty

Spiritual Objective: Noticeable characteristics of growth or color of flowers usually suggest a symbolism which people connect with them. So should children be led to see that by their **associations** and **attitudes** they too may become beautiful symbols of the religion God has entrusted to them.

Art Objective: To continue development of fine pencil rendering in flower interpretation and to teach flower symbolism.

Supplies: Sprays of flowers (if possible), paper, pencils

Procedure: Study the flowers on the page as examples of fine pencil rendering. They may be copied before attempting to make a pencil drawing of a real specimen. Note the delicacy of edges in full light.

Follow directions for the study of a single flower. Turn the specimen several ways until its finest aspect is visible. For this type of lesson each pupil should have an individual spray in order to really see its construction.

The sketch of flower spray may be used later as a source of design material. Have pupils look up symbolism of other flowers and compile a flower chart for the classroom.

BOOK VI, PAGE 39—THE VESTMENTS OF A BISHOP

Character Objective: Reverence

Spiritual Objective: To acquaint children with the office of a Bishop and an intelligent recognition of the special vestments connected with it.

Art Objective: To develop appreciation of fine craftsmanship in metal and needlework.

Supplies: Vestments (if possible), paper, pencils

Procedure: If possible, borrow real vestments while discussing their use and meaning. Explain the office of the Bishop as the governing power of the Diocese and the Bishop as one of the executives functioning in the Councils of the Church.

Spiritually he is the Shepherd of Souls. The Bishops are the links in the Apostolic chain, the pastors of Christ's flock.

The Miter is a headdress which is the distinguishing mark of the Episcopal office, a tall double pointed cap probably of Oriental origin, which can be traced back to pagan times. It did not come into use as a vestment until about the year 1100. The present double or cleft form was evolved gradually. It was first low and concave; the Gothic designers of the 13th Century gave it the straight lines and sharp point, while the 14th Century Italians gave greater height and curved lines, like the Miter photographed in the picture which belonged to the late Archbishop J. F. Regis Canevin. The two points or horns symbolize the Old and New Testaments, which the Bishop is supposed to explain to his people.

The Chasuble, Stole, and **Maniple** are the same for priest and bishop. See Book IV, Page 39.

The Crosier is the bishop's pastoral staff. It typifies his duties as the shepherd of the flock. It is a copy of the shepherd's crook, used for the guidance and restraining of sheep and has been looked upon as the restraining badge of the Episcopal office, since the fifth century at least, and is so mentioned in the ritual of a bishop's consecration. It signifies his power to sustain the weak and lead back the erring. The upper part is very beautifully moulded and enriched with symbolic ornaments.

The Pectoral Cross, so called because it is worn on the breast attached to a chain worn round the neck. It is of precious metal and contains a relic of the True Cross. For this reason it is transmitted from each bishop to his successor. It was introduced as a distinctive mark of the Episcopacy about the sixteenth century.

The Ring. In Rome of the classical period, rings were used as insignia of rank. The ring is mentioned in the early days of the Church and then not again until the 7th century. The ring represents the spiritual alliance between the bishop and the diocese which he has been called upon to govern and signifies faith or fidelity. It is worn on the third finger of the right hand.

The Gloves probably originated in the cold and cheerless churches of the early days of Christianity when they were worn to keep the hands warm. They took on a sacred character about the ninth century. The gloves of this period were richly embroidered and often a large jewel appeared at the back of each hand. They represent the respect for sacred things of which the bishop should give an example to his flock. They are of the same color as the vestments of the day.

The Stockings or Buskins were originally for Papal use only, but came into Episcopal use about the 12th century, as elaborately adorned silk stockings. They have now returned to original simplicity.

The Sandals. The Roman citizen of the early days for footgear wore mere soles secured across the instep by thongs of leather to protect the feet from stony roads. This sandal was worn by the clergy long after the introduction of Christianity. The extension of the Church into colder countries necessitated ankle shoes, which soon developed elaborate ornamentation. These slippers are worn only when the bishop is pontificating and they are the color of the vestments of the day.

The Processional Cross as its name implies, is only carried in solemn procession.

When the bishop is seated during the Mass, a sort of apron of silk called a **Gremiale** is placed upon his knees. Its original use was that in resting their hands they might not soil the sacred vestments. This is not shown in the photograph. Under his Chasuble, the bishop wears a thin silk **tunic** which is the vestment of the subdeacon and the dalmatic a similar vestment of the deacon. The tunic signifies joy and the **dalmatic** is the emblem of righteousness and charity. The **tunic** was originally the indoor garment of the Roman citizen while the dalmatic takes its name from the province of Dalmatia. By wearing these three vestments the bishop signifies that in his Episcopal office all the various orders find their culmination and perfection. The **tunic** and **dalmatic** are not shown in the photograph.

As this lesson has been especially prepared as source material for projection into the home, the page is to be carefully removed about a half inch from the binding in order to protect the other pages. Have it arranged page by page as lessons on these vestments are given. It is less confusing if they are not all given at the same time. Make each page arrangement show a knowledge of art principles already taught, in relating illustration to written work. Discuss the type of design with appropriateness found on vestments; familiar curves and beauty of texture.

If pages are planned to leave an inch margin at one side, they may be folded on this line later and fastened together with an appropriate cover.

BOOK VI, PAGE 41—BORDERS

Character Objective: Thoughtfulness

Spiritual Objective: To awaken in pupils love and devotion to Saint Joseph.

Art Objective: To continue the development of the principle of rhythm in design for a border.

Supplies: Flowers, crayons or pencils, doilies, silk string, flower pots, paints and brushes

Procedure: Study the flower composition analyzing its placing and arrangement exemplifying fine composition. Refer to Manual notes, Book V, Page 3, of flower spray drawn for lesson on Page 37. Using a flower motif from this lesson follow the method shown in the four steps at the top of the page, and described in the text.

Plan units in border form to show a **rhythm** of values in light and dark as illustrated in upper border. Plan a border to show a **balance** of values in light and dark as shown in second border.

Girls may transfer designs to doilies and fill in shapes with bright colored stitches of silk in pleasing color harmony. Boys may transfer design to flower pot bands for schoolroom decoration, painting them with poster paint. Keep designs simple.

BOOK VI, PAGE 43—THE ANNUNCIATION

Character Objective: Humility

Spiritual Objective: To help children to realize their complete dependence on God for their ability to do things, which they so often forget. Lead them to desire to keep Mary as their model in humility, and through controlling arrogance and conceit in classroom activities become ready to please God through greater service in the world later. Discuss other things that show a lack of humility.

Art Objective: To develop skill in effective poster making through the principle of contrast in light and dark.

Supplies: Posterboard, colored paper, poster paints and brushes

Procedure: After reading and discussing the text, ask individual questions to bring out the means employed by the artist to present a good poster. The large dark masses frame the figures. The bi-symmetric balance, shown by the large dark masses, centers attention on the small dark priedieu. The figure of Mary kneeling here is emphasized by **contrast**. The principle of **rhythm** has been used to give **dominance** to Mary by means of the angel's arm, the rays from the Dove, and the vertical lines of the dark masses. Also the gray shapes shown as openings at the top of the page are repeated in rhythmic sequence. The quiet space at the bottom planned for a simple line of heavy lettering allows the message to be read at a glance with no danger of confusion.

Suggest to pupils the appropriateness of using a Roman architectural setting when making an original poster arrangement. Ask pupils to find beautiful color schemes for the blank page which could be used to make a poster in color that would also show fine contrast in values. Read poem given in this manual, Book VIII, Page 15.

Make a poster advertising the School Picnic or Drawing Exhibition. Colored paper or poster paint is effective for carrying power.

BOOK VI, PAGE 45—PLAY PROPERTIES

Character Objective: Poise and Self Reliance

Spiritual Objective: To develop high ideals and a love of knightly virtues.

Art Objective: To develop craftsmanship and ingenuity necessary in making the properties for the play.

General Suggestions: Get a copy of Tennyson's "Idylls of the King," or a fine prose interpretation and read the story of the Holy Grail. Collect any pictures relating to knighthood or medieval times, and place them on the wall to create the proper atmosphere. Have pupils bring in any books from home to add additional illustrations or information relating to the period. As a background, a little of the story of King Arthur and the Round Table will add interest.

If two settings are used, a second one showing an outdoor set as well as the one in the book, two corners of the room should be used. An outdoor set similar to the one used in Book V will show the knights while on the journey. This second set will be a review of the drama work of the previous grade. A curtain to cover each of the sets is all that is necessary. The space between sets may hold untold dangers, according to the imagination of the players. The space curtained off and reserved as the outdoor set of trees, grass, and rocks shown on Page 45, Book V, will lend added interest to the dramatic meeting of the holy man with each of these adventures and also the meeting place for Galahad and Percivale.

Read suggestions in Manual for all the other plays in the series, to obtain additional hints for **this** play.

Remember that it is a classroom play devised to teach, and do not expect professional equipment or results although, with additional polishing up, a **second** production could be made part of an auditorium program.

Characters:

Sir Galahad, the Sinless Knight.
Sir Percivale, the Pure Knight.
Sir Lancelot, the Brave Knight.
Sir Gawain, the Boastful Knight.
Sir Bors, the True Knight.
King Arthur, an English King.
The Holy Hermit who helps the Knights.
Queen Guinevere, Arthur's wife.
The Princess, a friend of Percivale.
A voice, singing in the Castle Tower, which Lancelot braves the lions to find.
Two Lions, who guard the Tower of the singing voice.
The nun may be introduced if desired.
Ladies of the Court, **Knights**, etc.

Supplies: Chalk and blackboard (optional), curtain, cardboard, large sheets of paper, cloth, brightly colored scarfs or old smocks, crepe paper, silver paper or silver radiator paint, colored paper

Properties: The background may be drawn on the blackboard with large sheets of paper below, on which stone wall has been painted.

The high back of the chair may be planned from cardboard and fastened to the chair. If a chair with arms can be obtained, the sides may be covered with brown cardboard (from suit boxes) or pieces of cloth. The ermine used in the kingly robe may be made from cotton batting touched with black ink, or paint, and if cotton cannot be obtained, old bath towels may be treated in like manner.

Have pupils bring bright colored scarfs and other scraps of colored material to use in making costumes for the ladies. Mothers' old faded smocks are easy to get and with the addition of colored scarfs or crepe paper, make effective court dresses.

The style of the times requires a long dress touching the ground, fastened with a belt or girdle, to make a very short waist. Hair long and flowing or braided, bound to the head with a narrow band of ribbon or gold paper. Illustrations related to the story may be obtained at any library.

If silver paper is not available, silver radiator paint may be used on wood or cardboard. Boys usually enjoy making swords from wood, and then painting them. If more room is required in headsize of helmets, widen by inserting a strip of paper with laps on each side for pasting, between pattern sides. Use tough paper not easily torn. Use colored paper to decorate breastplate and banner. Long black stockings make effective leggings, dark sweaters trimmed with bits of silver paper make good chain armor.

Encourage pupils to visit the museum if possible, to study armor and heraldic designs.

STAGE DIRECTIONS FOR THE PLAY

Act 1: Curtain drawn shows setting as illustrated. Nobody on stage but two heralds. The heralds with borrowed horns or paper trumpets announce the approach of King and Queen. The queen's crown is like that of the King. Both wear ermine trimmed robes. They are followed by knights and court ladies. The event is to be the Knighting of Galahad (victrola music for marching, or a softly hummed air in march time adds interest).

The king requests that Galahad be summoned and he marches slowly before the king and bows low. Then ensues a conversation between the king and Galahad as to the meaning of knighthood, what it implies, and whether he is sure that he wishes to take the oath. Galahad answers affirmatively. Then kneeling, he solemnly repeats the knight's oath, which he has memorized, and Arthur then says, "I dub you knight. May you be as good as you are beautiful." He then hands him a sword.

Curtain lowered and raised immediately shows the same setting without the queen. They have just returned from the great room with the Round Table and all are excited about Galahad's bravery in sitting in the Seat Perilous and the resultant appearance of the Grail. Galahad is absent. Percivale quiets the commotion as all try to tell the king at once. Then he speaks and repeats the story of the Nun. Lancelot tells the story of the happening at the Round Table. Percivale reports that all have sworn to go. The king is sad, repeating that they have seen nothing and the Quest is not for them. Galahad enters and repeats that he has seen the Grail. (Actual lines from the poem may be used when it is desired to have them especially retained in the memory.)

The knights march away as **curtain** is lowered.

Act 2: Each knight in turn crosses in front of room from one setting to the other and **this space represents his journey** and what happens to him on the way. It is to be worked out in **pantomime**; each pupil shows his adventures as he wishes to interpret them. Ex.—**Sir Bors** imaginatively meets Lancelot, shakes him by the hand, points to himself and then to the sky, and then in direction from which he has come, indicating his willingness to return and sacrifice his wish to see the Grail for Lancelot. A downcast expression indicates it was useless. He then meets the pagans and preaches to them; struggles, and is overcome and then falls to the floor. He is now bound and in prison. Suddenly he shows surprise and raising on his elbow, sees the Grail. Next he shows that his chains are released, and escapes, going behind the curtain of the second setting. Sir Gawain and Lancelot enact similar scenes and then curtain is raised, showing the Holy Hermit who asks each one his mission. Each tells his story and when they have finished **curtain** is lowered.

Act 3: Curtain is raised to show Sir Galahad posed as in the picture by Watts, without the horse. The hermit appears from behind the trees and after a few words of greeting, bids him to follow to his house, as curtain drops.

Sir Percivale now crosses the space between the sets, enacting the pantomime of disappearing things and other adventures assigned to him before he also reaches the hermit's home; curtain is raised showing only the hermit. Conversation ensues about the other knights and then Percivale is told why he has failed. **This verse should be memorized.** Galahad appears and greets Sir Percivale. Then ensues conversation about their journey. Galahad shows happiness, Percivale is sad, but while he listens, grows more cheerful when Galahad promises he shall see the Grail.

They leave to see it as curtain is lowered.

Act 4: Action takes place as in first setting. The knights have all returned but Galahad. The King asks a report of each; he rebukes Gawain for his flippancy. Percivale tells what happened to Galahad, and the king has the final speech which holds the moral.

Music in the form of appropriate singing may be introduced in the court ceremonies in the first and last acts. Conversation may be introduced for queen. The voice, singing off stage heard by Lancelot in the castle tower, should accompany his pantomime. "Holy God" is appropriate since he describes the song as coming from an angel who guards the Grail, before he faints away.

A class game of pantomime may precede work on the play, in which pupil pantomimes an action and class guesses; sides are selected, scores kept.

CORRELATION

1. RELIGION: Elaborate on the spiritual objective showing the beauty of the ideals for which knights fought. Discuss Confirmation as suggested in text. Suggest formation of "Knights and Ladies of the Blessed Sacrament."

2. ENGLISH:
   (a) After story has been read have pupils reproduce it from topics covering the events listed on the board, giving special attention to capitals, punctuation, and clear concise sentences. Results will give best forms for dialogue.
   (b) Have class "try out" for parts repeating, orally from memory, corrected compositions, paying special attention to clear enunciation and freedom from common errors in speech. Pupil should be able to speak well for about two minutes.
3. HISTORY: Topics concerning English Government, people, customs, and early relationship with U. S.
4. GEOGRAPHY: Location of England; industries, possessions, etc.
5. ARITHMETIC: Problems in measuring and planning, related to sets for the play.
6. COLOR AND DESIGN: Principles of home decoration applied to "interior" setting.
7. COSTUME STUDY: English Costume of 12th century compared with modern.

BOOK VI, PAGE 47—THE QUEST OF THE HOLY GRAIL

Character Objective: Honor

Spiritual Objective: To develop in pupils an earnest love of the Blessed Sacrament.

Art Objective: An appreciation of Medieval English costume.

The complete story is to be read in either prose or poetry.

THE QUEST OF THE HOLY GRAIL

A classroom play adapted from "*Idylls of the King*" by Tennyson.

SYNOPSIS:

King Arthur was an English king who ruled part of England in the 6th century. He was so good and wise that tales of his greatness were handed down from generation to generation.

A writer named Mallory, gathered the stories of King Arthur together and published them under the title "*Morte di Arthur*" (The Death of Arthur). To make his stories more interesting, Mallory placed Arthur in a setting of feudal chivalry when knighthood was at its highest flower, about the 12th century. Later, the poet Tennyson, put the story in poetic form under the title "*Idylls of the King.*" Of the many interesting stories told of King Arthur's knights the one selected for the play has to do with the period when they left the castle on "The Quest of the Holy Grail."

An old tradition has been handed down that when Christ hung dying on the Cross, there came one Joseph of Arimathea bringing with him the cup used by Christ the evening before at the Last Supper, and as the blood dripped from the wound in His side, Joseph held the cup to catch the drops. Later, under persecution, Joseph fled to England bringing the cup with him, where it remained for many years, healing all whom it touched. Then the world became so sinful that the cup was caught up to heaven and none has seen it since.

King Arthur's knights were sworn:

"To reverence the King as if he were
Their conscience, and their conscience as their King.
To break the heathen and uphold the Christ
To ride abroad redressing human wrongs,
To speak no slander, no, nor listen to it.
To honor his own word as if his God's,
To lead sweet lives in purest chastity,
To love one maiden only, cleave to her
And worship her by years of noble deeds
Until they won her."

Chief among these knights was one known as Sir Percivale the Pure, others were Sir Lancelot, Sir Gawain, Sir Bors, and the youngest knight of all Sir Galahad, who "dressed in white and was pure as the driven snow." A saintly Nun, sister to Sir Percivale, had had a vision of the Holy Grail.

"Streamed thro' my cell a cold and silver beam
And down the long beam stole the Holy Grail,
Rose-red with beatings in it, as if alive
Till all the white walls of my cell were dyed
With rosy colors leaping on the wall."

At the Round Table of King Arthur there was one vacant chair called "The Seat Perilous." "Perilous for good and ill, for there no man could sit but he should lose himself." When all the knights were seated discussing the Grail, came Galahad saying "I lose myself to find myself" and sat in the Seat Perilous, to the great consternation of all of the knights. Immediately there were great noises as of thunder and a beam of light crossed the table and the Grail covered by a veil, passed slowly before them but Galahad alone saw it clearly.

Immediately all the knights took an oath to travel for a year, doing great deeds in order that God would permit them a clear vision of the Grail. Sorrowfully, King Arthur bade them go. The poem tells what happened to each.

Gawain spent his year in pleasure. Sir Bors, cousin to Sir Lancelot, wearing a pelican on his helmet, was grieved when he met Sir Lancelot in deep distress and offered to give up his chance of seeing the Grail, if God would permit Lancelot to see it. But later when he had been bound and cast into prison by the pagan people he tried to convert he lay thinking how he had failed, when a miracle happened; a great heavy stone slipped and while he gazed out at the starlit night the beautiful rose-red Grail moved past him on a beam of light followed by a deafening peal of thunder. Then a maiden of his own faith who worshipped in secret in the pagan tribe, came to him, loosened his bonds and helped him to escape.

Sir Lancelot, who never succeeded in conquering the evil in his nature, at one time almost saw the Grail after great hardship, but his strength failed and again he saw it covered by the veil.

Sir Percivale the Pure, traveled far and met many trials and did not find the Grail. Always when he thought he had reached success, things crumbled and disappeared. Then he met a beautiful princess who was his early love. She begged him to stay and he almost forgot the Quest. Then he suddenly remembered. He left and wandered on brokenheartedly. He met a holy hermit who listened to his tale and then he told him why he had failed, saying,

> "'O Son thou hast not true humility,
> The highest virtue, Mother of them all;
> For when the Lord of all things made Himself
> Naked of glory for his mortal change.
> "Take Thou my robe" she said, "for all is Thine."
> Followed Him down, and like a flying star
> Led on the gray-haired wisdom of the East.
> But her thou has not known for what is this
> Thou thoughtest of thy prowess and thy sins
> Thou hast not lost thyself to save thyself.
> As Galahad.' When the hermit made an end."

Galahad appeared in silver armor.

Percivale asked Galahad of his success, how he had fared, and was told that the vision of the Grail had been with him constantly, day and night. They attended Mass in the Chapel and afterwards Galahad told him that he saw,

> "The Holy Grail descend upon the shrine,
> I saw the fiery face, as of a child
> That smote itself into the bread and went."

Galahad told how he had conquered all evils, converted the pagans to Christ through the strength from the Grail, and now that his quest was over and his work done, and he was to go to the Spiritual City to be crowned. He promised that Percivale should see the Grail when Galahad left him.

His great faith filled Percivale with power and toward evening he followed Galahad up a great storm-swept hill, with thunder rolling and lightning flashing and below saw a great black swamp filled with dead men's bones. It would have been impossible to cross had not some ancient king built a bridge of piers and arches running out into the great Sea.

Galahad sped quickly over the bridge, but as he did so, each arch was consumed with fire and Percivale could not follow. And then he saw Galahad far away on the great Sea, his armor shining like a star and over his head hung the Holy Grail, veiled in a luminous cloud; then his boat seemed to speed with great swiftness and presently from the heavens shot a glorious light, and Percivale beheld the Sacred Vessel, shining rose-red, clear and pure over Galahad's head; Percivale gave a great shout of joy, for he knew the veil had been withdrawn. Then in the distance he saw the spires and gateway of the spiritual city, and saw Galahad move into it like a shooting star. Percivale returned filled with joy that his quest was over, and planned to spend the rest of his life in fasting and prayer. When they returned they told their stories. After King Arthur had heard them all he told them that he too had visions. "Many a time they come by night and by day until sometimes I am not sure whether this earth I tread on be earth at all, but still through all I feel the strength of my purpose to serve my God and my Savior, and then when the vision is at its highest, I know I shall never die, but live always."

And what he meant was that the most pleasing servant of God is he who follows not after any great quest, but faithfully looks after the unattractive duties that God has given him at home.

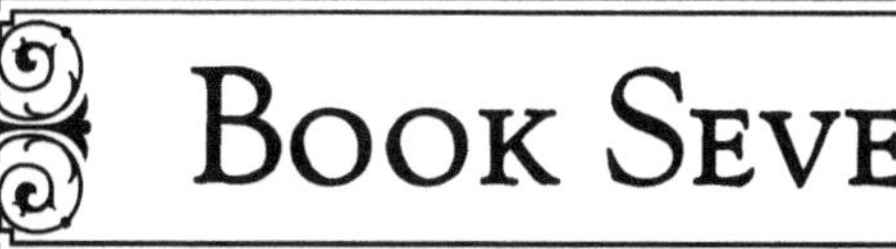

Book Seven

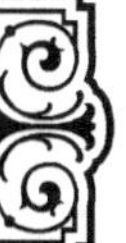

BOOK VII—COVER

See page 3 of this manual.

BOOK VII—END PAPER

Character Objective: Humility

Spiritual Objective: Humility was spoken of in the "Holy Grail" as the "Mother of all the Virtues," of which Christ, the King of power and glory, has left us the perfect example. Help pupils to see that the only way to counteract the deadly sin of **pride** so common to all is to motivate all work with this opposite virtue **humility**, that all service may be kept pleasing to God.

Art Objectives:

(1) To show the possibilities of striking effect possible in an all-over design through a fine balance of light and dark.

(2) To encourage interest in symbolism as a motive for design.

Supplies: Paints and brushes

Procedure: Read the verse and discuss the meaning of the lines as embodying the two Commandments given by our Lord which include the others—"Thou shalt love the Lord thy God with thy whole mind and thy whole soul and thy neighbor as thyself."

Have pupils memorize lines. Call for responses on the meaning of the symbols shown in the trefoil. The Hand with the two fingers raised in blessing was one of the earliest symbols for God the Father, when any representation of the figure of God was considered sacrilegious. Pupils will recognize the Lamb of God as the symbol for God the Son and also the dove as the symbol of the Holy Ghost. The whole makes a fitting illustration of the Trinity. Ask why this motive was used on the end paper for this book. Notice how the static quality of this pattern was avoided by the addition of the rhythm of curved shapes, added to the left side of each unit to give movement over the page.

Change the effect of the strong dark and light contrast by planning a color scheme for the page. Paint the design with a tint of one color and the panel a very light tint of an analogous color.

BOOK.VII, PAGE 1—JOAN OF ARC

Character Objective: Trust in God—Duty

Spiritual Objective: To the unlettered Joan came the **call** from God. Though timid and afraid, she recognized her **duty to her country,** her **duty to obey the command of God** and therefore unquestioningly placed her trust in Him and went forth. God still sends out His calls for **special work to be done by selected people.** Unlike Joan, people are often afraid and unwilling to hear God's call, **relayed** through **conscience**, instead of willingly placing full trust **in God and full strength in the work to be done.**

Art Objective: To continue development of picture appreciation through an understanding of mass analysis of color and form.

Teachers' Preparation: Study the picture before reading the text to realize its individual message to you.

The text gives much detail in the picture analysis but a knowledge of the history of the period is necessary.

In October of 1422, Charles VI died, leaving his kingdom with the hand of his daughter by the Treaty of Troyes, to Henry V, King of England. The French fought to keep their country. The Dauphin (Crown Prince), Charles VII was worthless, young, and indolent. War had desolated the country and the English had possession of the whole north and center. The besieged city of Orleans was the last obstacle in the south and it was on the point of surrender. The king was planning to escape. Never before had the liberty of glorious France been so menaced. National existence seemed about to be lost. And then God sent the obscure girl of sixteen, from the little town of Domremy, to save the country. She went to the king and received permission to lead the army, after she had shown her power by picking the king, whom she had never seen, from a group of people, passing by another who had been placed on the throne to fool her. She rode a white horse and she dressed in white; she wore silver armor, seeming to the people like some saint sent as an answer to their prayers.

The French gained new courage. She routed the English from Orleans and took their General prisoner. Victory followed victory for the French. Joan led the king to Rheims where he was crowned. Then jealousy of this young girl, on the part of the leaders, caused them to fail to carry out her plans. She was captured by the English. The king made no effort to help her. She was tried as a witch and condemned to be burned at the stake, the penalty in vogue at that time for witchcraft. She died with a prayer on her lips and a crucifix in her hands. And the people wept, crying, "We have burned a Saint." Joan of Arc is the patron saint of France for which she was martyred.

Bastien Lepage, the painter of the picture, loved his France as Joan did. He fought in the Franco-Prussian war. He has shown us his love for his subject by his knowledge of it. He made many trips to the lovely old garden where Joan lived to catch an inspiration from her environment. He knew her life and suggested its narrowness by placing her hemmed in by the old house and the trees. Her heavy figure speaks of toil, but he has shown in the face her magnificent soul.

Procedure: Have pupils study the picture for a few minutes in silence before reading the text.

Tell the story of Joan, weaving the spiritual objective throughout.

Encourage pupils to get the story of her life at the library. A translation from the French by Boutet de Monvel, the well known artist, is beautifully told and illustrated for children. Ask carefully planned questions to develop relationship of present day ideals. The scheme is analogous—yellow, orange, and green, emphasized through strong contrasts of light and dark. The browns in the picture are dark orange. Why is Joan called the "Maid of Orleans"?

For additional picture study see page xxx.

BOOK VII, PAGE 3—CONVENTIONALIZATION

Character Objective: Initiative

Spiritual Objective: As natural shapes must be conventionalized or changed to suit the material which they are to decorate, so must our personal desires be modified to conform to the work God has given us to do, if that work is to be made pleasing to God.

Art Objective: To teach the adaptation of nature to design through a regular progression of steps showing change of shape and value.

Supplies: Paints and brushes, dark paper, crayon, hot iron

Procedure: Have pupils render in color the illustration shown on plate to learn **method** of rendering. Remember that the **darker** accents of color are added when **lighter** color is **almost dry.** Review earlier lessons on flower rendering in Book V, Page 3. Follow this practice lesson with careful painting of any fall flower having broad petals such as **iris** or **cosmos**. When flower is finished, make a scale of the colors found in it, for future use in design. Use finders to make a good composition of the flower arrangement. Mount on darker paper.

Lesson 2: Read the text while studying its references to the plate. Explain that **Conventionalization** originated through the limitation of form necessary because of material used. Emphasis is placed on the **geometric shape** underlying the natural form.

Conventionalized forms should always show that the **intention is ornament** and **not the natural representation** of a plant.

The method of conventionalizing is clearly shown in plate. Take any part of the plant, or all of it, and begin by enclosing the parts to be used with a heavy line which is planned to eliminate the detail and emphasize the basic shape. After making several modifications of the basic shapes, try to obtain contrast of light and dark. Try new geometric shapes, making the unit conform to these. Many new units may be quickly created. Keep units very simple. When too much involved, they become confusing.

Lesson 3: Review the lesson on borders, Book VI, Page 41, and, using one of the units created, plan a border suitable for curtains. Paint the problem to show a good balance of light and dark either in color or neutral values. If desired, the problem may later be carried out, using real material for curtains as a lesson in home decoration. If crayola is used to color the design a hot iron will make color permanent.

BOOK VII, PAGE 5—SURFACE ENRICHMENT

Character Objective: Response to Beauty

Spiritual Objective: Careful attention to each little detail of the space to be decorated produces a beautiful design. Just as necessary is the careful attention we should pay to what seems unimportant details of everyday, such as courtesy, politeness, cooperation, and other habits, which are necessary to the enrichment of our service to God.

Art Objective: To emphasize fitness to purpose as shown in design motives used for chasuble decoration.

Supplies: Grapes or wheat (if possible), pencils, paper, brushes and ink, black paper, pictures of fruit, paste, blank paper

Procedure Lesson 1: Read the text slowly, relating it to the steps shown in the illustrations on the page.

Do not attempt a design so elaborate. This is shown as a fine standard of work. Study the upper panels as fine examples of pencil rendering. Observe the **lovely composition** of **flower and background** spaces while reviewing lesson on Book V, Page 3. Observe **placing of accents** to produce a **beautiful pencil line.** Copying these renderings will develop a feeling for beautiful line.

Using real models of either grapes or wheat, which are easily available at this season, make a good arrangement to be drawn and aim for fine pencil rendering.

Lesson 2: Make a copy of the first drawing on white paper, filling background with brush and ink, making a white silhouette on black to emphasize importance of light and dark contrast in producing balance. This will show the simplest **decorative** arrangement of the natural form.

Lesson 3: Follow procedure shown on page 3 to create a suitable border for a chasuble from any simplified forms made from pupils' drawings of grapes and wheat. The shape of the chasuble should be cut or drawn to have pupil understand the limitations necessarily caused by shape and the fact that design must be woven or embroidered with a needle. To keep designs simple, suggest simple arrangement of leaf and grape forms within a geometric shape to be repeated or modified; leaf shapes may be alternated with fruit to produce a rhythmical border. Find fruit pictures in color to paste on blank page.

BOOK VII, PAGE 7—POSTER LETTERS

Character Objective: Helpfulness

Spiritual Objective: As the poster letter must show strength and solidity in order that it may be read at a distance so pupils may be led to see that **strength** of will based on a **solid** determination to please God will **carry** a **good example** to others at a distance who may need help in learning the joy of service, or support in carrying it through.

Art Objective: To teach the arrangement of fine poster letters as an element of attraction in a poster.

Supplies: Chalk and blackboard (optional), gray paper, pencils, strips of paper, picture references, paste, blank paper, crayons

Procedure: Have pupils begin letter practice on the blackboard using the sides of short pieces of chalk. This permits errors to be quickly seen. Read the text and question pupils as to analysis given of poster shown on the page.

As a practice lesson, to aid in adapting letters to definite spaces, ask pupils to plan door or window signs to be used for offices of doctors or dentists. Each pupil should make his sign personal using his own name with the professional prefix. Initials may be used when names are long and **emphasis is to be placed** on making the **lettering conform to the oblong shape** of the sign which should be made on gray paper, not smaller than 9 x 12. Use strips of paper to plan the layout for size and balance, as they are easily changed. Letters may then be drawn to fill the layout strips and traced. Finish with brush and black paint. Add a well arranged margin line.

Lesson 2: Plan a poster on 12 x 18 paper to be used as a "car card" to aid in a campaign for "Kindness to Animals."

Have pupils find as many pictures related to the subject as possible. Paste good reference material on the blank page for future use. Have pupils suggest as many slogans as possible to list on the blackboard. Keep the poster as simple as the one shown in book. Permit pupils to work the problem out in cut paper or poster paint if it is available. Crayola may be used but it does not have strong carrying power. Aim for **originality, simplicity,** and **good marginal** spaces. Keep **letters thick and strong.** Thin letters look weak and do not carry.

BOOK VII, PAGE 9—COLOR HARMONY

Character Objective: Good Judgment

Spiritual Objective: Color combinations that are not harmonious produce ugliness. Original sin made the world ugly and inharmonious with Heaven. Christ harmonized Heaven and earth by joining His Heavenly Spirit with an earthly body, thereby relating man and God as they were in the beginning. Help children to see that if they would keep their souls in harmony with God, they must keep away from the **destroying** power of sin, so that their souls may reflect the beauty of God.

Art Objective: To teach the laws of color necessary to produce **Analogous Harmony.**

Supplies: Colored paper, magazine images, scissors

Procedure: Read all the color theory preceding the work in Book VII, and then review it with the class to be sure that they understand all previous steps.

Pupils have used in other color combinations, a **color with its tints** and **shades** and **intensities** which produced a pleasing harmony of **one color** for this reason called a **Monochromatic** Harmony. This is also a harmony of likeness, but is less interesting than Analogous Harmony. Follow suggestion in book for reference material to be pasted on the blank page.

Ask pupils to select from colored paper an **analogous** group of colors to be used in planning costumes. Read the story of Joan of Arc, if it has not already been read, and show as many pictures as possible of the costume of the time. The picturesque examples shown in the book will prove an inspiration for other costume arrangements.

A dramatization of Joan's story will permit individual color schemes to be worked into a whole ensemble. A large classroom poster could be made showing the coronation of the king.

Find costumes of today showing a relationship to this period.

Lesson 2: Ask each pupil to plan a school costume suitable for himself. Cut figure from magazine to insure correct proportions. Emphasize **simplicity** of design, as the keynote of good taste in dress. Other points to teach are:

1. Suitability for age and purpose (school, party, sport, dress).
2. Dress should be background for the face.
3. Color should be based on the color law of areas. (Sport costumes may be brighter because of larger background outdoors.)
4. Color harmony must include consideration of hair, eyes, and complexion which should be emphasized by similarity or contrast.

   Pupils with dark complexions and eyes may wear more brilliant warm colors than pupils with light hair and eyes and clear complexions who look better in light and cool colors. **Intermediate** colors grayed are best for pupils whose complexions are **sallow**.
5. The **larger** the person the more **inconspicuous** the color should be.
6. **Horizontal** effects increase shortness and stoutness.
7. Vertical effects increase **tallness** and **thinness**.
8. Principles of design must be applied to costume.

Ask pupils to plan costume to illustrate points discussed. If a costume book is decided upon, costumes for different seasons may be worked out with samples of suitable material added to illustrate color schemes.

This problem is even more important for boys than for girls because, having so little opportunity to use color in dress, they think it unimportant and become conspicuous through bad taste. The color page is planned as source material and frequent reference to it is advisable.

BOOK VII, PAGE 11—WINDOW ARRANGEMENT

Character Objective: Alertness

Spiritual Objective: When the **principle of rhythm** is present in fine window arrangement the **eye is led easily** through the whole display. God planned His Sacraments in a wonderful rhythm to supply us with grace necessary at different periods in our lives, so that our souls may more easily follow the path to heaven.

Art Objective: To teach Analogous harmony in relation to its use in attractive window arrangement.

Supplies: Paints and brushes, 12 x 18 gray paper, paste, blank paper

Procedure: Read the text. Read pages 9 and 11, Book VI. Discuss the principle of rhythm observing everything in the upper picture that tends to increase the line movement. Discuss the lower illustrations as separate arrangements, and then as one window. Call attention to pleasing proportions of background spaces by analyzing them. See Book V, page 3.

Assign the upper illustration as a definite problem in **analogous harmony.** Since the jacket in the center commands attention both by size and position, point out that its color should be neutral with brighter color for trimming. Neckties and scarfs may show stronger color. Remember that the addition of black always adds emphasis. Background should be a very neutral color or gray.

Mix color in lid of box and be careful when painting to not use too much water. Adjoining surfaces must not be painted while wet. The lesson of painting the lower illustration is to test the free use of color by the student. An exhibition and criticism is to be held at the end of the lesson.

Lesson 2: Ask pupils to find color arrangements showing a rhythm of color to paste on the blank page for reference material.

Have pupils discuss window arrangements they have observed since the previous lesson. Using colored paper, have pupils plan an interesting window arrangement within an oblong. Make a poster on gray paper, 12 x 18, using the window arrangement planned, combined with cut poster letters to advertise the subject selected by the pupil. Remember that a **well spaced margin line adds rhythm** and helps to keep the eye **inside** the poster.

BOOK VII, PAGE 13—SYMBOLISM

Character Objective: Understanding

Spiritual Objective: Posters and other signs are placed before us to interest us in various things in order that we may desire them and if we could not read these signs, we would be considered very ignorant. The **symbolism** of the Church is a means used by her to **show** her worship of God and, if we but **understand**, it will take us over every detail in the life of Christ, walking by His side, as it were the close companions of God. These symbols are sometimes seen and sometimes heard as they express form, color, or ceremony.

Art Objectives:

(1)—To arouse interest in symbolism as an aid to appreciation of beauty.

(2)—To awaken interest in symbolism as a motivation in design.

Supplies: Paper, pencils, crayons, paints and brushes, paste, colored paper

Procedure: After reading the text discuss symbols already learned in the lower grades. List these on the board with their meaning. Explain that the Church through her symbolism has beautified and perfected our prayers in order to present them before the throne of God. Be sure that symbolism is **not restricted** to pictured forms, but includes music, prayer, and ceremonies.

Most of the symbols on the page are familiar; others commonly used, may be added.

Plan a book from any of the models previously made to hold the explanations of the symbols drawn. This lesson will be **of value in the home,** where usually there is a dearth of knowledge on the subject and pictured symbols must be **seen** in order to be **recognized**.

The symbolism of the cross, used on the model book, is easily made and may decorate the cover in other ways. So other all-over designs may be planned to make a panel such as suggested in the illustration, where the beautifully spaced margins have received special consideration, to give emphasis to the panel as a decoration for the title. Each page in the book should show careful arrangement of illustration and explanation. Other symbols which should be explained are:

Sacramentals:

The Scapular—Meaning the Yoke of Christ.

Agnus Dei—Lamb of God (wax blessed by Pope).

Incense—Fragrance of Christian virtue and prayer ascending to God.

Ashes (burnt palm)—Palm signifies victory and ashes penance and humility necessary to gain victory over sin.

Holy Water—Purification or internal cleansing.

Ornamental Symbols:

Ship—The Church.

Lion—Our Savior.

Dragon—Sin.

Pelican—Christ.

Cross, Anchor and Heart—Faith, Hope and Charity.

Fish—Baptism.

The model page at the top of the plate shows six symbols. The second symbol is a monogram made from the Greek letters Chi and Rho, equivalent to the English Chr., which is an abbreviation of **Christ**. The monogram at the lower right is also emblematic of Christ, being the initial letters of the words "Jesus Hominum Salvator" (Jesus Saviour of Men). It may also be the abbreviation of the Greek word Iesous (Jesus) as the Greek letter E is shaped like our letter H.

BOOK VII, PAGE 15—STAINED GLASS

Character Objective: Industry

Spiritual Objective: The colorless and commonplace **leading** is shown to be the most important part of the beautiful window, as it **forms** the interesting shapes to hold the lovely glass firmly in place. The commonplace and colorless tasks of every day, when performed with our best efforts to please God, become the strong **leading** of habit formation which will fill our lives with rich, colorful service that will help to make the world happier, and prove eternally beautiful and enduring.

Art Objective: To teach the adaptation of landscape to stained glass and to awaken an appreciation of the industry of making stained glass windows.

Supplies: Clay, pencils, pictures of simple landscapes, white paper, ink, paints and brushes, black construction paper, razor blade, paste, thin paper

Procedure: If possible, obtain from the museum or from a worker in glass, a piece of soft leading to show pupils how the lead is made to hold the small pieces of glass. If lead cannot be obtained, use a coil of clay about as thick as a finger and flattened on two sides. Press the length of a pencil into the other two sides to make the channels that hold the glass. Several small pieces of glass may be inserted to show how the window is constructed by the artist following the design which has been previously painted on paper. Call attention to the fact that pieces of glass used in the design must not have edges too irregular and **leading must connect all parts.** Notice how the tops of trees when used are connected and how leading clears up all irregularities in sky and water spaces.

After pupils have read the text, have them follow carefully each step in the production of the window. Have pupils plan an analogous color scheme for the lower left panel and paint it, being careful to follow the **values** shown in the final panel. Ask pupils to find reference material for the blank page relating to the problem.

Lesson 2: Discuss real windows seen outside. Require each pupil to find a picture of a very simple landscape, or if landscape is too complicated, finders may be used to make a simple selection from it. Make a heavy outline around the most important shapes in the picture to eliminate details. Copy this drawing on white paper making it the size desired for window. Plan leaded lines and paint them with India ink. When dry, fill spaces with color to make a beautiful color harmony.

If black paint is used instead of India ink, it is better to paint the leaded lines last. If pupils wish to do so, they may trace design to heavy black construction paper and after planning the leading, cut out the spaces for glass, using a razor blade. This frame work is then pasted to thin paper which is painted to make a **transparency**.

BOOK VII, PAGE 17—A CHRISTMAS GIFT

Character Objective: Good Workmanship

Spiritual Objective: A blotter is used to absorb surplus ink, and after being used, it shows a reversed reproduction of what has been blotted. But because the blotter is so soft, the ink spreads and the reproduction is **heavier** and **deeper** than the original. Lead pupils to see that **bad companions** will have the same effect on them if they permit their souls to be that kind of blotter.

Art Objective: To develop skill and accuracy in the construction of a desk pad and appropriateness in its design.

Supplies Cardboard, paste, cloth binding strips

Procedure: Read the text, being careful to relate it to each step in the production of the desk pad. Printed directions close to the pictures were omitted in order to help pupils to carry the plan mentally. In pasting the writing pad for the center as well as envelopes, it is better to not paste **all over** in order to avoid having cardboard warp, since there is **no other pasting** on the opposite side to **neutralize** it. If cloth binding strips are available, they will provide a little more strength and durability for hinges.

The steps in the construction of the problem are so clearly shown that no other comments are necessary.

BOOK VII, PAGE 19—LEARNING TO SPATTER

Character Objective: Love

Spiritual Objective: The word **NOEL** is made up of two words and means NEW GOD. The Latin word for **New** is **Novies**. In the Hebrew word **elohim**, the first syllable el means God. (Gabriel means Messenger of God. Michael means like God.) The French put the Latin, No, and the Hebrew, El, together to make the word **NOEL** or **NEW GOD.**

Art Objective: To teach the technique of spatter in designing a Christmas card.

Supplies: Chalk and blackboard (optional), dark paper with poster paint or white paper and water color, water pans, toothbrushes, plain wallpaper, moth sprayer, blow pipe

Procedure: Have pupils practice at blackboard with ovals until proportions of the Baby have become familiar. Then follow directions given in text. If dark paper is used it will be necessary to spatter with poster paint. If white paper is used, pupils may use water color. When ready to spatter, place small amount of color in **flat bottomed small pan;** an ordinary water pan for painting lesson will do. Barely touch the tooth brush to the color, as only a **very small** amount is needed. While spattering, **do not hold brush directly over card**, in case surplus color should drop.

Interesting color effects may be had by using soft toned **plain** wall paper as background and using a moth sprayer, to spray a tone of darker color over the stencil. When this is dry, spray a second color that is analogous to the first. An ordinary blow pipe may also be used for spraying. Later in the year this lesson may be reviewed by making a flower stencil to be used as an all-over design for a textile.

BOOK VII, PAGE 21—WATCH YOUR SPEECH

Character Objective: Self Control

Spiritual Objective: To develop in pupils an appreciation of the wonderful organ of speech which God has given only to man, therefore, realizing that it should not be used to offer insult to God by making a jest of His Name.

Art Objective: To teach that fine letter grouping used for any commercial purpose is governed by principles of design.

Supplies: Paper strips, pencils, paints and brushes, banners

Procedure: Discuss the text while studying the illustrations. Before deciding shape of banner to be made, review the study of heraldic banners made in Grade 6 when studying the knights. Plan space arrangement of letters by using paper strips to represent letters and decoration as they are easily adjusted. When final sizes have been decided upon sketch words on "layout" strips. If this "layout" strip of sketched letters is placed directly above space allotted for the letters on the banner, it will serve as a guide for final placing of words.

Emphasize the importance of **light** and **dark** in planning the color scheme. Keep lettering bold and strong. Paint edges of letters sharp and clean. When lesson is finished, have a class criticism and if possible have banner selected by class made on real material for actual use.

Lesson 2: Continue letter practice on school room slogans arranged for use in a campaign for "Better English." These signs which may be changed every few days, should center attention on common errors of speech as "Gonna and Gonta." The making of the slogan does much to help the memories of pupils as aids in correcting errors.

BOOK VII, PAGE 23—WHEN RELIGION INSPIRED THE WORLD

Character Objective: Joy in Service

Spiritual Objective: The Gothic builders were motivated only by love of God, without hope of worldly fame or glory. People **offered their work as prayer.** We do not even know who made Gothic possible. No name is attached to any church. Yet of all churches these are the most beautiful and enduring.

"The conscious stone to beauty grew
They builded better than they knew."

Bernadette said "God works with those who work for Him." Show similarity of Gothic building in leading pupils to see that they should construct their lives on its principles if they wish to be sure of a beautiful creation for God that will last forever.

Art Objective: To develop an aesthetic appreciation of architecture through familiarity with and an understanding of the Gothic.

Supplies: Construction paper, pencils, crayons, paints and brushes, scissors or razor blade, paper

Procedure: From the library obtain as many pictures related to Gothic art as possible, as larger pictures will show beautiful details lost in the small pictures shown in the book. Quickly review leading characteristics shown in the Roman, Greek, and Egyptian. Pupils readily see that the **height of the dome** must be **limited because of its weight.** They will recall that the dome was built on intersecting **round** arches, upon which had been placed a round **collar type of base to help support it.** All this time the great Christian architects were trying to create a plan for **God's House** that would be completely Christian. So far everything had been an adaptation from something earlier and of course the very first types were **pagan**. In the first Christian churches the roofs were wood, but these took fire so easily that they had to be replaced with stone and in order to support this very heavy weight the walls had to be made very thick, with few windows. Even then at certain places on the wall **outside** an **extra thickness** of **masonry** was **added to help support the wall.** This extra part built on the wall was called a buttress, because it had to bolster up the wall.

One day somebody had a great idea. He discovered that by making a **point** at the top of the **round** arch, two of them could be made to fit together much better than round arches, when **intersecting** to make a ceiling. Then by **adding** a **rib over the place of joining** in these **pointed** arches they were made strong enough to be built **higher** when supported on either side of the arch by **columns**. But he knew that even though he supported the slanting roof **inside** by these columns, the **outside** wall would be bulged or **pushed out** because the added weight of the roof, which architects call **the thrust of the roof,** was not evenly distributed or balanced. And then he had another **great idea.** He figured out that by making stronger the little **buttresses** supporting the little outside walls of the aisles, they could be made to support the **big main wall** or **clerestory** (clear story) and roof rising high in the center of the church, by **inventing** a new buttress planned much like a post leaning against a door to hold it shut. One end of this new buttress was fastened at the **top** of the little aisle wall buttress resting on the ground, and its other end was fastened to the big **main wall** near the roof. Because it seemed to **leap** or **fly** from the edge of the slant roof down to the little buttress standing on the ground, it was called a **flying buttress** and it **was entirely new.** This allowed height and strength together. Because of these **two new** ideas in construction, 1st., the **pointed arch** which permitted the beautiful high **vaulted ceilings** and 2nd, the **flying buttress** which **supported** the **outward thrusting weight** of the roof, these early builders were enabled to build God's most glorious churches. This new form of buttress or support permitted height never before thought possible, which, added to the beautiful **rhythms of vertical lines** necessary in Gothic construction, carried the eyes and thoughts of the people to heaven and to God. Gothic architecture now showed the **three essentials** of all good architccture, **Strength, Beauty,** and **Fitness.**

The early Romanesque churches had shown the first step in Christian planning by being built in the form of a Latin cross. The Gothic churches were also planned on a Latin cross. The Sanctuary or part enclosed at the **top** of the cross is called the **apse**; the **length** of the cross **below** the arms is called the **nave**; the arms of the cross right and left are called the **transepts** (north and south) The early churches were planned to have the apse **face** the **rising sun**, so that the priest would face the **light**, symbolic of **God.** This is the reason the opposite part of the church having the main doors is usually alluded to as **"the West Front."**

This front view is also called the **facade** or face. High above the slanting roof rise **the spires,** soaring heavenward like **fingers pointing to God.** At their base are **little spires** called **pinnacles** which add support and emphasize to the **beauty of line.** Pinnacles are also found elsewhere on the building.

Because it was no longer necessary to have thick walls without windows to support the roof, the Gothic churches showed great large window openings, impossible before. These windows were filled with beautiful colored glass, that the sunlight might add glorious color to the interior by painting the cold gray stone. The windows were also made to tell stories of Christ and the Bible to those who could not read.

In architecture the arrangement of windows in a building is called **fenestration** from the Italian word "finestre" or window. The **ornamental stone framework** of the windows developed from an attempt to arrange beautiful space relations at the top of the spaces planned for **lights**. This stonework is called **tracery**. These ornamental shapes take their names from Italian words for numbers. Trefoil (tre—3), Quatrefoil (quatre—4), Cinquefoil (cinque—5). For Rose Window, see notes on window page 23.

For the sake of greater beauty **inside**, instead of the heavy Romanesque pillars formerly used, the pillars of **columns** were made very slender, adding to the effect of height by their vertical lines, and this made it necessary to group them in clusters around a central one for sufficient strength. These **clustered columns are characteristic of all Gothic architecture.** On the ribs in the ceiling, and decorating the gables found over windows, we find little curled ornaments shaped like the top of a shepherd's crook. These are called **crockets** and are intended to remind the people that the pastor is the shepherd of their souls. The little ornaments holding the ribs where they meet are called **bosses**.

Notre Dame Cathedral is the oldest of the Gothic Cathedrals, being built in the 12th Century. Many of the French cathedrals were built with towers on the West Front instead of spires. The towers are designed to give dignity to the building and to hold the heavy set of bells to be rung for service. Spires were added for height. Notice that both horizontal and vertical divisions of the **facade** or face of the church shows the symbolism of the Trinity; its composition in light and dark and fine space relations is one of the finest in the world. (Have pupils analyze these points.) Its statuary has been made

subordinate to the architecture and **treated as a pattern** to be seen from a distance, hence, viewed separately and near at hand, looks crude and inhuman. This is true of all Gothic sculpture. The **clerestory** or main wall rising over the nave is pierced with windows filled with some of the finest stained glass in the world.

Cologne Cathedral is considered the finest specimen of German Gothic; it has one of the highest naves in the world as well as being one of the largest churches. It is about 500 ft. long with spires over 500 ft. high. The wonderful rhythmic lines of its high slender columns, almost lost in the high vaulted ceiling, have been likened to music in stone.

An elaborately carved shrine marks the supposed resting place of the "Three Kings," whose remains are said to have been brought to the Cathedral when built.

Giotto's Tower is one of the architectural treasures of Italy, as also of the world. Built in the 13th century by Giotto, an Italian artist, who, when planning this tower to hold the bells of the Cathedral, showed a knowledge of especially fine space relations on the facade. Notice how the **fenestration** has been planned to show increasing sizes from the ground to the top. He planned much as did the Greeks to overcome the effect of perspective on the eye.

The building is gorgeous with beautiful inlays, mosaics, and veneerings; when glistening in the morning sunlight, reflecting its iridescent hues of rose, violet, and green, it seems like some exquisite jewel casket. The tracery of its windows is graceful and varied. This beautiful tower is the essence of Italian Gothic decorative art. It is the pride of the city of Florence.

Miserere Seat. The carved wood seat from Wells Cathedral in England is one of about a hundred similar seats in the sanctuary, no two of which show the same motive. The picture shows one in which the dragon, symbol of sin, is shown consuming himself in very shame, before the Divine Presence. This wood-carving is done on **hard** wood and shows very great beauty. These seats were used by the Monks in the sanctuary when they sang the "Miserere," hence the name. They are movable and any pressure causes them to close with a noise. It has been said they were jokingly called "Misery" seats by the Monks, who when suddenly awakened from sleep to attend services sometimes during the night, unconsciously leaned upon them for support when they should be standing upright, only to be embarrassed by the tell-tale noise of the seat.

The carved wood of the sanctuary furnishings in all of the Gothic churches was beautiful beyond words. We must remember everything was done to give honor to God and each person did the work he could do best. The nobles hauled stones with the peasants.

The Rose Window shown belongs to the French Cathedral of Chartres, which has the finest stained glass in the world. The Rose Window was originally a wheel window symbolical of the wheel on which St. Catherine was martyred. It also suggests the great eye of the Church forever looking after the good of her children.

Gargoyles were wonderfully carved grotesques, planned for use on the building as waterspouts. The gurgling sound of the water may have given them their names. A learned bishop has suggested the meaning of these grotesques to be an appeal to all creatures to praise the Lord "dragons and all deeps, beasts and all cattle, creeping things and flying fowl." It is a beautiful thought. The picture shows the gargoyles in place at the base of the towers of Notre Dame, looking out over the City of Paris.

The Cathedral of Learning. Gothic architecture was planned for religion, therefore its symbolic spiritual idea is best suited to churches. Education and religion should each strengthen the other. The University of Pittsburgh, adapting the symbolism of Gothic to a modern temple of learning, has made its soaring mass decreasing in a rhythmic sequence like a spire, to lead the eyes upward to God as true education should do, each section on the upward climb representing the various **accretions of knowledge in the educational journey.** The building is a beautiful example of rhythm, both in **line**, and in **light and dark.** It is surmounted by a huge aviation light which changes at Christmas to a colossal star which, at this great height, is truly a reminder of the Star of Bethlehem.

The following outline is from a demonstration lesson given to her 6-A class by Miss Eleanor McConville, teacher in the Larimer Public School of Pittsburgh. The lesson was given for the Elementary Principals, Supervisors, Associate Superintendents, and Superintendent of Schools. At its close they were unstinted in their enthusiastic praise. The most impressive thing to them was the **intense interest** and **reverence** of the children and their keen reactions as the lesson progressed.

I—**General Topic:** Appreciation of Architecture.

II—**Objective:** To develop in the pupils aesthetic appreciation, or the response to the beautiful in the works of man.

III—**Content:**

1—**Specific Objective**: Appreciation of Gothic Architecture.

2—**Materials:**

(a) Pictures

(b) Sketches (many were made on blackboard)

3—**Principles to be emphasized:**

(a) Line

(b) Form

(c) Proportion

(d) Balance

(e) Fitness (Harmony)

(f) Rhythm.

4—**Aids—references—devices:**

(a) Charts

(b) Paper cuttings (Showing tracery development, etc.)

IV—**Lesson Presentation**:

1—**Introduction:**

(a) Short review of architecture from Egyptian through Greek, Roman, and Romanesque to Gothic.

2—**Suggested Procedure:**

(a) Origin of Gothic

(b) Characteristics of Gothic Style:

(1) Pointed Arch

(2) Vaulted Roof

(3) Buttress

(4) Flying Buttress

(5) Spires—pinnacles—towers (Line)

(6) Clustered columns

(7) Stained glass

(8) Rose window

(9) Traceried window

(a) Trefoil, quatrefoil, etc.

(10) Gargoyles.

(c) Employment of rules of design:
   (1) Balance—Fenestration
   (2) Proportion—Facade
   (3) Fitness to purpose:
      (a) Uses
      (b) Church
      (c) Commercial Building
      (d) Domestic Building.
      (e) Summarization.

3—**Final application:**

(a) Local examples.
   (1) Churches
   (2) Commercial buildings.

(b) Assignment for next lesson: Bring to class pictures of Gothic buildings and Gothic decoration.

The Gothic project may be carried through the whole semester if desired. The class should discuss and analyze each of the pictures on the page and then plan an interesting composition of picture and notes concerning it. These pages should be planned for later binding by having a line drawn 1 inch from the long edge, on which to fold the sheet lengthwise and stitch. The cover may be stiff as shown in model, Book 4, page 17, or cover may be heavy construction paper. A suitable design should be used with the title. Cut text book page about a half inch from the binding to protect the other pages. This lesson is planned for special home projection.

BOOK VII—PAGE 25—APPRECIATION

Character Objective: Sincerity

Spiritual Objective: The Gothic builders showed more than anything else **sincerity** in their work and even though the ornament was high on the building, out of sight of people, it was beautifully finished "For the eye of God sees everywhere," and the **work was done as prayer.** Lead children to see that **sincerity** is the mortar that will hold their "stones" of character **firmly together**, and **God will not accept imitations.**

Art Objective: To vitalize the teaching of architecture through the concrete knowledge gained from modeling in clay.

Supplies: Clay, string

Procedure: Read all the references to clay made for the preceding books to know what steps have been accomplished as pupils have progressed through the grades.

Ordinary pottery clay is **very much cheaper** than the many forms of plastic material on the market under various names. An important thing about this type of modeling is that pupils should have **plenty of clay** with which to work. A watchful eye should be kept for the talented pupil who shows **special ability** in order that he may be **conserved for more advanced training.**

The **new** step in modeling to be learned is **modeling in the round** illustrated in the Holy Water font and the Gargoyle.

The Quatrefoil symbolizes the Four Evangelists and when a quatrefoil shows a circle inside it means God (eternal) and the Four Evangelists. The fleur-de-lis, which is the national flower of France, means **purity**.

Previous lessons on tiles, leave nothing new but the subject matter. The fleur-de-lis may be traced **on** and **dug out** or **built on** like the trefoil and Cathedral of Learning. The Notre Dame tile is drawn and traced on and then dug out. The **coils rolled out** for the Holy Water font should be about as thick as the index finger, and about four times as long, for comfortable handling and building. Scratch the parts of the coils that must touch to help strong welding. **Widen** the bowl as it rises by allowing each **new coil** to extend a little bit **outside** the one **under**. Weld coils smooth by running finger over place of joining. When of desired height, separate by cutting **with a cord** through the center. Weld firmly to background. Ask pupils to model something related to their local parish church, following any of the suggestions shown on the page.

These pictures may be included in the Gothic booklet if desired.

BOOK VII—PAGE 27—LEARNING TO SEE

Character Objective: Judgment

Spiritual Objective: As all receding parallel lines meet in a point on the eye level, so the daily acts we leave behind us line up parallel, one beside the other, the good with the good and the bad with bad. and they all meet the Eye of God.

Art Objective: To teach pupils to correctly interpret in pencil rendering objects in parallel perspective.

Supplies: Paper, scissors, strings, books, pencils, chalk and blackboard (optional), stiff paper, crayons, scissors, paste, blank paper

Procedure: Recall experiments made in Book 6, page 33, to review the effect of **distance** on **size** of objects. Have each pupil make the paper oblong with an inside oblong cut on **three** sides. Have pupils experiment with this, **keeping it on the eye level.** Have it opened and closed like a window or door, noting the changed direction of lines enclosing the smaller oblong when compared with opening. Note effect when opened in opposite direction. This experiment proves the first assertion or **principle** stated in the text.

Do not use the term **perspective**. It is apt to confuse pupils and is not necessary to their correct **seeing**. When this principle of convergence is **given** mechanically as a **rule of perspective** instead of being **discovered** through experiment as the **cause for appearance,** the visual alertness of pupils is retarded and objects are mathematically **drawn according to rule** instead of being **records** of what the pupil **really sees**. This problem is particularly concerned with developing **correct observation.**

The second experiment with the string and the book emphasizes the first experiment and completes it by showing that if **converging lines** are continued they will **meet in a point on the eye level.**

When sketching an angular object the **amount** of convergence is easily estimated by comparing the **space** of **front** and **top**, finding **corners of back edge** as shown in the picture and then connecting front and back edges.

Have pupils practice at blackboard with a fairly thick book, making quick sketches of it in various positions **above** and **below** the eye level. On the eye level the result will show only the **oblong** of **back** of book.

Finish lesson by having each pupil sketch one of his own books, placed directly facing him, on the front edge of his desk. Emphasize the necessity of **keeping eyes centered** in the **middle** of the book while estimating **back** corners of book.

Lesson 2: Begin lesson by making the experiment oblong from stiff paper. The inner oblong is **cut on two edges** and **diameter** connecting them. This makes two doors or casement windows. **The point to be developed** is the use of principle just learned in drawing book when applied to more complicated problems. Holding paper with eyes located at center of opening, open the doors in the oblong until they are at **right angles** with the paper; notice that if the slants of the **tops and bottoms** of doors were continued they would **meet in** the **middle** or **on the eye level.** This may be shown on a large classroom model on which a string has been fastened diagonally over the opening.

Lesson 3: Have pupils find pictures similar to picture shown in book in which all objects in the picture have **one** side **directly facing** the observer. With colored crayola extend all **receding** or converging lines **to meet** at a point on the eye level which is the **center of their vision.**

Paste these reference pictures on the blank page. Give pupils a series of pictures to test their ability in finding **where** the artist was located while making the picture.

Lesson 4: Have pupils copy picture of street shown in book for method of approach in **blocking in** correct lines for buildings and details. Also have them study the pencil technique of rendering. Follow this lesson with pencil rendering from similar photographs and pictures in color. In this problem be watchful of placing of doors and windows and elimination of detail as shown in illustration in text. Notice the **interest** added by **accents** on windows and doors.

Encourage pupils to try sketching outdoors and when these are brought in for criticism exhibit them to encourage others. **Do not expect fine results.** Our problem is particularly **concerned with teaching pupils to observe.**

BOOK VII, PAGE 29—FLAG STUDY

Character Objective: Patriotism

Spiritual Objective: As the American flag should be **held sacred** by every American because of **what it stands** for as well as being his safeguard at home or abroad, the powerful sign which the world understands to mean **liberty** and **independence**, so pupils should be led to see that the **powerful sign** God has given us to keep our liberty and independence from sin is the **Sign of the Cross.**

Art Objective: To study the color and design of various flags.

Supplies: Scissors, pencils, crayons, paints and brushes, colored paper, paste

Procedure: Discuss the flag and its history. The dictionary will show its evolution. A series of flags showing this may be worked out for the classroom as a decoration for a Washington program.

Lesson 2: A flag booklet may be planned to include the flags of all nations as a correlation of the geography or history lesson.

The Papal flag which is the newest of the national flags, should be discussed from **that** standpoint first and then as the **symbol spiritually** of the Head of the Church. Pupils should be made to clearly understand the difference between the **temporal power** of the Pope and his **spiritual** power as Christ's representative. Have them realize that the Pope proved his indifference to worldly power by refusing to accept the costly palaces and valuable ground which the Italian Government wished to give him, keeping only that part in which he lived. The meaning of the symbols used by the Pope are:

The pallium or scarf signifies his rank as Primate and the tiara or triple crown signifies his threefold office: that of teacher, lawgiver, and judge. It is also said to mean his supreme authority in spiritual things; his jurisdiction over the Church as a human society and his dominion as a temporal monarch. It also means his threefold authority, Doctrinal, Sacramental, and Pastoral. The crossed keys symbolize his power to "loose and bind." Teach the quotation "Thou art Peter and upon this 'rock' I shall build My Church and shall give to thee the keys of the Kingdom of Heaven. And whatsoever thou shalt loose on earth it shall be loosed in heaven and whatsoever thou shall bind on earth it shall be bound in heaven. Feed My lambs. Feed My sheep."

BOOK VII, PAGE 31—FIGURE DRAWING

Character Objective: Duty

Spiritual Objective: The artist looks first for the **action line** of the figure when he wishes to make an interesting sketch from life. Action always adds interest to life. Great leaders have always been men and women of action. Lead pupils to see that God, the Great Artist, also looks for **action** on the part of His children while doing His work on earth. He will **not** be satisfied with the lazy lifeless servers who always think of **personal comfort first** whether action is needed in helping another or in visiting our Lord in the Blessed Sacrament. **Action is a duty.**

Art Objective: To continue the development of figure drawing, emphasizing the necessity of action and correct proportions.

Supplies: Chalk and blackboard (optional), pencils, paper, scissors, paste

Procedure: Read the text while studying the drawings on the page. Have pupils work on the blackboard from books until they have memorized the proportions of the head, by drawing the ovals in several positions. It is easy to see and correct mistakes at the blackboard. At desks have pupils copy the pencil technique while learning the proportions. Review figure drawing, Book 5, Page 29, to see how the **balance** of the figure may be correctly estimated.

Muscular drawing of the action line in the air helps to give the "feel" of the action. Notice how much of the figure is located on the **right** side of the **vertical through the head** and how much is on the **left** side. This helps to estimate "placing" of the sketch. Notice the "station points" on the figure or **bending places of joints,** where **direction of line changes.** Look for **points of contact** as in still life drawing, where the hands touch the knee with parts of the feet almost touching.

Details are not added until layout of figure is completed, as **action** is the **important** thing in the lesson.

Ask pupils to find fine examples of action to be pasted on the blank page for illustration references. After sketches on the page have been copied, pose a pupil in a similar position **reversed**, possibly whittling. This creates an easy step to the next pose which should be more difficult. No two children will **see** the model in the same way. Be watchful to see that drawings show **individual seeing.** Continue lessons in figure drawing as often as possible, developing good pencil accenting of folds, shadows, etc., shown in details of model.

BOOK VII, PAGE 33—LEARNING TO SEE ANGLES

Character Objective: Tolerance

Spiritual Objective: The angles of a book change as rapidly as the book is changed. Every situation in life has as many angles as a different viewpoint may give it. Lead pupils to desire to avoid belonging to that class of people who do not make use of the fine intelligence God has given them to enable them to see many angles of every subject, and so become intolerant. Our Lord left a perfect example of **tolerance**.

Art Objective: To teach pupils to correctly interpret, in pencil rendering, objects in angular perspective.

Supplies: Large dictionary, pencil, pictures of angular objects, paste, blank paper, chalk, posterboard

Procedure: Find the largest dictionary possible to use as a model. Have pupils read the text, relating it to illustrations as they read. Demonstrate for the class, with a pencil and the dictionary, each step as the class proceeds with the analysis.

Emphasize the fact that when measuring with a pencil it is necessary to **brace the back** against **chair back** and **stretch** arm at **full length** with pencil in order to always **keep pencil** at **same distance from the eye.** Otherwise, measurements **cannot** be true.

Make it clear that measurements on pencil are for **proportions** and **not size;** a postage stamp and a building may have the same proportions. When sketching the real model have a large dictionary for each two rows placed on a board across aisle. The right corner is **located** as suggested in figure, by holding the pencil perfectly horizontal with its **under** side touching the **point of contact** between the **right corner** and the **ground** on which it rests, and noting **where** the **under side** of the pencil **makes a point of contact** with the **near edge.** In this instance we find it a little **above** the **middle**. The sketch at (b) shows how this observation has been recorded in constructing the book.

When measuring the width of the book from the **near edge** to the **right** corner, it is most important, after having measured the apparent size **on the pencil** that this **size be kept** and **measured into** the space being estimated, while keeping the pencil **parallel with the eyes** and at a right angle with the hand and arm.

The tendency of pupils is to allow the pencil to **follow the direction of** the book. When a pupil has great difficulty in realizing this point, a clear pane of glass held before him will help him to get muscular control necessary. Make him realize that his drawing of a **three dimensional** book must be shown on a **two dimensional** sheet of paper. Be watchful of this same error when **testing angles with the folded paper strip.**

In step 3 the pencil is **held** to **cover the back corner.** Make it clear that it **does not** touch the **side** of the book but is **nearer** the observer than the **front edge.** A small chalk mark placed on the back corner of the classroom model helps pupils to locate this point more easily. The rest of the procedure is sufficiently clear in the text book to need no further comment.

Ask pupils to find pictures of angular objects placed at an angle to test distant edges for correct foreshortening, and receding lines for true convergence. Paste these test pictures on the blank page.

Make a poster to advertise the library, using books as a decoration.

BOOK VII, PAGE 35—FREE BRUSH DESIGN

Character Objective: Initiative

Spiritual Objective: Commonplace shapes are placed together according to laws of design, unlike shapes are harmonized, accents are added and a beautiful unit or rhythm of units is the result. In much the same way commonplace and irksome duties are given to us through God's plan and when **harmonized** with the joy of service and **accented** with love and God's grace, become a beautiful pattern of life which may be the example needed by an associate.

Art Objectives:

(1) To teach the combination of simple shapes made directly with the brush, into beautiful design units showing balance, rhythm, unity, emphasis, and subordination.

(2) To teach the adaptation of these units to textiles and other industrial products in order to develop aesthetic appreciation of the products of these industries.

Supplies: Chalk and blackboard (optional), pencils, samples of textiles, poster paint or chalk, paints and brushes, pens

Procedure: Discuss the text and illustrations with pupils. List on the blackboard all the simple geometric shapes given in pupil responses. These should include square, oblong, circle, semicircle, triangle, oval. Keep shapes geometric and simple. Pupils may select any shape and follow steps shown on page. **Balancing** masses may be **any shape** and **not limited** to two. They may be placed above, below or either side of main mass. **Growth** lines should show an **uneven number** for the sake of variety and should harmonize the balancing masses with the main mass, by showing something common to each. The strong accents added give variety and interest. Have pupils practice making units planned on the axes, to keep them balanced. These practice units are best done with black in order to concentrate on form. Make practice sheet suggested in text.

Lesson 2: Ask pupils to bring as many samples of textiles as possible. Study the units and their arrangement to make the pattern. Analyze the color schemes found in samples. Notice that striking effects are obtained by combinations of light and dark in color, while subdued effects are the result of color combinations much closer in value.

Plan an all-over pattern for a textile. Review Book VI, page 3. Plan the structure of the pattern by placing the axes for repeats. Continue pattern with direct brush work. The rhythmic lines connecting units are added last.

The color harmony should show a beautiful analogous scheme of neighboring colors, having one primary color that may be used in **full intensity** on **small spots for accent.** If design is painted on paper of a neutral tone, the color scheme should harmonize with the tone of the paper. If poster paint is not available, a touch of chalk on the spots to be accented will keep accents stronger. Encourage pupils to show in their results the pure joy of using color.

Lesson 3: Plan an interesting Easter card using a suitable decoration made directly with the brush, and an added greeting of simple lettering made with the pen. **Use all capital letters.**

BOOK VII—PAGE 37—SURFACE PATTERNS

Character Objective: Trustfulness

Spiritual Objective: As the ugly earthbound caterpillar is magically changed into the beautiful butterfly, so our souls were changed from ugliness of Original sin into the beautiful reflection of God through the Sacrament of Baptism. Help pupils to appreciate the great goodness shown by God, when they, through indifference to that beauty, have lost it through sin, He is ever ready to welcome them back through the Sacrament of Penance that their souls may again grow beautiful.

Art Objectives:

1—To continue development of color appreciation through painting a butterfly.

2—To continue the study of textile design through application of an interesting arrangement of dark and light by means of a stencil.

Supplies: Real butterflies (if possible) or colored images, stiff paper, construction paper, scissors, paste

Procedure: If possible use real butterflies for the lesson. If children attempt to make a collection they should be instructed how to preserve them with chloroform.

If real specimens cannot be obtained, use colored pictures. The library will have a collection of these; the Geographical Magazine supplies many lovely colored photographs.

The problem is a test of **keen observation** and **color interpretation.** The second butterfly is an excellent example of the **conventionalization** of the **first butterfly**. Notice the liberties taken to adapt its parts to the design motif, while simplifying it and giving it additional beautiful rhythms grouped in an orderly arrangement of lines and valucs.

Lesson 2: The all-over pattern, lower right, shows a still more highly conventionalized form planned to fill the light space in an interesting way. The pattern shown at lower left has become almost abstract, showing only the most important elements of the butterfly. This motif is suitable for a stencil as the spaces enclosed by the heavy dark lines could be easily cut out.

From the butterfly painted make a conventionalized design in a square or oblong. Transfer to stiff paper for a stencil. Cut out the background as suggested on the page, and add bridges or ties where needed. Leave sufficient paper (at least an inch) around the oblong to protect the adjoining material. Keep unit very simple.

Plan a color scheme showing strong contrast and apply design to decorate a sheet of 9 x 12 construction paper. When finished, construct from it a box with attached lid for Easter eggs. Measurements on long edge of paper for horizontal divisions 2"—3"—2"—3"—2"; measurements on short edge of paper for vertical divisions 2"—5"— 2". Crease and fold on lines. Cut horizontal division on long edges, from edge to vertical line. Paste laps and fold. Estimate size of two long strips and three short strips to make supports for 12 eggs.

BOOK VII—PAGE 39—BEAUTY

Character Objective: Faith

Spiritual Objective: The early Gothic craftsmen gave their finest service to honor God and left us as an evidence of their faith this beautiful Chalice of St. Remi. It should remind us of what the Chalice means to us and the necessity of the grace received through the Sacraments to keep us strong in the service of God.

Art Objective: To develop an aesthetic appreciation of beauty as expressed in fine craftsmanship in metalwork.

Supplies: Pictures of fine jewelry, paste, blank paper

Procedure: Read the text and study the picture which is a photograph in color of one of the most beautiful art treasures in the world. If possible, borrow a small example of cloissoññè decoration often found in small vases to exhibit.

This Chalice of St. Remi shows a refinement of form with greater elegance in shape and proportion than was shown in earlier chalices. It has a certain regularity and precision of details that show the intellectual development of the people. Earlier chalices did not have as much surface decoration. The deep luminous tones of the enamels, the rich color of the stones, the shimmer of the gold and the light and shade of the filigree make this Chalice one of the finest Gothic examples of the goldsmiths' skillful art.

In shape chalices are divided into three classes: Roman, Gothic, and Renaissance, so named from the art period illustrated in the design.

The Roman Chalice is constructed on circular lines in the shape of cup and foot, with handle consisting of a short stem whose center forms a round knob.

The Gothic Chalice has a cup fashioned in form like a tulip and sometimes oval like the larger half of an egg. Its handle is longer than in the Roman chalice, with sharp corners which are also introduced into the molding of the knob and foot having ordinarily six and eight sides.

The Renaissance Chalice is a more or less graceful blending of the Gothic and Roman. The most practical chalice is one in which the cup gradually widens toward the lip without ending in an abrupt edge. The knob should be smooth and round and not too large, as the celebrant must hold the Chalice, at the Elevation and Communion, between the index and middle fingers, and the sharp corners of the Gothic pattern give pain when the chalice has to be lifted in that position.

Safety demands that the foot of the Chalice be broad and heavy to avoid the danger of overturning. Inscriptions of a personal character, such as monograms, cannot be placed on the outer surface of chalices, but may be engraved on the bottom. The chalice must be consecrated by the bishop and after consecration may only be touched by a priest. The chalice is used in the Mass because Christ used a chalice at the Last Supper when He instituted this wonderful Mystery.

At first it was probably an ordinary drinking goblet of those times. See Book IV, page 39. Ask pupils to find pictures of fine jewelry or other craft work to paste on the blank page. Have pupils notice beautifully decorated hinges found on many church doors which are examples of fine craft work in iron.

BOOK VII—PAGE 41—PENCIL SKETCHING

Character Objective: Response to Beauty

Spiritual Objective: The interesting accents that cluster round an old weather-beaten shed that has withstood the storms, make it worthy of the artist's pencil when he wishes to make a beautiful picture to show to the world. Old people are interesting for the same reasons and should be treated as thoughtfully and carefully as the artist treats his picture. On the last day the Great Artist may show their lives as beautiful pictures. **Be kind to the aged.**

Art Objectives: To teach pupils the technique of pencil sketching as a means of developing aesthetic appreciation of landscape.

Supplies: Pencils, sandpaper (if possible), images of landscapes, scissors

Procedure: Have pupils read the text while relating it to the illustrations. Review lesson, pencil sketching Book V, page 43 for pencil handling.

Copy the small sketches in the panel paying careful attention to the **weight** and **direction of line** in each. Notice how **strong and vigorous** the lines look. Every stroke has a **definite beginning and ending.** Notice that pencil **strokes follow the contour** or shape of the particular space where placed. Have pupils analyze where pencil has been **turned on edge** to give **fine sharp accents.** See that each pupil has a small piece of sandpaper if possible, to **keep pencil point flat and broad.** Emphasize value of **omitting detail** which tends to clutter up the drawing. Notice how the **strong darks accentuate the light** sunny places. Copy the large sketch by adding darks as shown in the three steps.

Lesson 2: Ask pupils to find snapshots of landscape to render in pencil.

To draw correct angles use method taught on page 33. Be careful to have snapshot **fastened firmly** to edge of paper to **keep it in same position when testing** with the paper angle. Notice how effectively the white paper may be used as part of the drawing as shown in the white spaces left for the window frames in third picture of the house.

Lesson 3: If views from the classroom windows are interesting, have pupils cut small square frames (an inch square cut out of a two inch square) and use them as finders in selecting a simple subject, as a corner of a roof with chimney, or a tree in the school yard. Keep subject very simple for successful result. Encourage sketching of any type when at home. The making of a small sketch pad about 2 1/2 x 4" is a reminder and an incentive to home sketching which primarily means **outdoor seeing.**

BOOK VII, PAGE 43—CIVIC BEAUTY

Character Objective: Good Citizenship

Spiritual Objective: When God made man in His image, He implanted in him a **sixth sense,** which is the **Aesthetic** sense, or a love of the beautiful. Only the **use** of it will make it grow strong, and it is the duty of each one to develop his own sense of beauty by always trying to **leave behind him a bit of beauty where it was not before,** whether the seed planted has been a kindly word or a kindly act or a beautiful flower.

Art Objective: To develop an appreciation of the values of color as a means of creating a beautiful analogous harmony of contrasting light and dark.

Supplies: Posterboard, poster paints or regular paints, 12 x 18 gray bogus paper, colored paper, scissors, paste, chalk and blackboard (optional)

Procedure: Discuss the text and help pupils plan a campaign for Civic Beauty. Discuss ways and means of making it successful. Discuss the things that go to make a good citizen both in school and outside. Read suggestions given for Book VI, page 43, and continue discussion along lines given there.

Lesson 1: Before planning an original poster have pupils plan a color scheme to paint poster drawn on the page. What is the most important thing in the poster? Should the lettering be made most important by using brilliant color or should it be emphasized through strong contrast of light and dark? The second suggestion is better, as brilliant color would detract from **legibility**, and it is most important that a poster be **read easily**. The background is the largest space; should it be intense or neutral, very light or very dark? Dark lettering will carry farther than light lettering, and a light neutral background will be more easily harmonized with the rest of the decoration.

The small spots decorating the letters may wait until the last. Decide on the color harmony to be used; if **blue** is selected its neighboring colors will be found to be blue-green and green on one side and blue-purple and purple on the other, each having different values and intensities. If **red** is used its neighbors are red-orange and orange on one side, and red-purple and purple on the other, and if **yellow** is used its neighboring colors are yellow-orange and orange on one side and yellow-green and green on the other. It is unwise to use too many colors. Why must pupils be careful to **not use two primaries** in this scheme? (They have no relationship.)

If a light neutral blue is used for the sky a dark neutral blue will be effective for the lettering with the decorative spots of two values of green and a brilliant spot of light blue-purple. White, gray, and black may be used. Be sure that dark masses are balanced with each other and with the light masses.

Lesson 2: For the original poster find suggestive figures, flowers, etc., to be pasted on the blank page for reference material. Do not attempt more than one figure. Plan poster on 12 x 18 gray bogus paper. It may be carried out with cut paper or paint. If poster paint is available, it is more effective as it is opaque, and keeps its brilliancy on neutral paper. Place on the blackboard a list of subjects for decoration and a list of slogans suggested by pupils to stimulate the less inventive pupils.

BOOK VII, PAGE 45—AN EXTERIOR STAGE SET

Character Objectives: Ingenuity and Self Reliance

Spiritual Objective:

> Who seeks for heaven alone to save his soul,
> May keep the path, but will not reach the goal;
> While he who walks in love may wander far,
> Yet God will bring him where the blessed are.
>
> *Dr. Henry van Dyke.*

Have pupils memorize Dr. van Dyke's beautiful thought against the time when selfishness may choke good deeds.

Art Objectives:

(1) To develop a discriminating sense in the use of color.

(2) To develop interest in historic costume as shown in Oriental dress.

(3) To develop constructive skill necessary in making the setting for the play.

General Suggestions: It is most important that the original story *The Other Wise Man* by Dr. van Dyke be read in the classroom in order that pupils may absorb its unusual beauty. As the book is very inexpensive, pupils should be encouraged to **buy and own their own copies for re-reading.** Have pupils get from the library illustrations showing the costume of the period with characteristic decorations.

Discuss the beautiful word pictures of the story as suggestions for an additional setting. The set shown in the book may be sufficiently changed to answer for Acts 3 and 4. A second **outdoor** set might show the desert, Artaban's home, or any of the many scenes suggested that would review the earlier work in stagecraft. Read suggestions for the other plays as a basis on which to build the new work. As in previous plays where two sets are used, have them **both** planned in opposite corners of the room and covered by separate curtains. The space between the two sets, through the use of the blackboard, may be turned into a magical realm of imagination, in which the players will enact their parts.

Always remember this is a classroom play devised to teach, and do not aim for professional equipment or results. The imagination of the pupils will supply deficiencies as planned in the early Morality plays of the Church.

Supplies: Chalk and blackboard (optional), loose long dress, pointed hat made of paper or cloth, shoes, heavy paper, cotton or fringed rope

Properties: The illustrations in the book need no comment.

The problem offers a fine review of perspective problems for the grade. Instead of painting door solid, it may be cut out and dark material hung over it on **inside** of set. This permits using it as a door. To change this set for the last scene a readjustment may be made by removing vases or other movable accessories used in act.

For desert scene see Books III or V for suggestions. Slight modifications on blackboard will also transpose the space between sets into Artaban's home, in which the teacher's desk covered with dull dyed material may become the roof of his house, where he studies the stars. The arrangement of the stage near a robery door is always convenient for entrances and exits.

The costume for the priest is a long loose dress bloused and belted at waist and with elbow sleeves. It has ornamental bands at bottom and at sleeves; a pointed hat similar to that of a bishop is worn with bands extending down the side of the face to the chest.

The hat may be made by cutting two sheets of paper like a pointed arch and pasting about an inch of curved edges together. If cloth is used, cut paper pattern and sew cloth over it for strength and stiffness.

Decorate with a winged circle of gold on front.

Bedroom slippers may be used for shoes by adding a long point of heavy paper to extend the toes about 3 inches. Add paper top to fit as in moccasins, Book III.

The costume for women and peasants may be found in any pictures of the Nativity.

The Three Wise Men should be in rich costume, carrying their traditional gifts for the Christ Child.

Read suggestions for making armor for soldiers given in this Manual for 6th Grade play.

Use brilliant colors for costumes of priests. Bright scarfs or colored paper will do. A small sheet may be draped for the long white robe worn by them over the color beneath. Beards may be made from cotton or fringed rope, dyed black.

Characters:

Artaban—A Persian Priest and Astronomer.

Abdus, **Rhodaspes**, **Tigranes**, **Abgarus** (Priests of the Magi)

Caspar, **Melchior**, **Balthazar** (The Three Wisc Men)

A Jew—Found ill on the desert.

A Jewish Mother—Living in Bethlehem.

A Roman Captain—In Bethlehem.

An Aged Philosopher—In Egypt.

A Young Girl—In Jerusalem.

The Voice—On Good Friday.

Soldiers, peasants, beggars.

STAGE DIRECTIONS

Act 1: (The action takes place in the open space in front of classroom outside curtain, in the home of Artaban.) Artaban is standing waiting for his guests, the Three Wise Men. They arrive singly, and as he greets them in Oriental fashion, they seat themselves on low stools. (Small boxes covered may be used). They discuss the signs they have found that cause them to think the new King is to be born shortly. They make plans for their trip to find Him. Decide where they shall meet and when. They depart. Artaban goes to the roof and studies the stars. He returns and again stands and waits for the rest of the priests, who have come to hear the important news Artaban wishes to tell them.

(Here the story may be followed for substance of dialogue.)

They depart, leaving Artaban alone, and again he goes to the roof to watch. He sees the Sign. (**Curtain.**)

Act 2: (If second set has been made the sick man will be behind the curtain; if not, action takes place outside curtain.) As Artaban rides on his horse he describes the country he is passing through. The business may be partly pantomime. His horse stops and he finds the Jew. Dialogue with Jew suggested in story.

He arrives at meeting place and finds the paper telling him to follow. He talks aloud to himself regretting what he must do. Sell the sapphire to buy equipment.) (**Curtain**.)

Act 3: (Action takes place before the door of Jewish home.) A mother and baby are sitting before the door as he approaches. Dialogue following is suggested in the story. They enter the house. Noise is heard off stage and Artaban reappears at the door. Soldiers appear and demand entrance. He bars the door, calmly looking them in the eye. Dialogue is suggested in the story. The soldiers march away and the woman blesses him. Curtain is dropped on Artaban standing with bowed head asking forgiveness of God.

Act 4:

Scene 1—Action takes place in the space between the two sets across front of room and **outside** curtain. Most of it is pantomime. Artaban begins his search for the Holy Child—on the way he meets the aged philosopher who tells him to search among the poor and lowly.

The search suggests prisons, hospitals, etc.

Scene 2—(Same as Act 3)—Groups of townspeople are discussing the Nazarene. Conversation should include the dramatic incidents leading up to His arrest. Artaban appears, old and bent with white beard. He talks to the people. (Conversation suggested in story). The crowds pass on and he is alone. He thinks aloud as he looks at his precious pearl. Screams off stage attract him and he stops and comes back to center of stage. Soldiers appear, dragging a girl. She frees herself and rushes to Artaban. Dialogue is suggested in the story. Artaban turns his head away and hesitates. Then he puts his hand into his breast and pulls out the pearl which he gives to the captive, who blesses and thanks him. (Classroom shades maye be swiftly drawn for the darkness if a pupil is placed at each window. A flashlight may be used for lightning. Boys will devise a noise for thunder).

The soldiers disappear as a "stage stone" falls on Artaban. He drops to the floor while the girl wipes his face and holds his head. A voice off stage is accompanied with very soft music. (Music is made by the soft sound of several pupils' voices humming any selected suitable music). The music alone precedes Artaban's answer and then the music softens to a whisper while the Voice speaks. A flash light should be thrown on Artaban as the vision appears to him. (**Curtain**.)

CORRELATION

RELIGION: As the production of the play proceeds, use every opportunity to elaborate on the enrichment of life possible through love of one's neighbor and unselfish service. Help pupils to realize that God is love.

ENGLISH: Work in English has now progressed through the grades, far enough to expect more refinement in sentences; sustained interest in longer speeches; creating suitable **conversation to interpret** what has been shown through **description** in a story.

As a "tryout" for parts in the play, have each pupil select a character and compose three or four well rounded speeches to be delivered by the character at definite intervals in the play.

Preceding this lesson it is well to have the entire class create one definite speech, the substance of which has been assigned by the teacher.

This type of assignment which must be done quickly and enunciated clearly, will give pupils confidence in planning their own dialogues and prove an aid to poise and self-reliance in delivery.

Each character is responsible for his own dialogue, but may have the assistance that any class lesson may afford.

Pupils should assume responsibility for individual and group rehearsals to precede a cast rehearsal. Aim for clear enunciation, soft, clear voice, and intelligent accent.

HISTORY: A brief knowledge of the country of the Wise Men and the surrounding countries. Government, customs, dress, religion, etc. The Roman government of the Jews and its effect upon them.

GEOGRAPHY: Parallel information to supplement the work in history.

What desert did the Wise Men have to cross? What would be the nature of the trip from Bethlehem to Egypt?

Compare with country of today. Compare with travel of today.

ARITHMETIC: Problems necessary in estimating scenery, costumes, etc.

COSTUME STUDY: Call attention to the similarity of the Oriental costumes to many of the vestments used today. Have pupils find pictures in newspapers and fashion magazines showing points of likeness to these costumes. Pupils should know that one source of modern costume design motivation has always been a study of historic costume.

On the blank page paste pictures of Oriental costumes (any type) and if possible modern costumes showing a relationship. From cut paper or with pencil and color, design a coat or dress suggested by costumes shown on page 47.

COLOR AND DESIGN: If pupils are working with tempera, which is poster paint, they must be careful to keep it in the proper consistency which is like cream. When too thick it does not spread easily. It may be diluted with water. Small amounts of color should be taken from the jar carefully to keep balance of color pure. These colors are brilliant and opaque, and permit painting light colors over dark which simplifies the correction of errors. Several jars may be purchased for the room for special use. White is usually added when mixing these colors.

MUSIC: Music may be correlated as needed in the play.

BOOK VII, PAGE 47 THE STORY OF THE OTHER WISE MAN

Character Objective: Love and Sacrifice

Spiritual Objective: As Galahad "lost himself to find himself," and the Other Wise Man "lost the King to find the King," so pupils should be led to see that only through being willing to **give the best of themselves** to the service of others when possible, can they expect to finally present to God the pleasing jewel of a rich and fruitful life. And as the hot flame is necessary to produce the fine tempered steel, so **sacrifice and service** are necessary in the production of fine character.

Art Objectives:

(1)—To develop skill and ingenuity necessary in making an exterior set for a play.

(2)—To show that principles of design are necessary in fine stage arrangement.

(3)—To develop an appreciation of historic dress as shown in Oriental costume.

THE STORY

A school room play adapted from the story by the same name, written by Dr. Henry van Dyke. (Harper & Bros. New York.)

Synopsis: Four philosophers of the East, Casper, Melchior, Balthazar, and Artaban, had carefully calculated the time for the appearance of the promised Messiah through the lore of the stars. When the star that had been foretold appeared in the heavens, they planned to travel together across the desert to pay homage to this new King.

Artaban converted all his wealth into three exquisite jewels, a sapphire, a ruby, and a pearl, as gifts for the King, and started on horseback to meet his friends at the place appointed. On the way he found a dying Jew and stopped to care for him. The delay caused him to miss his friends and it was necessary to sell the sapphire to purchase equipment to cross the desert alone, and the first jewel meant for God was gone. The Jew had told him that the Messiah would be found in Bethlehem. He arrived in the little town and stopped at a small house to make inquiries. A young mother and her baby boy were the only occupants. She told him his friends had been there three days before and had given costly gifts to a child and his young mother, the wife of Joseph the Naz-arene. They had all left as suddenly as they had appeared and it was rumored they had gone to Egypt. She gave him food and while he was eating there was wild disorder in the streets and cries, "They are killing our children!" The mother, terror stricken, cowered with her baby in a corner, while Artaban went and stood in the doorway. He said, "There is no one in this house and I am keeping this jewel for the wise captain who leaves me in peace." The greedy captain craved the gorgeous ruby held out to him and ordered his soldiers to pass by. Thus the second jewel meant for God was given to man. Artaban bowed his head and prayed for forgiveness. He followed every clue he could find in his search for the King.

He was told to search for Him among the poor and lowly and there he would find Him. Meanwhile, his knowledge of medicine made it possible for him to care for the sick and poor when he found them suffering.

The years passed swiftly, filled with deeds of love and service, until thirty-three had been counted and Artaban's head was white. His quest had been unsuccessful. He traveled back to Jerusalem and found the city crowded, for it was the time of the Passover. He wondered why all were traveling toward the Damascus Gate, and was told that they were on the way to Golgotha where a Naz-arene was to be executed for having proclaimed Himself the Son of God. Joy filled his heart that he still possessed the wondrous pearl, for he thought he could reach the King in time to save Him by giving this pearl as His ransom. As he climbed up a narrow street he met a group of rough soldiers dragging a young girl to the slave market to be sold for her father's debts.

As she saw him she broke away from her captors and clasping him around the knees piteously begged him to save her. It was the old conflict and this was his last chance to present his tribute to the King. But the choice w.as inevitable. He took the lustrous pearl from his bosom and laid it gently in the girl's hand. "This is your ransom." His heart was crushed as he realized the failure of his quest.

Then suddenly the sky grew dark; earth shocks rocked the buildings. While the soldiers fled in terror, a huge stone toppled from above and struck Artaban on the head and he sank to the ground as the girl wiped the streaming blood from his wound. She heard a voice like music of unearthly sweetness, but saw no one. Then the old man's lips moved and she heard him answer, "Not so my Lord! For when did I see Thee hungry and fed Thee? Or thirsty, and gave Thee drink? When did I see Thee a stranger and took Thee in? Or naked, and clothed Thee? When did I see Thee sick or in prison and came unto Thee? Three-and-thirty years have I looked for Thee; but I have never seen Thy face nor ministered to Thee, my King."

And then the girl heard the sweet music of the voice again, and this time she understood the words: *"Verily I say unto thee, inasmuch as thou hast done it unto one of the least of these my brethren, thou hast done it unto Me."*

Joy lighted the face of the dying Artaban; he gave one gentle breath and he was gone. His journey was ended. His gifts had been accepted. The other Wise Man had found the King.

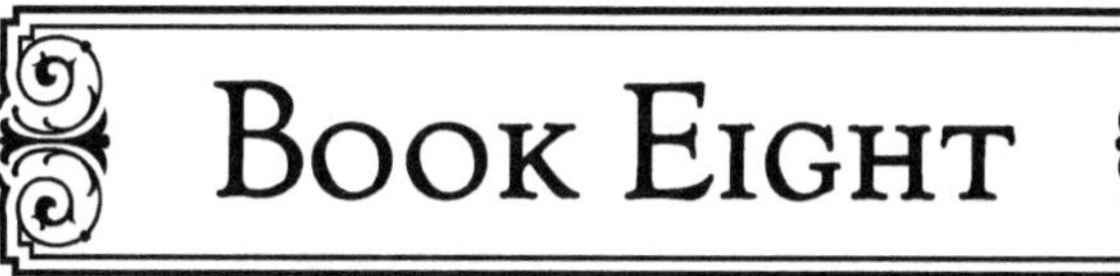

Book Eight

BOOK VIII—COVER

See page 3 of this manual.

BOOK VIII—END PAPER

Character Objective: Faith

Spiritual Objective:

"Into each life some rain must fall,
Some days must be dark and dreary."

When a rainy day disappoints us for a picnic, we seldom think of the untold blessings of rain and do not thank God for it, but He, realizing the limitations of our judgment, sends us what we need. The lovely poem prayer in the text book belonged to a very old lady who carried it in her prayer book during her lifetime. Its author is unknown but it is a very fine thought to store away.

Art Objective: To teach the use of symbols in an all-over design emphasizing movement, with strong contrast of dark and light.

Supplies: Paints and brushes, paper

Procedure: Read and discuss the poem and memorize it. Turn to end paper at back of the book to study meaning and suitability of symbols used.

The mood of the poem suggested the Crucifixion, as a comparison that would illustrate victory over apparent failure. The symbols of the Crucifixion were used to decorate the poem.

The cross and crown suggest the victory of Christ, the King.

The crown, nails, and scourge suggest His suffering.

The dice suggest the soldiers casting lots for His clothing.

The money suggests the price of betrayal.

The zigzag lines suggest the lightning and the tumult of nature at His death.

These unlike motives were modified until they harmonized in shape. The chaos of the hour was kept as the dominant rhythmic motive of diagonal movement. To form a contrast to the diagonal movement, the horizontal movement of the money and crown were introduced and again for variety a subordinated downward movement was added through the dice and the thongs on the ends of the scourge.

The Balance of black and white was carefully planned to give a striking contrast.

With brush and color plan a color scheme to decorate the poem. Use very light tints of the colors used. Mix color in the lid of the box and paint.

Lesson 2: Using two or three of the symbols shown on back cover, plan an all-over design in black and gray suitable for use on a Lenten booklet.

BOOK VIII, PAGE 1—SISTINE MADONNA

Character Objective: Love and Devotion

Spiritual Objective: In the glimpse into heaven shown by Raphael we see the Queen and her Son coming toward us, as Mary is about to present her Son to us. With what assurance may we approach her when we wish her to intercede for us with this Son Who denies her nothing!

Art Objective: To continue development of aesthetic appreciation of pictures through an analysis of line, color, and textural qualities of a picture.

Teachers' Preparation: Study the picture and analyze its effect upon yourself to better understand the effect it may have upon your students.

It is not only an unusually great picture but it is an unusual Madonna, since Mary and her Son are shown in Heaven instead of upon earth.

Raphael, the "divine painter," was asked by the Monks of San Sisto to paint for them an altar piece which would show the dream of Pope Sixtus IV, who dreamed he saw the Blessed Virgin appearing in the clouds holding in her arms the Divine Child, while before her knelt Saint Barbara.

The result was Raphael's greatest masterpiece. He planned his composition in the form of a pyramid, in what was known as the "Grand Style," to give great dignity and stability to the picture. He achieved interesting space relations at the top by introducing the dark curtains which also gave strong contrast of dark to emphasize the light of Heaven behind the Virgin. They gave a dramatic appeal of partly drawn curtains, surprising us with an unexpected view of Heaven. He realized the value of curved lines the beautiful rhythms of which intrigue the eye to travel through the picture. So we find flowing lines in the veil and dress of our Blessed Mother, the series of **ovals** in the whole figure of St. Barbara, the curves of the clouds and the rhythmic folds of the cope, with its touch of red curving out to catch the foot of the Virgin.

The color, which is also symbolic, has been beautifully spotted at the Virgin's feet and echoed in a lighter tone in her waist, preventing any possibility of detracting from the center of interest—the two faces.

Notice the gold tone of the Virgin's veil echoed slightly in the flesh tones, caught again in St. Barbara and enveloping the figure of St. Sixtus, so that the eye is carried down to the insignia of his office, the Papal Tiara or triple crown. Notice the material of the cope; even in a reproduction we can feel its weight and richness. Compare it with the softness of the Baby's hair or the thinness of the scarf around St. Barbara's arm. This is what is meant by the **textural qualities** in a picture. Compare other materials in the picture.

Aside from his composition, of which he was a master, Raphael painted a picture that has always been the despair of other artists who have tried to copy it. The beautiful Virgin seems scarcely to touch the clouds as though borne by an unseen power. To give his idea of Heaven he has filled the light background with a multitude of baby angels barely discernible, as delicately painted as a morning mist, painted as only he could paint a background for Divinity.

The eyes of both Mother and Son have a marvelous expression of wistful wonder as they look far into the future at the many who do not care that their redemption has been won at such a price. There is a hint of sadness in the eyes of the Child as though He had been denied that which He desired most.

In contrast to the majestic calm of these expressions is the earnest appealing face of Pope Sixtus who begs help for his people on earth, while St. Barbara looks benignly down upon them before adding her prayers to his. The counterpart of the Divine Infant is seen in the little cherubs guarding the entrance. It is said these cherubs were not originally planned for the picture, but they came and watched Raphael while he worked, much as they keep watch in the picture, and he immortalized them just where they were.

The colors used are symbolic. The emphasis of green at the top urges us to have hope since our Blessed Mother is willing to mediate for us. The red on the Virgin symbolizes love while on the two saints it symbolizes martyrdom. The gold signifies a wealth of heavenly grace.

Supplies: Pictures by Raphael (if possible)

Procedure: Have pupils study the picture in silence in order that it may make its own appeal without interruption.

Call on pupils for reactions and these will form a nucleus for the discussion of the picture.

Review all the points of analysis made familiar through other lessons.

Have pupils analyze the color harmony which is a double complementary harmony of blue and orange with green and red.

Raphael Santi was an Italian who painted many beautiful Madonnas. He is one of the most beloved painters the world has known. He died at thirty-six, but left sufficient work for a completed life.

If possible, get from the library a number of pictures by Raphael in order that pupils may become familiar with his work. Recall the Madonna of the Chair studied in Grade I.

For additional picture study see page xxx.

BOOK VIII, PAGE 3—PENCIL RENDERING

Character Objective: Cooperation

Spiritual Objective:

"Like leaves on trees the race of man is found
Now green in youth, now withering on the ground.
Another Spring, another race supplies
They fall successive and successive rise."

Homer

Lead pupils to see that the longest life when considered with eternity is as short as the life of a leaf. As each leaf has helped to make the whole tree beautiful and useful through cooperation with many other leaves, so boys and girls may help the whole community by cooperating with every movement for good in which they are asked to help.

Art Objective: To develop a response to the beauties of nature, while teaching their interpretation with good pencil technique showing fine relationship with lettering.

Supplies: Pencils (2-B and 2-H, if possible), paper

Procedure: Discuss the text while studying the illustration. Explain that the word **texture** means the structural quality of the surface of materials.

Notice that the type of pencil stroke used in the trunk is different from that used in the foliage. The artist tried to show the quality of each. Notice the vigorous freshness of the lines and the crisp dark accents shown in the shadows. Notice how the light gray masses of foliage come forward while the trunk stays back where it should be. This has been emphasized by the edge of dark accents dividing the foliage from the tree. A beautiful pattern of light shapes has been introduced along the branches, due to a careful study of the tree structure and wise elimination where necessary. Emphasis has been given to the leafiness of the edges of the whole tree and the smaller masses within the large mass. Notice how well the distance recedes **back** of the tree because it is framed by the dark branch and ground.

If possible have students use two pencils, one very soft, 2-B, and one very much harder, 2-H. The use of two pencils will permit the pupil to handle the pencil as it should be used. **Light masses** should be put in **with the hard pencil with a strong pressure** by pupil, sinking into the paper and making clean sharp edges. The **darks** are put in **with the 2-B** in the same way. When a pupil is compelled to get both light and dark from one pencil, he must necessarily change the strength of his pressure and the result is a stroke having an uneven edge which gives a "woolly" appearance, **considered poor pencil technique.**

Study the lettering in the lines of poetry which the tree sketch was made to illustrate. It is beautifully spaced and artistically decorated, making a beautiful harmony of lettering and illustration.

Have pupils copy tree and lettering as an aid in acquiring good pencil technique. Follow directions given in text. Ask them to sketch some lovely old tree in the neighborhood, searching for its most beautiful aspect. Ask them to place beneath it a line from some tree poem they think as lovely as the tree.

Lettering should be added as an exercise after study of page 7.

BOOK VIII, PAGE 5—THE SANCTUARY WALL

Character Objective: Self Control

Spiritual Objective: Grapes are a symbol of the Blood of Christ shed for all sin, and this thought should be uppermost in our minds when temptation threatens from alcoholic wines, that inevitably kill will power. We should remember this always while developing habits of self control.

Art Objective: To make an all-over surface pattern in light and dark developed from a nature motive.

Supplies: Pencils, crayons, paints and brushes, colored paper, scissors, paste

Procedure: Study the panel of grapes for fine quality of line in the rendering of light and shadow. On account of the use for which the design is planned grapes, because of their symbolism, are appropriate.

Analyze the fine space arrangement of the composition. In selecting the elements for the conventionalized design any parts of the natural growth may be used. In the lower panel notice that the parts used were the most interesting aspects of the grape composition.

The chalice has been made the center of interest by being made **the dark accent** of the design and without this addition to the leaf and grape composition, the pattern would be in danger of becoming monotonous. The light area back of the chalice emphasizes its symbolism and gives a rhythmic line of white that encircles all the shapes and gives movement to the pattern.

Have pupils suggest other symbols appropriate for a design for the wall of a Sanctuary. When the design motive or combination of motives has been selected, decide which plan of repeats is to be used. (Read notes for Book VI, Page 3.)

Plan repeat to give variety of sizes in background spaces.

Notice changes that were made in the motive shown at lower left. The upper leaf was enlarged to give sufficient support to the heavier grapes and the lower part of the grapes was shortened to fit into a more interesting shape in the leaf. Ask for criticism of the elements of design as planned in lower left panel. (Successively increasing shapes are not interesting, Book V, Page 3.) The final arrangement has more variety.

When design has been traced, plan a color scheme giving thought to the balance of dark and light. Since design is to be used as a wall covering the colors of large spaces should be kept neutral. The design for church walls may have stronger color than house walls, as the decorated walls are an important part of the complete decoration and as a rule they are not intended as a background for pictures or people.

A similar design may be made as an all-over decoration for the booklet on page 35.

BOOK VIII, PAGE 7—ROMAN LETTERS

Character Objective: Carefulness

Spiritual Objective: The ancient letterers, in stone and with ink, discovered the need of the serif to keep the wayward chisel or pen from going beyond the stopping place, thus causing their letters to be imperfect. God knew that strong human desires would carry His children **beyond the point of safety in conforming** to the **letter of His Commandments** and so He instituted for them the Sacraments of Confession and Communion to act as "serifs" to keep His grace within them.

Art Objective: To teach technique and appreciation of fine Roman lettering.

Supplies: Chalk and blackboard (optional), pencils, ink, pens, rulers

Procedure: Have pupils carefully study the formation of the letters, their beautiful proportions, and variety of line. These letters are especially valuable to the designer because their varying widths lend themselves easily to space filling.

Have class aim to recognize the **medium letters, the narrow letters, the wide letters,** the **size** and **thickness of serifs,** as well as **half serifs.** They have previously learned to connect a circular form with things that are Roman and the illustrations show the relationship of the circle to this new alphabet.

In beginning practice it is well to work large on the blackboard with individual letters to emphasize the placing of the thick and thin strokes. Select the letters beginning with a simple vertical down stroke and having no upstrokes, B D E F H I J L P T E. Use a short piece of chalk which is to be **kept horizontal at all times.**

This helps pupils to see reasons for thick and thin lines on these letters due to material used. Continue lesson with letters A M N U X Y to show treatment of letters with upstrokes. The early letterers began A M and N with upstrokes of pen; have pupils make them the same way, remembering the rule of width or pressure on the down strokes. Keep chalk vertical going up and the slanting down strokes will show the **width**. Without changing the position of the chalk emphasize placing of slants in these letters so often incorrectly made by pupils. The circular letters C G O Q may be made by keeping the chalk in a horizontal position. This blackboard practice lends interest while permitting the teacher to quickly detect errors and enables pupils to **concentrate on thickness of line only.**

Lesson 2: Continue the lesson at desks with pencil and paper. A stiff card will serve to draw construction lines (see Book IV, Page 7). **Urge pupils to keep very sharp points on pencils** when constructing letters. Use India ink to fill in letters carefully. The procedure for construction is clearly shown in illustration of letter N. In finishing serif emphasize working **from end of serif toward the letter** to keep it thin to make a graceful joining with the letter.

When ruling ink lines, **use a brass edge ruler turned upside down.** This prevents ink collecting on edge causing blots. On cards apply letters to titles for books to advertise good reading.

Lesson 3: Using broad pen or filed stick, have pupils experiment with freehand Roman letters. This procedure will be much like the practice work with the chalk as far as **position of pen point** is concerned. Ability to letter freehand makes this alphabet valuable because of beauty possible in planning light and dark spaces.

During the work on lettering urge pupils to visit a printing shop or, if possible, a newspaper office to see how this wonderful industry is carried on. Commercial people are always glad to cooperate with schools. Ask pupils to find fine examples of Roman lettering to paste on the blank page. Adaptations of the Roman may also be included.

BOOK VIII, PAGE 9—HARMONY OF CONTRAST

Character Objective: Judgment

Spiritual Objective: Complementary colors enrich each other by contrast when properly related and, with additions of light and shade, give our most beautiful color harmonies. In the same way we should consider work and prayer. Each complementing and emphasizing the other. Both offered to God as a spiritual harmony accented by the lights and shades of disappointment and fulfilment. The more difficult harmonies are always the most beautiful.

Art Objective: To develop a knowledge of Harmony of Contrast and an understanding of color relationship that will function in better color selection in dress and in the home.

Supplies: Colored pictures of birds or flowers, colored paper or paints and brushes, scissors

Procedure: Review color notes given for all previous grades and be quite sure that these are clear in the minds of the pupils. The color chart shown on the upper left of the page is a review of Page 9, Book IV, with additional values added of **highlight** and **low light, high dark** and **low dark**. The color scale at the right shows the amount of light or the reflective power of each color in its normal state. It will be noticed that the **two normal colors on the same level** in the color circle **have the same value in gray** between black and white.

Give each pupil a colored picture of either bird or flower and require him to reproduce it with pencil showing the **proper value for each color** reproduced. At the bottom of the sketch a small scale should be made to show colors found and corresponding values used.

Lesson 2: The color circle in the center has been so arranged to review all the color information previously learned and place it in a convenient form. The color circle has not been used earlier in order that children should not be made to understand **complementary colors as colors opposite on a color wheel,** which is **a very common error made in teaching this subject to young children.** After complementary colors and their uses are clearly understood, the arrangement in a circle is a convenience and shows complements as having greatest contrast because most widely separated, being at the extreme ends of the diameters of the circle. Review Book V, Page 9, to be sure that complements and their uses are clearly understood.

The color circles on the **inner** part of the wheel show the normal color on the **outside after it has been neutralized.** These colors are sometimes alluded to as **tertiary** colors since they are related to **the third property** of color which is **intensity**. Continued graying of these tertiary colors will end in neutral gray.

The color wheel also shows the **warm colors including yellow,** arranged on the **left side of the circle,** and **the cool colors including purple** on the **right side of the circle.**

Paint an original landscape showing only warm colors (skytint of orange, deepening to stronger orange and red, with trees or ground dark red purple).

Repeat the same landscape to show only cool colors; (sky a tint of blue deepening into blue violet and violet with trees or ground values of green and blue green).

Lesson 3: Discuss harmony of contrast and remind pupils that when they neutralized the complementary colors in Grade 5 they created complementary harmonies, because of the pleasing relationship created between the colors.

The landscape shows a complementary harmony of yellow-orange and blue-purple which is also the **dominant harmony** but it shows several **subordinate** complementary harmonies which enrich and add interest. Ask pupils to find them. Notice how the black accents add brilliance to the colors. This is a purely decorative landscape in which the nature forms have been highly conventionalized and carefully planned for beautiful space arrangements. Call attention to the rhythmic lines of the landscape which offer an interesting contrast to the horizontal lines of the sky.

Using colored paper or brush and paint, plan a decorative landscape using a single or a double complementary scheme with black.

Lesson 4: Experiment with color washes on sheets of paper using complements. Cut several bowl and vase shapes aiming for beautiful curves showing good proportions. Cut from sheets just painted decorative flower shapes to be planned in an interesting arrangement.

Points to observe:

1—Vase and flowers to make a color harmony.
2—Stems cut on a diagonal to get variety of sizes.
3—Interesting contour of mass.
4—Avoid too many in vase.

5—Aim for center of interest.
6—Pleasing distribution of color.
7—Short stems in low, broad containers and vice versa.
8—Single flower in slender container to suit type.

Refer to Book V, Page 11.

Obtain a collection of fresh flowers and seed pods by asking children to bring them or perhaps a local conservatory might contribute them. Obtain a number of containers of different shapes and colors.

Have pupils experiment in arranging them beautifully, according to rules of design and color learned in the progress through the grades.

Problems to be assigned to pupils are:

1—Emphasizing harmony of shapes.
2—Emphasizing a center of interest in group, by balance.
3—Center of interest in room contrasting harmony or analogous harmony.
4—Harmony of likeness in color.
5—Harmony of contrast in color.

The following outline is from a demonstration lesson given to her 8-A and 8-B class by Miss Katherine Mooney, teacher in the O'Hara Public School of Pittsburgh. The lesson was given before the Elementary Principals, Supervisors, Associate Superintendents, and the Superintendent of the Pittsburgh Schools. At its close they were unstinted in enthusiastic praise of its relative value to other school subjects through initiative, self-reliance, thoughtfulness and responsibility developed by class through the problem, and particularly because of its direct linking up with life.

The class was divided into committees of four and the chairman of each group after consultation, selected the problem they wished to solve and then they proceeded to solve it through selection and arrangement of flowers and container, being permitted to take anything they wished.

I—General Topic: Flower Arrangement.

II—Objectives:

1—To develop in pupils aesthetic appreciation or the response to the beautiful in nature and the works of man.

2—To develop in pupils judgment in the selection and arrangement of objects and materials used in every day life according to the principles of art.

III—Content:

1—Specific Objective:

(a) Ability to judge, select, and arrange cut flowers, berries and seed pods in suitable containers, according to principles of art.

(b) The decorative use to be made of composition.

2—Materials:

(a) Berries, seed pods, cut flowers of different values, hues, and intensities.

(b) Bowls and vases of various sizes and shapes.

(c) Lantern (Used to throw shapes on screen).

(d) Colored mica or glass.

3—Principles to be Emphasized:

(a) Balance.

(1) Subordinates

(a) Rhythm and harmony.

4—Aids, references, and devices:

(a) Reference material such as pictures containing flower arrangements with appropriate containers, good color, form, line, and composition.

IV—Lesson Presentation:

1—Introduction:

(a) Discuss problem with pupils.

(b) Review color theory—list color terms (questions).

(c) Review bowl and vase forms for size, form and color (paper forms).

(d) Teach meaning of laws of proportion and relationship to the proper arrangement of flowers (center of interest).

(e) Discuss texture of flowers and containers.

2—Suggested Procedure:

(a) Make trial flower arrangement.

(1) Analysis of composition for:

(a) Color.

(b) Proportional relationship.

(c) Arrangement of light and dark.

(Pupils gave reasons for choice and suggested its suitability for a definite place.)

(b) Select best compositions.
   (1) Pupil discussion.
      (a) Show effect of colored lights on composition and practical application of same.
         (Flowers on an altar; flowers on a table; flowers in a window.)
      (b) Shadow pictures with lantern of the best composition to bring out the outline, show massing and shape relationship.

3—Final Application:

(a) Encourage pupils to arrange flowers brought into school room from time to time.

(b) Encourage practical application at home, church, office, etc.

BOOK VIII, PAGE 11—COLOR TEST

Character Objective: Friendship

Spiritual Objective: To make pupils understand that a nation is only as great as the people of whom it is composed just as a chain is as strong as its weakest link. Friendly good will in every day contacts, added to a sincere prayer for understanding and wisdom will make the boys and girls of today, with fine ideals, constitute great nations of the future, who will understand the utter folly of war.

Art Objective: To develop a discriminating color sense in the use of a complementary color scheme in commercial advertising.

Supplies: Paints and brushes, scissors or razor blade, heavy paper

Procedure: Read and discuss the text to be sure pupils understand what is to be done with the problem. Look up flags in dictionary to be sure of correct color. Keep black and white balanced in doves and flags. Keep colors light, as darker values may be easily added but cannot be removed. Do not use much water.

Problem should be painted as an exercise for Armistice Day, mounted on heavy paper and taken home. Cut page about a half inch from the binding to protect other pages.

BOOK VIII, PAGE 13—INITIALS

Character Objective: Charity

Spiritual Objective: The little advertising folder shown on the page is to remind pupils of thousands of brave men and women all over the world sacrificing every pleasure in life that they may bring a knowledge of God with the joys and consolation of religion to the millions of people in the world who are living hopelessly without it. Christ has said "Go ye and teach all nations." The field is great and the workers are few. These workers are giving the best of themselves to their fellowmen. Arouse pupils to give them thoughtful consideration.

Art Objective: To develop an appreciation of illuminated letters and the value of decorative lettering applied to advertising art.

Supplies: Paints and brushes, images of modern advertising, paste, blank paper

Procedure: Compare lower case Roman letters with lower case Gothic or poster letters. Notice that the Roman are more decorative, and spacing can be planned in the same way as in Gothic, as most letters are based on a circle.

Study the decorated initial letters noting that the **letter must be kept more important than the decoration.** Make initial about 3 inches square in order to work out details comfortably. Decorate it and paint with a pleasing color harmony.

Plan a folder to advertise anything of interest to the pupil. The folder shown on the page is rendered in a modern style, showing an interesting decoration of title and a fine balance of title and place.

The rhythmic bands of the decoration carry the eye up to the title and over the top to the inside when the rest of the information has been placed. The band at the right helps to strengthen the outside edge and the small black dot finishing it balances the word "AFAR."

Observe following points in criticising all cover designs.

1—Title most important.

(a) Other information subordinated.

2—Ornament should echo title or be abstract and subordinate to title.

(a) Should have same movement as enclosing form.

(b) All lettering should be of same style and emphasized by strong contrast.

3—Spacing to show interesting variety. **Lower margin always greatest.**

Ask pupils to find fine examples of modernistic advertising to paste on the blank page for future reference in advertising design.

BOOK VIII, PAGE 15—TO MAKE A LINOLEUM BLOCK

Character Objective: Love and Reverence

Spiritual Objective: Careful tracing, accurate cutting and firm pressure produce a clearcut beautiful impression of a block print. Lead pupils to see that they may consider themselves as human printing blocks.

Attention to good instruction is the tracing being made; practice in prompt response to duty is made possible through strong pressure on the part of the will. The result is a beautiful impression pleasing to God. Aim to make good block prints.

Art Objective: To develop fine craftsmanship through manual skill required in cutting a linoleum block.

Supplies: Scissors or razor blades, linoleum, paste, wood

Procedure: Read and discuss text before pupils decide on the subject they wish to use in the design for the linoleum block.

The process as shown on page needs no comments. Keep design and lettering very simple. Any symbol suggestive of the Christ Child may be used, as an example a star with rays. Regular cutting tools may be purchased, but old razor blades are good substitutes. **Cut on a slant away from line.** Be sure that **design is reversed on the block.** It is safer to glue linoleum to wood in order to keep it level for printing. When printing, pressure must be very heavy on block. A strong blow with a mallet, while keeping block firm, brings out a clear impression.

A few experiments in printing develop necessary skill.

Read the following poem to help pupils appreciate the full import of the birth of the Christ Child.

THE WONDERMENT OF MARY

He came to me out of the darkness;
    He passed on a shudder of pain;
He burned with the heat of summer
    And chilled with fall of the rain—
Strange did it seem that His eyes had seen
    The Cherubs in clouds of gold,
Eve in her garden of roses
    And Abraham growing old.

He bled when the blade of Joseph
Lay sharp in the path of His feet;
He wept when the breasts of His mother
Denied Him their fountains sweet—
Strange did it seem that the little lips
That blundered in childish song
Had called from a mountain of thunder
The law of the right and the wrong!

Weary of bauble and playmate,
Or sick of the journey afar,
He lay in my arms, a baby,
And guessed at the evening star—
Strange did it seem that the baby hand,
So weary and helpless, then
Was God in the sword of Judith,
And Christ in the faith of Men!

He came to me out of the darkness,
He passed on a night of pain,
One with Barrabas, the robber,
And one with Barrabas, slain!—
Grief stricken I knew that because
His blood Ran red on the cold gray clod,
Men would awake and the sons of men
Would hail Him the Sovereign God!

Aloysius Coll

BOOK VIII, PAGE 17—CHRISTMAS GIVING

Character Objective: Generosity

Spiritual Objective: A beautiful screen is made to cover something not beautiful that may be a necessity. True love of God is a beautiful screen that acts in an opposite way, a **screen of safety against** sin.

Art Objective: To develop skill in craftsmanship and appreciation of home decoration.

Supplies: Construction paper, paste, cardboard, scissors, various images, paste

Procedure: Discuss the text to have children feel the true spirit of Christmas giving.

Steps given on page showing the process of construction need no further comment. Use soft toned construction paper and spread paste evenly all over surface then place cardboard pattern.

Turn cardboard toward desk and after placing sheet of thin paper over construction paper to keep it clean, press firmly with palm of the hand to get rid of air bubbles. Trim, allowing about a half inch to turn over cardboard. Lining is pasted in the same way only shape is first cut to fit about ¼ inch **less than cardboard shape** and pasted later. The warping of the cardboard caused by moisture of paste on one side is counteracted by the lining but it is necessary to place the completed screen under a heavy weight for several hours after hinges have been pasted. As soon as hinges have been pasted, rub the smooth **handle** of the scissors at the place of hinging to make them fold easily when dry.

A dark line around the edge of the decoration is effective. Decoration may be traced to the screen and painted directly or made on a separate sheet of drawing paper and applied with all-over pasting. The landscape problem planned for page 9 may be used for this problem.

Ask pupils to find reference material suggestive of shape or decoration to paste on the blank page. Reference material may include suggestions for other gifts which pupils may wish to construct.

BOOK VIII, PAGE 17—THE HOLY NAME

Character Objective: Self Control

Spiritual Objective: To arouse in pupils a sense of responsibility to become members of the great group pledged to stamp out profanity. Have them realize that in unity there is strength.

Art Objective: To teach the use of the paper layout in commercial advertising.

Supplies: Advertisements cut from magazines, colored construction paper, water-color paints or poster paint and brushes, crayons, chalk

Procedure: Discuss the poster first to elaborate on the spiritual objective to enthuse pupils in a spiritual and material crusade against misuse of the Holy Name and other forms of speech defilement. When interest is strong, pupils will feel the need of posters in a campaign to advertise it in the school.

Have class analyze the model poster shown in the book. The poster makes its bid for attention through strong contrast of light and dark.

The young and vigorous knight in the foreground suggests the strength of the Army of Youth in the distance. The white banner provides the strong contrast necessary for the slogan, while the white letters on the black background at the bottom are sufficiently subordinated to emphasize the center of interest without detracting from it. Call attention to the beautiful freehand Roman lettering used on the poster.

Call attention to the strong movement shown in the poster emphasizing the movement shown in rhythmic lines of banner, army, and lettering necessary in the campaign to make it a success. Notice interesting background shapes caused by having the various elements cut the edges of the poster.

Study the different layouts of the poster shown in the panel below to stimulate originality. The first block shows how to represent quickly the action of a figure. The second block shows the layout used by the artist in making the completed poster shown. The balance of the layouts show various arrangements of decoration and lettering planned, while experimenting with different ways of creating balance.

Notice, in every case, that the lettering has been considered as a definite decorative shape. Have pupils plan slogans and cut from magazines fine arrangements of advertising conforming to the laws of good arrangement. Paste on the blank page any reference material that may stimulate ideas in arranging an original poster not less than 9 x 12 inches. If colored construction paper is used, poster paint is more effective. If water color or crayola is used, the addition of chalk to the paper, where needed, will help to keep colors bright.

Lesson 2: Make a poster to advertise a local community or school campaign using Roman letters and an appropriate decoration. Require **thinking** all along the line in every art lesson.

BOOK VIII, PAGE 21—BOOKPLATES

Character Objective: Thrift of Time

Spiritual Objective: To acquaint pupils with the beauty of the "Little Flower's" philosophy of love that they may realize how easy it is to follow her "little way" to the Heart of God. She made commonplace duties radiant with an intense love of God, spending her life in sacrifice for others. That her "little way" pleased the Master has been shown us by the many manifestations of His miraculous power that He has exercised in her name. Interest pupils in her life culminating in the fulfilment of her desire that "After death I may spend my heaven on earth in the service of others."

Art Objective: To develop in pupils an appreciation of fine books and ingenuity in relating themselves personally to the book through designing an original bookplate.

Supplies: White paper, ink

Procedure: The solution of the bookplate problem shown on the page was planned for the Little Flower because bookplates are comparatively a modern invention and the Little Flower in her childhood could have been required to solve the same kind of problem confronting the pupils of this grade. Since the bookplate is planned as a personal thing to express the personality of the Little Flower, it cannot be copied if the problem is to show the personality of an individual pupil. The page is intended to show clearly each step in the solution of a design **which shall be the individual expression of each pupil,** since no two pupils will have the same data for use in the design.

Study the two bookplates carefully. Both show beautiful arrangements of Roman lettering and decoration. Both show the name as the dominant interest.

The first solution of the problem shows an informal arrangement of design material showing points of 1, 2, 3, 6, were used as decoration for her bookplate. The second solution shows a much more formal arrangement with the design materials used in an enclosing border, the corners emphasized by special symbols. Material under points 2, 3, 4, 5, and 6, were used in this decoration. The panel at the left shows the steps in flower conventionalization while the panel at right shows similar steps in conventionalizing the goat which was her zodiac sign.

Have pupils list their individual material, not forgetting the symbol of their patron saint which may be used in the bookplate, and then select that which they intend to use. They should aim to make this problem express all the rules for beautiful arrangement that they have learned. The problem should be finished on white paper with India ink. If planned for use as a **block print, avoid thin lines** and keep design very simple.

Pupils will be interested to know that one of the favorite books of the "Little Flower" was a French translation of "Evangeline." This book is placed with her other keepsakes in the bedroom of her home. At her convent in France are shown her palette and paint brushes beside her last picture, a figure of Our Lord.

BOOK VIII, PAGE 23—WHEN LOVE OF LEARNING INSPIRED

Character Objective: Alertness

Spiritual Objective: The period of the Renaissance meant the awakening of the Italians to the fact that they had in their midst countless art treasures of which they had not been conscious and lack of specific knowledge made it hard for them to distinguish the real from the copies. This should remind us that we too may become unconscious of our great treasure, the soul, if we permit conscience to be "put to sleep" by sin. God foresaw this danger and sent us the Sacraments of Penance and Holy Communion so that His grace might awaken new life in our souls. Encourage a slogan "Don't go to sleep."

Art Objective: To develop an aesthetic appreciation of architecture through having pupils become familiar with the characteristics of the Renaissance.

Supplies: Architectural images, scissors or razor blade, crayons, paints and brushes, paste, colored paper

Procedure: Have pupils bring from the library as many pictures as possible to bring to the lesson the atmosphere of the period. Large pictures show many interesting details lost in the small reproductions.

Read all previous work on art history given in earlier grades and then quickly review Egyptian, Greek, Roman, and Gothic, having pupils explain characteristics.

Emphasize the fact that the Gothic style did not become popular in Italy owing to the fact that it did not suit the climate. The steep roofs were not needed as they had no snow. The many windows were unwelcome since Italians needed thick walls and narrow windows to protect them from the hot southern sun. They had continued building their Romanesque churches while the outside world flowered into the glorious Gothic. Then came the great St. Francis preaching the service of God through love of one's neighbor. His teaching awakened the people to a realization of the duty they owed to one another. They became interested in learning more about one another and about the beauties of nature with which God had surrounded them. The invention of printing about this time made the diffusion of knowledge possible for the first time.

Old Italian architects had continued building in the old style, building their dome shaped buildings as high as they could. Printing made it possible to study the writings of the ancients and they began a close study of the Roman monuments all around them, measuring them, and erecting new ones like them.

Another important event that helped in this Renaissance was the capture by the Turks of Constantinople, the city which had been a center of art and letters since the great Constantine had first conquered it. Immediately all the great scholars fled to Italy with their precious manuscripts which, until then, had been hidden away in libraries from the world. The new industry of printing soon made this knowledge available to the people and education became the popular desire. They became proud of their ancestors and the ancient classic ruins, almost covered during the centuries, were now excavated by the architects and artists in search of inspiration. Some of the pieces of sculpture they found were Roman copies of original Greek sculpture and others were real originals. To the Italians they were all Roman as they knew nothing of the glorious period of Greek history with which we are all familiar. It will be remembered that the Romans often borrowed Greek ideas and used them badly; one of these ideas was the use of the column as a decoration instead of as a support. In copying these classic ideas to the new modern style of that day they did not discriminate, but mixed up the Greek and Roman, thinking it was all one.

The style of architecture which we know as the Renaissance shows features characteristic of both classic Greek and Roman.

The Renaissance showed really a type of decoration rather than style of architecture since it added nothing new to real construction.

We can recognize it by the dome, by round top windows, heavy projecting cornice sometimes crowned with statuary, balustrades, broken pediments, engaged pillars (meaning pillars attached to the wall as ornaments and not supporting a weight), rusticated masonry, (very rough stonework).

The small decorations show scrolls, garlands, wreaths of fruit, flowers, cupids and angels, masks and musical instruments, and lions' heads, examples of all of which you may see on the streets of your own city.

The Strozzi Palace. The Renaissance developed immediately into a type of architecture for domestic use. The intrigues of politics caused noble families to make war on each other and strong fortress like palaces were needed for protection. Notice the small barred windows on the street floor and the heavy rustic stone. The palace was built with a hollow square inside which contained lovely Italian gardens that are still popular today. The hot Italian sun suggested the very broad cornice to cast a much needed shade, and the very thick walls kept out the intense heat of the day. Call attention to the fine space divisions shown on the facade of the building emphasized by the string courses at the bottom of the windows.

These palaces are as well preserved today as when they were built; this one is considered one of the noblest in Italy.

Library of Oberlin College presents a modern example of the Renaissance at its best period. Notice the fine balance of dark presented by the large door and window on the first floor and the group of windows in the center on the second floor. The quiet simplicity of the design suggests the use of the building as a college library.

The Bambino is an example of **glazed terra-cotta**, a fine contribution to the Renaissance sculpture by Luca della Robbia.

Previous to this time all statuary was marble and too expensive for ordinary people. Della Robbia invented a glaze which could be put over a type of clay, easily modeled and very cheap. This was done on a large scale and used extensively in building. The colors used were a lovely dark blue and creamy white, the figures modeled in relief were light and the background painted blue.

The Bambino shown is one of a great many babies composing a frieze about six feet wide encircling a foundling asylum in Florence, called the Hospital of the Innocents. This Bambino or baby represents the Christ Child and is placed over the main entrance. The other babies are very similar, but no two are alike.

Singing Boys. These two panels are taken from a choir loft, made by Luca Della Robbia, one of the finest things in Italian sculpture.

The Pope was expected to visit the great Cathedral; della Robbia and another sculptor, Donatello, (whose pupil made the fine horse and rider shown on the page), were asked to make two galleries for the choir boys. When finished, that of della Robbia was pronounced the more beautiful of the two. In the left panel notice the arrangement of the seven boys singing. No two are the same size and yet how well they group together. How earnestly they are singing!

Notice how the little fellow with the book beats time with his foot. The artist has eliminated detail, emphasizing rhythmic lines and a feeling of life. The panel on the right shows a contrast in position and grouping but emphasizes the life and youth of the singers. The figures are about half life size.

The Colleoni Statue is considered the finest equestrian statue in the world. It was modeled by Andrea Verrocchio, who was once a pupil of Donatello. Colleoni was a wealthy Florentine nobleman who was famous in his country's wars.

The statue emphasizes a life-like quality of both horse and rider. The general is in full armor; his strong erect position, almost rising in the saddle, gives strength and power to his personality. The horse is a marvel of truthful modeling, a fitting horse for such a rider.

The Pieta. This beautiful group was modeled by the great Mi-chaelangelo when he was only twenty-four, and the spiritual quality with which he has infused the marble is uplifting. The beautiful modeling of the Christ in its nearly horizontal position forms a contrast with the rhythmic folds of Mary's gown on which it rests.

Here we find no violent grief, only the calm resignation we expect in the Mother of Sorrows. He has made the Mother much larger in proportion than her Son, evidently to emphasize Mary as being great enough to bear the sorrows of all her children as easily as she bears the body of her Son.

The Moses is another masterpiece of Michaelangelo, the greatest sculptor the world has ever known. This statue is in the church of St. Peter in Chains, in Rome. It was originally made to decorate the tomb of Pope Julius, never completed. The figure is colossal in size and shows Moses seated but with foot drawn back as though about to rise and hurl angry words at his faithless people. The horns on his head are a symbol showing that he was a prophet; the curling beard that he was a poet; tablet of stone that he was a law giver.

The marvelous modeling of the body and hands, the alert expression of the deep set eyes, the turn of the head, all express his great qualities of leadership.

Michaelangelo could express life and character in stone as no other sculptor has ever been able to do.

St. Peter's Cathedral in Rome is one of the finest churches in the world and also the largest. It was originally designed by Bramante but the plans were later changed by Michaelangelo, who designed the glorious dome which is unrivaled and is its most striking feature. It was originally planned on a Greek cross but was changed by Michaelangelo to a Latin cross, which improved the interior by giving it greater length. Its interior shows an impressive size without seats, as we are accustomed to find them, filling the church. There are only a few chairs before each of the many altars.

The tomb of St. Peter is located directly under the dome in the space beneath the church. An impressive portico was planned as an entrance to the church by Bernini, and this helps to give it a splendid setting. Two fountains play in the courtyard and between them is an Egyptian obelisk, a present from the Egyptian Government.

The Vatican is on the right, the entrance being at the end of the portico. The Pope's apartments are facing the churchyard and here he holds audiences daily. The back part of the building houses the Vatican library and the Vatican Museum.

Remove the page carefully, about a half inch from the binding, and plan a beautifully arranged page of picture with description for each of the pictures shown, and bind them into a book with a nicely designed cover. Have pupils look up more information if possible, to include in the book.

BOOK VIII, PAGE 25—APPRECIATION

Character Objective: Purity

Spiritual Objective: The Renaissance palace was made strong against the enemy on the outside and the beautiful gardens were within. We should keep our souls in a Renaissance palace of Grace with the beautiful gardens of purity kept safe within for the visits of the King of Heaven.

Art Objective: To vitalize the teaching of architecture as an aid in the development of an aesthetic appreciation of the allied arts.

Supplies: Soap, matches, clay, toothpicks, wire

Procedure: Soap modeling is cheap and convenient, and is suggested because it is possible to do it at home.

In modeling the palace at the top of the page it is necessary to use two bars of soap. To fasten them firmly together use two matches or other pieces of wood. Allow both pieces of soap to become slightly soft. Put pieces of wood in one bar and then press the other bar firmly to it. Rub outside, smooth with fingers, and allow it to harden again before beginning to model. Trace main divisions of building to soap and remove surface until cornice has been made sufficiently prominent. Add window spaces and model. Hollow center for courtyard. Try soap modeling as an assignment to reproduce a simple local building. In all modeling keep studying the model on all sides.

The second subject shown at the bottom of the page shows clearly how Verrocchio may have begun the modeling of his great Colleoni statue.

The horse is **built up** to insure sufficient support for the weight when finished. As the modeling proceeds, small rolls of clay are added where needed as shown at 2. A piece of picture wire or a toothpick will help to support the body of the rider. Find pictures to use as reference material. If desired, the pictures on this page may be included in the Renaissance book after clay work has been completed.

BOOK VIII, PAGE 27—FIGURE SKETCHING

Character Objective: Modesty

Spiritual Objective: "They work not, neither do they spin, yet Solomon in all his glory was not arrayed like one of these."

For the boy or girl who carefully guards the laws of health, good taste, and religion, we can also say "Solomon in all his glory was not arrayed like one of these."

Art Objective: To teach the balance of light and dark masses in figure sketching.

Supplies: Pencils, gray paper

Procedure: Read figure drawing in Book V, Page 29 and Book VII, Page 31. The vertical line on the first sketch shows the balance of the figure. The curved line shows the action of the figure.

Call attention to the few details shown in the first sketch. **But all necessary proportions** are there for use in the second sketch to which interest is added through strong light and dark.

Notice how carefully and freshly the dark lines are added. A softer pencil was used for the skirt. Instead of drawing the edges they have been **emphasized by not drawing them.** Notice how accents are shown by stopping the pencil before it reaches the edge. The addition of collar, cuffs, and book pages with white chalk gives attractive contrast.

Have pupils copy the sketch in the book to learn the technique. Follow this lesson with a lesson from a real pupil posed in a simple position, sitting, kneeling, standing, sweeping, etc. Follow all hints previously given and when proportions are good, add masses of dark and light. In selecting a pupil to pose, be sure to select one whose costume will show definite contrasting values of dark and light.

Sketch on gray paper.

Discuss modesty in dress as lesson proceeds.

BOOK VIII, PAGE 29—THE HOLY GRAIL

Character Objective: Purity

Spiritual Objective: This beautiful picture suggests to us Christ at the Communion rail, where "o'er our heads" in the hands of the priest there is a "Holy Vessel hung" before we receive the Adorable Guest. Like Galahad we should be faithful in our quest for that which is pleasing to God.

Art Objectives:

1—To teach the use of the figure in illustration.

2—To teach the relationship of beautiful lettering with illustration.

Supplies: Charcoal, crayons, paper

Procedure: The play produced in the 6th grade presents a fine informational background for illustrations based on this subject.

Study the simplicity of the picture and its fine balance of light and dark. The medium used by the artist in making the picture in the book was charcoal and chalk. The capital letter is the relating element in color between the picture and the lettering. The colored line of the panel around the lettering also relates it and gives unity to the whole illustration. The rays around the chalice were added with an eraser.

Have class discuss the various incidents in Sir Galahad's life which would suggest an interesting composition. Have entire class sketch a boy posed in some attitude easily adapted to any of the illustrations.

Plan the illustration, using this sketch as the central figure. Make illustration an expression of all the laws of composition learned through the grades.

Letter a line of poetry suggestive of the illustration with an illuminated initial letter similar to one shown in picture.

Illustration may be made in charcoal or colored crayola about the size of the picture in the book.

BOOK VIII, PAGE 31—PERSPECTIVE

Character Objective: Judgment

Spiritual Objective: Finding pictures to illustrate the rules or laws of perspective, to be placed in the booklet, may be made to remind pupils that there will come a time when the Great Lawgiver will ask them to produce **deeds to illustrate** their understanding and following of **His laws.** Their Book of Deeds should be made beautiful for His sight.

Art Objective: To review facts discovered while learning to "see" and interpret them as rules of theoretical perspective.

Supplies: Paper, string/cords, cardboard, pencils

Procedure: Read text and ask pupils to review what they have learned about various objects they have drawn in their progress through the grades. These are:

1—A circle or other shape held horizontally on the eye level appears to be a **straight line;** as it is **raised** or **lowered** it becomes **wider from front to back.**

2—The appearance of the circle above or below the eye level is called an **ellipse**.

3—Two objects **cannot** occupy the same space at the same time.

4—**Spouts and handles** are usually placed **opposite** each other.

5—**Distance** causes objects **to appear** smaller and this is called **foreshortening,** (the cause of convergence).

6—Objects **farther away** are shown **higher up** in the picture and vice versa.

7—All **receding parallel** edges **appear** to **converge** and if **continued** will **meet** at a point **on the eye level.**

8—Receding edges of **objects parallel with the eye,** appear to **meet at a point on the eye level directly opposite the eye;** this is called the **center of vision.**

9—Horizontal lines parallel with the eye **remain horizontal.**

10—**Vertical** lines are **always vertical.**

11—The direction of receding edges constructing an angle which faces the eye may be tested with a movable angle, **one side of which is kept parallel with the eye.**

The rules of theoretical perspective as usually taught in all art text books, belong to an advanced subject necessary in professional work, which when taught to children, suffice as rules for mechanically **drawing** "type" objects **without observation. This defeats the purpose of** this phase of art which **is observation.** This course is planned to have pupils **discover facts** through **seeing** them and **formulate rules** as a result. This gives a solid foundation for advanced work when they are ready for it. Meanwhile, **observation has been made to function truthfully** and pupils have been made familiar with the "joy of drawing" and **the value of "seeing."**

Make a book as shown in illustration as follows:

Follow directions for construction of book on Book IV, Page 17. Cut as many leaves as desired for the rules to be illustrated.

Measure, on cover, points for holes as shown on Book VIII, page 31, by placing one in center and one on either side of center, halfway between top and bottom.

Punch these holes and use them as markers for **back cover** and **leaves**. When punching is completed with pages and covers in position, push cord through the **top hole** from the **underside** with a pencil, **down front cover to second hole, through to back cover, down back cover to third hole, through to front cover down over both covers at bottom to nearest hole on back cover, through to front cover, over the back** to **same hole on back cover,** through to **front cover, up front to middle hole,** and **through to back cover around back to middle hole on front cover, through to back cover, up back to top hole through to front cover, over back to same hole, through to back cover, over both covers at top, and tie** firmly to loose end.

If cord is started **between** covers and final cord is **ended at the same place,** the knot will be **inside** and the binding be more neatly finished. This is known as **Japanese binding.** It is wise to make the teaching of this binding a separate lesson, using two small strips of cardboard through which holes have been punched with a pencil and a short piece of string. **Use a punch when making the books.**

Design suitable cover and on each page letter one rule placed beside a picture of anything that will illustrate the rule. Each page is a problem in fine arrangement of illustration and lettering. Call attention to the beautiful arrangement of the model page, where lettering and pictures make one complete shape harmonizing with the page and showing well spaced margins.

BOOK VIII, PAGE 33—PICTURE STUDY

Character Objective: Fearlessness

Spiritual Objective: If you look carefully at the faces in the picture you will notice there is but one Disciple whose face shows no distress or concern. That one is John. Through the nearness of his hand to that of Christ he seems to have felt an electric touch all sufficient to banish any fear of blame. Frequent visits to the Blessed Sacrament will help us, through the electrifying touch of grace, to calmly face any adverse criticisms of our associates, so long as we know we are doing what is right and, therefore, pleasing to God.

Art Objective: To develop aesthetic appreciation through an analysis of the principles of beauty.

Supplies: Charcoal or black crayon/ink,thin colored paper

Procedure: Each pupil should be provided with a **fine** color reproduction of the original of the picture for reference as the lesson progresses.

The lower panel shows a pencil tracing from the original picture reproduced in the upper panel in "half tone" or in tones of a photograph. The tracing was made to show only very important shapes and the rhythmical arrangement of these shapes has been emphasized by the dotted lines and arrows which all lead the eye to the head of Christ, which is the center of interest.

Rhythms of shape have also been made to lead to Christ. These may be found in the sequence of decreasing sizes shown in the windows on both sides of the room and the rows of rhythmic shapes in the ceiling. A bisymmetric balance of both sides of the room was used to emphasize Christ. To avoid monotony, the artist used occult balance in arranging the figures on either side of the figure of Christ.

In the colored reproduction Christ is garbed in a beautiful rich red, showing color has been used to emphasize His figure. The top of the door showing in the picture was cut in the wall for convenience by one who lacked aesthetic appreciation. The picture was painted directly on the wall of the refectory of a monastery in Milan over four hundred years ago, by Leonardo da Vinci, who is considered one of the greatest artists the world has known. Although much of the color of the picture has faded, thousands of people visit it each year because it is still a model of unusually fine arrangement. (An excellent study of the picture is given in "Great Pictures and Their Stories," Book VIII, by Lester—Mentzer-Bush & Co.)

Using the original in color if possible, make a tracing of one of the pictures assigned for picture study in the grade. Let the tracing show whether the picture emphasizes rhythmic line or strong contrast of light and dark masses. If contrast of light and dark is to be shown on tracing, use solid black and color of paper for light to show solution of problem. Make tracing on thin paper and trace to drawing paper by going over lines accurately on reverse side and then re-draw in original position.

BOOK VIII, PAGE 35—LITURGY OF THE CHURCH

Character Objective: Understanding.

Spiritual Objective: Any profession or business to be successful requires long hours of careful study and attention to details in order to improve the business or advance the profession. The most important business in life is saving one's soul for God and the most important profession in life is a sincere profession of faith in your religion. To be sure that both these aims have had one's best efforts a study of Church liturgy is essential.

Art Objective: To emphasize symbolism of color while developing skill and accuracy in painting.

Supplies: Paper, paints and brushes

Procedure: Much of the liturgy of the church has been touched upon in the correlation of Religion and Art through the preceding grades. Review the work to be conversant with what pupils should now know. Add to the information given other important necessary information in detail concerning the divisions and meaning of the liturgical year which lack of space prevents. A convenient small book for desk use is "Explanation of the Catholic Liturgy for the Laity" by Rev. A. M. Cheneau, John Murphy Company, Baltimore.

The chart is very comprehensive and needs no comment other than to emphasize careful painting showing sharp clean edges. Be careful to avoid painting adjoining spaces if one is still moist. Use tints of color for the seasonal year. Blue for Winter, yellow for Spring, green for Summer, and orange for Autumn. Do not paint the outer rim of circle. Paint the color rim with pure color of full intensity. Paint black circle about 1/8" wide on the **inside** of circle at center to show use of black vestments all through the year.

Meaning: The Liturgical year is divided into three cycles. The Christmas cycle is the period of Preparation; the Easter cycle is the period of Fulfillment, and the Pentecostal cycle is the period of Expectation.

Advent—The liturgical year begins with Advent, the four weeks of preparation preceding the birth of Christ and representing the four thousand years which preceded the coming of Jesus Christ upon earth.

Christmas—Celebration of the mystery of the birth of our Lord Jesus Christ the Son of God made man.

"And the word was made flesh and dwelt amongst us." (Jn 1:14)

Circumcision—The day on which our Lord received the name Jesus, meaning Saviour.

Epiphany—It is the feast of the **manifestation** of our Lord to the Gentile or pagan world in the person of the Magi. We should thank God on that day for the great grace of being called to the Catholic faith, in the person of the Magi to whom Christ revealed His Divinity.

Septuagesima Sunday occurs within a period of **70 days** before Easter. **Sexuagesima** is within the period of **60 days** before Easter.

Quinquagesima is within the period **50 days** before Easter.

This was caused by some churches not keeping the fast of Lent on Thursdays, Saturdays, and Sundays and the penitential season had to be lengthened to cover the forty days.

Ash Wednesday—Ashes of burnt palm of the preceding year are blessed and put upon the foreheads of the people in the form of a cross, to remind them of death and the necessity of penance.

Lent—A period of forty days devoted to prayer and penance in preparation for the feast of Easter.

Passion Sunday is the fifth Sunday of Lent on the eve of which all the crucifixes and statues in the church are covered with a purple cloth as a sign of mourning and penance as the time of the crucifixion approaches, and to commemorate the time when the Saviour no longer showed Himself to the people but, according to the words of St. John ending the Gospel for Passion Sunday, "Jesus hid Himself and went out from the Temple."

Palm Sunday is the first day of Holy Week, commemorating the triumphant entry of our Lord into Jerusalem, when the crowd strewed palms before Him. The people pray that they may keep from sin and that they may not be like these Jews who, after honoring Him, crucified Him.

Easter Sunday—Sunday on which is celebrated the Resurrection of our Lord Jesus Christ.

Paschal Time—The forty days of joy during the time our Lord stayed on earth with His disciples after His Resurrection. It ends with Trinity Sunday.

Feast of Ascension—Commemorates the glorious ascension of our Lord into Heaven, forty days after His Resurrection. The Paschal candle, the figure of Christ, which has burned since Easter, is extinguished at the words of the Gospel, "He was taken up into Heaven." It is not lighted again until the next year.

Novena—In preparation for Pentecost is held the nine-day prayer to the Holy Ghost for the grace of wisdom and understanding.

Pentecost—The church celebrates the descent of the Holy Ghost upon the Apostles. It is, after Easter, one of the greatest and most solemn feasts of the Christian year. The word Pentecost means **fiftieth day** and is celebrated fifty days after Easter.

Trinity Sunday—The feast of the Holy Trinity follows the Octave of Pentecost and in it the Church honors the three divine persons in one God.

Corpus Christi—The feast of Corpus Christi (Body of Christ) or the Blessed Sacrament, falls on Thursday after Trinity Sunday, but in the United States is solemnized on the following Sunday. It always includes a solemn procession of the Blessed Sacrament. It is planned by the Church to pay especial honor to our Lord in this Sacrament of Divine Love and to repair the outrages which He receives in the Holy Eucharist.

The time between Corpus Christi and Advent represents the period of waiting and expectation of the Messiah.

This problem is **planned especially for projection into the home where this information is very much needed.** After it has been painted, it should be carefully removed from the book and made into book form, with necessary information about the liturgy and then taken home.

BOOK VIII, PAGE 37—A CIRCULAR WINDOW

Character Objective: Carefulness

Spiritual Objective: Comparison by the early Christians of the Rose window with a great eye in the church should remind us that the eye of God is always on our every act and thought.

Art Objective: To continue development of interest in architecture and a responsiveness to beautiful color in glass through the construction of a Gothic Rose window.

Supplies: Construction paper, thin paper, paints and brushes

Procedure: Read Gothic art given in notes for Book VII, page 23, and review the work with pupils. Borrow as many pictures of rose windows from famous churches as possible. Assign pupils to report on how glass is colored by painting and burning; see process given in next lesson. The procedure is clear enough to need no further comment.

Pattern may be folded and cut from thin practice paper, traced to heavy construction paper, and cut for the sake of fine skill in cutting acquired through cutting separate openings. If thin paper is used for painting, the resulting transparency is more effective in showing beautiful color combinations. Review glass making on Book VII, Page 15.

Study local church windows and reproduce one as a community problem in a larger size than class lesson. Refer to structure and color of the beautiful windows on page 39.

BOOK VIII, PAGE 39—BEAUTY

Character Objective: Sincerity

Spiritual Objective: Lead pupils to realize that as the designer subordinates the figures in his window to the use for which they are to be used, that of scattering beautiful rays of light, so they should aim to subordinate themselves to the use God expects them to make of themselves, that of scattering joy and helpfulness as they pass through life.

Art Objective: To interest pupils in art in industry as illustrated by the photograph in color of the beautifully designed windows.

Supplies: Pictures of local windows, scissors, paste, blank paper

Procedure: Ask pupils to carefully examine the windows in their local church in order to see the actual construction of a large stained glass window.

These windows are first planned in black on light paper to show the distribution in light and dark; heavy black lines are drawn to show the iron bars necessary to hold window firm, as lead and glass alone would be too pliable to withstand the weather. The entire plan of the window must show unity. These large drawings are called "cartoons." They are working drawings for the use of the glass worker. Next a small layout in color is made to be used with the large cartoon. The glass is colored by dropping different amounts of pigment into the hot liquid glass which, as it is rolled into the large sheets, shows gradations of the color from the richest dark shades to palest tints. This large sheet is then cut into smaller sheets and a great variety of colors are given to the glass worker who constructs the window. The glassworker now begins to build up his window by cutting with his hot iron or diamond point small pieces to fit into his design. These he places in the lead channels which are soft and pliable, and, where the strips join, he solders. He must be careful always of the effect on the colors he uses, of the light when it penetrates. He must think of a beautiful design in color to be seen from a distance rather than the naturalistic details of each separate design. For this reason it may be necessary to make details in color very unreal as illustrated by the various colors shown in the haloes on the figures. We noticed when studying Gothic sculpture that it, too, was considered first as part of the architecture, and when viewed separately, seemed quaint and inhuman. Good decoration will always be subordinated to the architecture. The figures used in all beautiful Gothic windows were treated as decorative human symbols used to tell a story and fill a definite space. **Color balance** is always the chief concern of the worker and at the same time a **constant interchange of color** planned for scintillating lights. Because the sunlight is so strong as it penetrates the glass, it is necessary to use rich deep tones of glass which, mixed with brilliant sunshine, seem to flame and sparkle like a living fire. Often if the worker wishes to produce the effect of purple instead of using purple glass, he may use a red piece of glass next to a blue one, allowing the color to mix in the eye, getting a richer color, much as the Impressionist painter does with paint. But we must remember that these ancient Gothic workers in glass discovered this plan several hundred years before the Impressionist painters heralded it as their invention. Pieces of glass used for hands and faces of figures are carefully drawn upon first with brown enamel and then the glass is fired and the enamel is burned into the glass and made permanent.

Painted colored glass, like all imitations, is not considered good, as it is pretending to be what it is not and the outstanding characteristic of the Gothic workers was sincerity.

The windows on page 39 are beautiful examples of real stained glass, designed and made as the Gothic craftsmen planned them.

They were planned for St. Peter's church in Lexington, Kentucky, so we find St. Peter prominent in the design. The upper left circular medallion shows St. Peter receiving the Keys from Christ; the upper right medallion shows Peter as the Head of the Church, inspired by the Holy Ghost; the lower left medallion shows Pope Gregory sending St. Augustine to England; the lower right shows St. Francis of Assisi with the Infant, St. Agnes, and St. Anthony of Padua. Notice the fine space arrangement in each of these medallions. Notice the fine interplay of color in the two windows which gives great iridescence and a beautiful harmony. Notice that the designs in both windows, with the exception of the medallions, are the same, yet the distribution of color has made their appearance quite different. Notice how the brilliance of the two medallions on the left window balances the red border in the window on the right, where the medallions have been subdued. Notice the Gothic symbols in the jewel-like pieces of dark blue glass; have pupils recognize other symbols at **the top** of the windows. Call attention to the semi-circular designs in red on the long blue panel which have been placed to carry the eye from one window to the other, lacing them together as it were, to add to the unity of the whole. Have pupils analyze the windows for major color harmonies and minor harmonies, noting particularly the effect that the colors have on one another. This is the keynote of all good color effects, whether in paint, textiles or glass. Color area and color relationship must always be carefully studied.

If pictures can be obtained of local windows, either in color or in black and white, they will prove valuable if pasted on the blank page for comparison and study.

BOOK VIII, PAGE 41—CIVIC BEAUTY

Character Objective: Social Attitudes

Spiritual Objective: The campaign for Civic beauty will naturally suggest a similar effort to produce **soul beauty,** as a preparation for the **Feast of Corpus Christi. Conscience** will help find all the unsightly things, **confession will clear them away** and leave the soul rich with grace to nourish the new seeds that will blossom into beautiful and loving devotion to the Blessed Sacrament.

Art Objective: To stimulate originality and good arrangement in designing a poster from definite specifications.

Supplies: Posterboard, poster reference material, paste, blank paper

Procedure: Read the text and appoint a committee to make plans for the campaign. One group may plan the publicity and another group may outline the procedure of the actual work in cleaning up. Start with the school yard and its environs, carry the campaign into the home, and make its influence really felt.

Study the model posters. All show a specific problem of illustrating a slogan of not more than five assigned words. "Plant, Paint, and Clean Up."

The four posters shown on the page solve the problem, but each in a different way. The top and center bottom are more nearly alike. Call attention to every device that has been used in these problems to emphasize rules of design already studied. Call attention to the block of letters carefully planned as a design element to harmonize with the shape of the poster.

Notice elimination of details in order that shapes may be painted in flat color (no gradations). The first and third posters at the bottom of the page are similar in plan but different in illustration and lettering. Both have lettering placed in a panel and both have emphasized the words **"Clean Up."** Both of these posters show interesting problems in **angular perspective.** As practice work for original poster, plan color schemes for these posters and carefully paint them, emphasizing with color what has been indicated by line and shape.

Plan original poster for Civic beauty on sheet of gray or white paper preferably about 12 x 18 inches. Use any suggestions given for previous posters to develop good rendering. Ask pupils to find suitable poster reference material related to this problem to be pasted on the blank page.

BOOK VIII, PAGE 43—TRELLIS DESIGN

Character Objective: Love of Home and Orderliness

Spiritual Objective: In Book VI, pupils planned **to make their bodies each "A living house of God."** The lovely rose-covered trellis to be placed at its portal should be a **pleasant smiling countenance** with shining teeth to **beautify the smile.** This body house should "become **a harmonious unit"** in its neighborhood of other **"houses" by cooperation with all its neighbors.** A well-kept garden of **joyous service** in the soul within will be pleasant to greet **its frequent Guest, the King of Heaven.**

Art Objective: To develop discriminating taste in home decoration both interior and exterior.

Supplies: Paper strips, dark paper, colored paper, pictures of homes, pictures of furniture, carpets and wallpaper, paste, blank paper, heavy paper, cardboard

Procedure: Have a class discussion of the text, discussing the value of landscape design or landscape gardening and its results in aesthetic satisfaction as well as increased property value. Using cut paper strips, plan a design for a trellis to emphasize fine space relations. Make trellis white and mount on dark paper. Small bright spots of colored paper may be added to suggest flowers. The first and third panels show the side view of a trellis. Problem should show both views as working sketches for actual construction of trellis.

Lesson 2: Draw an oblong representing a building lot that may be arranged to illustrate good landscape gardening. Show location of house and arrange the rest of the ground in flower beds, borders, hedges, trees, etc., to make an interesting garden. When plan has been approved, paint to show color scheme of flower arrangement. Color of house must be considered as a part of the color scheme.

Lesson 3: Find pictures of simple beautiful homes to paste on the blank page for reference. With cut paper, design the front view or as it is called the **front elevation.** Aim for a fine balance of windows and **center the interest on a well designed door.** Consider as part of the plan the roof and chimney. In planning the color scheme, remember that the roof is an important area. Add spots of colored paper in the garden as flower decoration to harmonize with house.

Lesson 4: Review Manual notes, Book VI, page 23, and Book V, page 41, for suggestions on interior decoration.

Plan a sheet 12 x 18 to show a color scheme for a selected room. Mount on a large sheet of heavy paper pictures of furniture and carpets and wall papers clipped from catalogues, samples of textiles planned for draperies, and a painted sample of the suggested color of woodwork. Mount on same sheet a short description of the suggested room. An alternate for this problem is the construction of the floor and sidewalls of a room planned on cardboard with paper strip hinges to fold. The plan and color scheme of the room is carried out in much the same way, only each sidewall is definitely planned as a design.

Emphasize the fact that the completed problem must show unity if the design is to be good. If pictures are used be sure to have them harmonize with shape of wall on which they hang.

BOOK VIII, PAGE 45—SYMBOLISM

Character Objective: Ingenuity

Spiritual Objective: To emphasize the efficacy of prayer.

Art Objective: To develop imagination, originality, and skill in making costumes, motivated by Symbolism.

Supplies: Chalk and blackboard (optional) or large sheets of paper, curtains, colored paper, scarves

General Suggestions: Read the notes given for all previous plays to get additional help for this play.

Always keep in mind that the play is planned for the classroom as a means of teaching ideals and developing character.

Place responsibility for everything in the hands of pupils and permit them to experiment in working out simple stage effects.

Remember that the imagination must be allowed full sway and as in the case of the old Morality Plays, this play is planned to be given without scenery. For the sake of experience in illustration, it will add interest to place a scene on the blackboard similar to that shown in the text book if the blackboard extends across the front of the room; if not, the scene may be painted on large sheets of wrapping paper and tacked up. Enough material for curtains should be used to cover the scene so that it may be shown only when needed as the proper background. The two corners of the room may be used respectively to show the school and the home at the beginning and the home at the end of the play.

Curtains should be down when these sets are not in use. The principal action of the play takes place in the open space across the front of the room. If possible, arrange for convenient entrances and exits. In the old Morality Plays the actors were summoned from the audience and made entrance from the crowd, returning to the audience when the part was finished.

Colored paper and scarfs add beauty and interest to these costumes, each one of which is to be planned by the pupil representing the character.

Music necessary may be supplied by violinists who may be in the class but more probably by victrola records. In case neither is available, substitute suitable songs for the carnival or otherwise rearrange to suit conditions.

The work is planned to stimulate originality on the part of the teacher as well as pupils. Pupils are not critical and enjoy the planning and production. Appointing committees for various phases of the work to consult with the Director and the Property Man enables the teacher to place definite responsibilities.

Characters:

Everychild, the Boy.

His Mother
The Guardian Angel } Who watch over him (same person).

The Nun
Prayer } Who direct him (same person).

Pride
Selfishness
Carelessness
Neglect
Greed
Money } The Vices (who ruin him).

Adventure, a Knight of the Road.

The King and Queen of Pleasure.

The Doctor, who saved him for his mother.

Faith with the White jewel—Purity
Courage with the Red jewel—Love
Duty with the Yellow jewel—Wisdom
Self-Control with the Green jewel—Hope
Loyalty with the Blue jewel—Truth
Humility with the Purple jewel—Penance
Service with the Orange jewel—Thoughtfulness

} The Virtues (who help him).

Properties: The bed for the first and last acts may be made from three chairs placed side by side against the wall and covered.

A stone on which to sit in second act may be a box covered with unbleached muslin dyed dull purple and squeezed tight while wet and allowed to dry in that condition.

For dyeing any materials, have pupils use a cold dye. (Waldcraft dyes are easily used.)

Rocks of Loyalty may be planned from covered chairs leading up to the desk. Some of the material for covering should be dyed as suggested.

Use colored paper on a flashlight to throw colored lights on carnival dance (window shades down).

STAGE DIRECTIONS

Act 1—Scene 1: The schoolroom shows Everychild at his desk (chair) but with his head raised to listen to the conversation outside the door (off stage) in which he hears himself lauded. He repeats aloud what he hears and adds comments to show he is being possessed by Pride.

The Nun re-enters and talks to him about his work, giving him needed advice. He leaves to go to the athletic field.

Scene 2: Everychild has been injured and is lying in his bed at home. The doctor tells his mother how it happened and works over him. The Nun enters and kneels beside him, holding her rosary. His mother bends above him. He opens his eyes for a moment and looks at them all but does not speak. He gives a great sigh and closes his eyes. The doctor does not seem hopeful but promises the mother that he will not leave. The Nun continues praying (curtain).

Act 2: In the Land of Free Will (curtains may now be drawn from pictured setting), which lies in the space between the two curtained corners, Everychild appears rubbing his eyes and looking around. He wonders where he is and how he may get home. He suddenly remembers his Guardian Angel and repeats the little prayer he learned in first grade. The Angel appears and conversation ensues suggested by story. Prayer appears, (conversation suggested by story). They leave him. He sits to read his directions and Pride, Adventure, and Greed appear. (Conversation suggested by story.)

They all leave the stage. Curtains drawn over background.

Act 3: In the Land of Pleasure. Bands of brightly colored paper may be fastened to curtains to suggest festivity. (Each character should have a handful of confetti to use during the carnival.) The four characters appear and wait for the merrymakers. (Conversation suggested by story.)

The merrymakers appear, Neglect, Carelessness, Selfishness, Money (and any others desired). They are introduced and greet him as one of them. He does not like his new friends. They announce the King and Queen and conversation follows about the gift for tribute.

The King appears and the carnival is introduced by music. The dance begins and grows more furious as it proceeds. The maps of Everychild drop one by one from his pocket and are lost in the confetti. Money and Greed quarrel, the other vices take sides, and a riot ensues. Everychild is knocked down apparently striking his head. The carnival is dispersed by the King and Queen, and Everychild is left lying. Greed returns, steals the jewels, and, thinking he is dead, drags him off the stage.

Act 4: Curtain is drawn to show pictured background of Land of Free Will (same as Act 2). Everychild appears walking dejectedly and searching for his treasures. Again he thinks of his Guardian Angel and repeats the prayer. The Angel appears and conversation follows.

She helps him to remember and following the story there appear in order as he remembers each prayer. Pater Noster and Ave Maria —Faith, with the jewel bag. Contrition—Humility; Morning Offering—Courage; Grace—Self Control; Angelus—Duty; Conversation of each is suggested by story. Everychild now starts on his journey and reaches the Rocks of Loyalty without his safeguard, the blue jewel. He meets the dragon (or ogre) and gives battle, but gradually loses. Again he calls for help and this time Prayer appears and gives him the name he needs for the prayer, The Apostles Creed. She kneels to say it for him and Truth appears with the blue jewel and the enemy disappears.

He rises from the ground and then sits to regain his strength. He is afraid even now, with only one more hazard to meet, that he will fail without the last jewel. He sits and thinks of all that has happened. How wonderfully he has been helped along the way 1 Immediately he realizes that God has taken care of him through his wonderful Guardian Angel. He begins to say an Act of Love and immediately comes Service, bearing the flaming orange jewel. And Everychild knows that he is safe. Just before he reaches the gates of the Fields of Service he hears a hum of voices and again he meets his one time friends on the way to the Land of Pleasure. Pride appeals to him to come, telling him Adventure and Money await him. But he is strong now and bids Pride begone, since Pride had been the cause of all of his misfortunes. He tells him he never wishes to see his face again.

While he talks the Angel and Prayer appear and stay near him.

He enters the Fields of Service and falls asleep, off stage after describing the tree under which he plans to rest.

Epilogue: In the home of Everychild taking up the story exactly where it stopped in Act 1, with the doctor using the same sentence he was using at the close of Act 1.

The doctor is not sure he will recover, but hopeful. He puts his ear close to hear the faint murmurs of the boy who is still unconscious. He tells the mother that the boy is mumbling something about a bag of jewels. But his pulse is growing stronger and he seems better. Everychild suddenly opens his eyes and then raises himself on his elbow (his head is bandaged). He seems puzzled as he looks first at the Nun and then at his mother. They are exactly like the Angel and his good friend Prayer. The doctor warns them not to talk to him but assures them he will be well in a few days. Everychild then repeats the last lines of the story as the curtain drops.

CORRELATION

1. ENGLISH: Read notes given for play in Book VII and continue development of English dialogue for the play as planned there. Finer sentence structure and better delivery of lines may be expected. Keep the imaginative type of conversation uppermost, especially in having descriptions given of what characters are supposed to see.

   Aim for additional comments on value of the different prayers mentioned which may be named but need not be repeated.

Have speeches planned for the Virtues and Vices in the form of a description in the first person, each giving his characteristics and what he intends to do.

2. RELIGION: May be used to develop the spiritual objectives.
3. DESIGN AND COLOR: Use all the principles of color and design learned, to plan a colorful grouping of characters for each act. Plan definite harmonies showing good balance of dark and light with proper Emphasis.
4. COSTUME DESIGN: The most difficult costume is shown in the book and represents the most common vice, the first of the Seven Deadly Sins.

   Other costumes should be worked out by pupils. Money might be shown by dollar marks tacked to clothing or as shown in picture with bags.

   Greed should be grotesquely fat and rather humorous, but crafty. Carelessness may be always losing something and have her conversation emphasize this characteristic.
5. MUSIC: For the dancing in Act 2, suitable music would be:

   "The Witches Dance"—MacDowell

   "In the Hall of the Mountain King" from Peer Gynt—Greig.

   Other music may be substituted as suggested in notes.

   Allow pupils to make up the dances as suggested by the rhythm of the music.

BOOK VIII, PAGE 47—EVERYCHILD

Character Objective: Humility

Spiritual Objective: To arouse in pupils a desire for good rather than evil, through holding before them a mirror showing their own reflections.

Art Objective: To develop originality in design and color through the creation of a play based on Symbolism.

EVERYCHILD

A Symbolic Morality Play for the Classroom

SYNOPSIS

Everychild was a modern boy ready to graduate from the 8th grade. He was the pride of the school in athletics and kept well up in his class. But he was careless about many things. One day he overheard a conversation between his mother, who was visiting the school, and his teacher, the Nun who had always been his friend in need.

Not knowing he could overhear them, they praised his work and his many fine points and the Nun expressed her belief that he would have a very brilliant future. Pride rose strong within his breast as he pictured himself when he could follow his own will, greater than all his companions. Then he would show them something!

When school was out he went to a ball field for practice. On the way home he carelessly ran in front of an automobile and was struck. His companions led the way to his home. He opened his eyes once to see his mother and a doctor bending over him, while the Nun knelt by his bed and then all was dark.

Suddenly a light seemed to break through the great darkness and he found himself in a strange queer land in which he could make out nothing clearly.

He had only one great overpowering desire, and that was to go home to his mother who always waited for him at the gate of the lovely old garden.

While he was wondering he thought of his Guardian Angel and repeated the little verse he had said every day. He heard a sweet sound like the soft low tones of the organ at church and turning he saw his beautiful Guardian Angel, who told him he was in the Land of Free Will. She told him he must be very careful if he wished to return to his home and mother as the paths were full of danger and hard to find, and wicked dragons held the entrance to each new road. He asked her if she could accompany him and show him the way. But she said she could only help him, so long as he could hear her voice through conscience, since he would not be able to see her. She said he would have other guides on the way. Just then he heard a small voice at his elbow and looked to find a lovely white clad figure who smiled sweetly at him, telling him her name was Prayer. She told him she would give him seven maps to direct him on his way; that he must carefully read the directions and guard them. Then she handed him seven beautiful jewels, one white, one red, one blue, one green, one yellow, one orange, and one purple. They glowed and sparkled in his hand and while he looked, she handed him an exquisite bag of glistening gold so fine and sheer that he thought it must disappear when he touched it. She told him it was very rare, having been spun from the threads of conscience to remind him of the precious wealth he carried; that so long as he guarded it, his jewels would be safe. She told him that on the way he would meet a wicked dragon at each of the places where he was to follow a new map, but that he should be fearless because when the dragon saw the jewel, if he used the proper one, he would immediately disappear. Again urging him to guard them and to remember when to use the jewels so that nothing might harm him, she disappeared and he was left alone. He stowed the bag of jewels carefully away and sat down to look at his maps. At the top of the **first** one he read: "The true road of **Faith** is just ahead of you if you follow the **Pater Noster** and the **Ave Maria,** and when the dragon appears you will vanquish him with the **white jewel** which is called **Purity**."

On the **second** one he read: "To help you to mount to the **high road of Courage** which you will know, for there you will find **"The Morning Offering"** waiting to assist you. When you meet the dragon take forth the **red jewel** which is called **Love** and the dragon will vanish."

On the **third** map he read: "You will come to the **River of Self Control** which is swift and wide, but you will find a bridge and at one end will be waiting for you **Grace before Meals,** and he will take you to **'Grace after Meals'** at the other end. When you meet the dragon who guards the entrance, hold high the **green jewel called Hope,** and you may cross in safety."

The **fourth** read: "You have now come to the **lonely valley of Humility,** but do not falter, for you will have for your guide the **Act of Contrition,** and when you meet the dragon, take forth the **purple jewel, which is called Penance,** and you will be safe." He opened the **fifth** one and read:

"Six days must you travel and so that you may know the days, the **Angelus** will tell you when it is **your duty** to eat and rest, and if the dragon attacks you, conquer him with the **yellow jewel, which is called Wisdom."**

He opened the **sixth** map and read: "The high **Rocks of Loyalty** will now bar your way, but waiting for you will be the **Apostles Creed,** strong and broad, and he will help you to scale the rocks. But before you reach him, have ready **your blue jewel called Truth** to vanquish the dragon." And now he had come to the **last** one and noticed it was lettered in gold and read:

"Your dangers are almost over. You have now reached the Gates of the Flowery Fields of **Service** where the **Acts of Faith, Hope, and Charity** are waiting to receive you, to conduct you to your mother who is waiting for you in her garden. One dragon remains to be overcome by the **orange jewel of Unselfishness.** Like all true knights you must bring to your Lady Fair your bag of precious jewels as your trophies from your adventures." When he had finished reading he again took out the jewels to be sure they were all there, and while he admired them, he saw three queer looking people coming along, dressed for a fancy dress party; one looked like a peacock; the second had a broad hat, a bright red sash and dark knee trousers, and a long swinging sword; the third seemed all stomach, he was so fat. His head was small and his eyes sharp. They greeted Everychild in a friendly manner, and to his great surprise the peacock slapped him on the back shaking his hand, saying, "Hello old friend, I'm glad to see you. My name is Pride. We were great friends in your school days." And Everychild had a guilty feeling, knowing that what he said was true. There was something about him he didn't like. "Here Adventure," said Pride to the one with the wide hat, "you will find Everychild to be somebody like yourself. I know you will be boon companions." Turning to the third one he said, "Now Greed, don't look so longingly at Every child's jewels. He is our friend and we must take care of him." They all urged him to go with them to the carnival. It would not delay him long and he would never see the like again. He liked the one called Adventure, and allowed himself to be persuaded. In a few minutes they came to the great carnival in the Land of Pleasure. They spoke truly when they said he would never see the like again. Costumes of every kind and variety, strange wild music that made him want to join the wild crowd in their dance, weaving out and in through bands of colored ribbons, while the light seemed to change every minute. "We must not go far," said Pride to Adventure, "the King comes this way and Everychild must be presented." Adventure turned to him to tell him that all must pay tribute when presented. Everychild began to wish he had not come as he had no tribute and he said so. "Give him one of your jewels" said Greed. "They are for my mother," he answered. "Well," suggested Pride, "give him the empty bag, it is fit for a king." Everychild decided that was the easiest way to solve the problem. And he disliked Pride more than ever. Just then the King was announced and Everychild was introduced and gave him the bag. That was not mentioned in the maps and he could get along without it. He was then introduced to Money, Selfishness, Carelessness, and Neglect, who were ringleaders in the fun.

Before he knew it he was whirling madly around with the rest and as he did so one after another, his maps dropped out of his pockets and were swept away.

He forgot everything, even his dislike of Pride, and was glad he had come. Somebody started a quarrel and before he knew it he was in the middle of what seemed like a riot. The din was awful and then a blow on the head and he knew no more. The crowd dispersed and he was left lying on the ground. But one returned who had seen the jewels. Greed had seen where they were put and, helped by Carelessness, quickly found them.

Everychild awakened and found himself alone. He had nothing and was frightened at the terrifying noises he could hear. He suddenly thought of his Guardian Angel and wished she were there. Immediately she appeared, looking at him sorrowfully. He ached with homesickness as he saw her because she looked so much like his mother. He begged her to help him but she told him she could not; she could only advise him to help himself. She urged him to remember some of the directions on the lost maps but it was no use. He tried to remember, but gave up in despair. Gently the angel urged again, telling him to call on Mary, the Queen of Angels. Immediately his face lighted, part of that first map was a prayer to Mary and that gave his memory the key; then he remembered all the rest, but the jewel was gone. While he sat in dejection, Faith appeared, having rescued the jewel.

He began to tell the Angel he was sorry for going to the Land of Pleasure and as he did so the words seemed familiar and he found himself saying an Act of Contrition, and then he remembered the purple jewel. Even as he did so there stood Penance holding the jewel toward him. His confidence began to return and Penance promised to help him. The Angel told him the day was breaking and habit made him repeat the Morning Offering. Immediately came Courage with the red jewel he had rescued and Every child began to feel less afraid every minute. He began to feel hungry and wished he was at the table at home listening to the Grace and he remembered the green jewel. He repeated Grace and, before he finished, Self Control appeared bringing the green jewel to him and behind her came Conscience bringing his golden bag. Overjoyed, full of hope and courage, he then decided to start on the trip since he had recovered more than half of his treasures. He found the sign posts as foretold, and after he had grown weary traveling he began to wonder what time it was and that made him remember the words "time to eat and rest." Looking up he saw the sun was directly over his head. "It must be twelve o'clock" he said, and then he heard sweet bells ringing and he stopped and stood with bowed head repeating the Angelus. When he finished there stood Duty, holding the yellow jewel of Wisdom. Everything went well until he came to the Rocks of Loyalty and then he grew fearful as he had not remembered the prayer, and had no jewel. He knew he must fight the dragon alone. His Guardian Angel, through his conscience, urged him to be brave. But he had no weapons and the fight was going against him when suddenly Prayer appeared and repeated the Apostles Creed while Truth came with the blue jewel just in time to save him. He sat down to rest and think. Only one more hazard before reaching his mother.

He tried hard to think of a sure plan of safety. And while he sat came Thoughtfulness with the orange jewel to keep him safe at the last barrier; as his memory was now quite clear, he knelt and said the Acts of Faith, Hope, and Charity. As he marched along with head held high he heard shouts of laughter ahead that sounded strangely familiar.

Looking down the road he saw the group of merrymakers who had caused him so much distress. They called him by name, casting silken ribbons about him, but he would have none of them, calling them false friends and bidding them go away. Especially did he wish never to see Pride who had caused him all the trouble. And now that the last dragon was gone he entered the Flowery Fields of Service, and continued happily along, plucking the flowers as he went, to bring them to his mother. As he neared the end of the field he felt a strange sweet drowsiness enveloping him. He saw a tree under which was comfortable shade and decided to rest before going on. And again all was darkness.

He heard a strange voice he did not know, saying, "He is out of danger now," and was quickly on guard to protect his precious jewels. He opened his eyes but there was no tree; his mother was bending over the bed, no, it was his Guardian Angel and there was faithful Prayer kneeling at the bedside, no, it was the Nun his teacher, but again he was sure it was Prayer, for how could he ever forget her sweet smile? Yes, he was sure she was Prayer. But things were terribly mixed. And this Guardian Angel who was bringing him something in a cup couldn't be a Guardian Angel for she hadn't any wings.

So he said, "Sister Prayer, I will not forget again but I have saved all the jewels for mother, and she is my Guardian Angel."

Bibliography

GENERAL

Brown, Harold H. .... Applied Drawing ....Mentzer, Bush & Co.
Charters, W. W. .... The Teaching of Ideals ....Macmillan, N. Y.
Furniss, Dorothy .... Drawing for Beginners ....Bridgeman, Pelham, N. Y.
Jacobs, Harry .... The Drawing Teacher ....Binney and Smith, N. Y.
Kirby, C. V. .... The Business of Teaching and Supervising the Arts ....Prang Co., N. Y.
Koch .... Pencil Sketching ....Prang Co., N. Y.
Mathias, Margaret .... Beginnings of Art in the Public Schools .... Scribners, N. Y.
Soper....................... Elementary Drawing ..... Scott, Foresman Co., N. Y.
Sullivan, Rt. Rev. J. F. ... Externals of the Catholic Church ...... Kennedy, N. Y.
Trilling and Williams ..... Art in Home and Clothing ....Lippincott, N. Y.
Whitney .... Blackboard Sketching ...... Milton Bradley Co., N. Y.

ART HISTORY AND APPRECIATION

Caffin, Charles .... Art for Life's Sake..................Prang Co., N. Y.
Cockrell, Dura .... Introduction to Art .... Richard Smith, N. Y.
DeGarmo .... Aesthetic Education .... Bardeen
Daniels .... The Furnishing of a Modest Home ....Mentzer, Bush & Co.
Goodyear, William .... History of Art ....Laidlaw, N. Y.
Goldstein, H. I. and V. .... Art in Every Day Life ....Macmillan, N. Y.
Hamlin .... History of Architecture ....Longmans, Green, N. Y.
Lester .... Great Pictures and Their Stories ......Mentzer, Bush & Co.
Marquand and Frothingham ... History of Sculpture ....Longmans, Green, N. Y.
Parsons, Frank Alvah .... Interior Decoration ....Doubleday, N. Y.
Poore, Henry R. .... Pictorial Composition ....Doubleday, N. Y.
Reinach, Saloman .... Apollo ....Scribners, N. Y.
Richards, C. R. .... Art in Industry ....Macmillan, N. Y.
Van Dyke, Henry .... The Meaning of Pictures ....Scribners, N. Y.
Van Dyke, Henry .... History of Painting .....Longmans, Green, N. Y.
Wynne, Gladys .... Architecture ....Nelson & Sons, N. Y.

COLOR AND DESIGN

Batchelder .... Design in Theory and Practice .... Macmillan, N. Y.
Branch, Eliz. G .... Illustrated Exercises in Design .... Prang Co., N. Y.
Chase .... Decorative Design ....Wiley & Sons, N. Y.
Crane, Walter .... Line and Form .... Bell & Sons, London, Eng.
Dow, Arthur W. .... Composition .... Doubleday, N. Y.
Littlejohns .... Art for All (Color) .... Pittmann, N. Y.
Parsons, Frank A. .... Interior Decoration .... Prang Co., N. Y.
Parsons, Frank A. .... Psychology of Dress .... Doubleday, N. Y.
Weinberg .... Color in Everyday Life .... Moffat, N. Y.
Sargent, W. .... Enjoyment and Use of Color .... Scribners, N. Y.
Traphagen, Ethel H. .... Costume Design .... Wiley & Sons, N. Y.

COMMERCIAL

Guptill, Arthur L. .... Rendering in Pen and Ink ....Pencil Points Press
Guptill, Arthur L. .... Sketching and Rendering
in Lead Pencil ....Pencil Points Press
Parsons, Frank A. ... Principles of Advertising Arrangement ....Prang Co., N. Y.
Wallace, C. E. .... Commercial Art .... McGraw-Hill, N. Y.
Young, F. H. .... Advertising Layout ....Covici, N. Y.

INDUSTRIAL

White .... How to Make Pottery .... Doubleday, N. Y.
Buxton .... Paper and Cardboard Construction .... Menomonie Press
Mijer, Pieter .... Batiks and How to Make Them .... Dodd-Mead & Co., N. Y.
Watson, Ernest W. .... Linoleum Block Printing ...... Milton Bradley, N. Y.
Winslow, Leon L. .... Elementary Industrial Arts .... Macmillan, N. Y.

MAGAZINES

Catholic School Interests
School Arts Book
Art Digest

Notes

www.ingramcontent.com/pod-product-compliance
Lightning Source LLC
LaVergne TN
LVHW061219100826
845148LV00004B/801

* 9 7 8 1 6 4 0 5 1 1 3 5 4 *